"This astonishing book is a scholarly inventory of everything to do with the Mediterranean, from ships to maps to vocabularies to ocean currents to fish to warehouses to people. But it is far more than that: it is as though a lyric poet had distilled in his very words the entire essence and meaning of the Inner Sea and set us wonderingly afloat upon it."

Jan Morris, author of *Fifty Years of Europe: An Album*

"A voice from Central Europe, from the continent, the broad Pannonian plains of Croatia, has masterminded a brilliant and totally original book about the Mediterranean, a book that enriches cultural historiography as well as the literature of the sea and a thousand-year-old tradition of treasures as varied as those resting in the briny deep. . . . *Mediterranean: A Cultural History* tells a story, but a story that brings facts alive and seamlessly grafts culture onto fantasy."

Claudio Magris, author of *Danube*

"A divine mass for a sea whose boundaries defy definition."

Le Monde

"Required reading for everyone who loves the Mediterranean."

Lu

"Matvejević has succeeded in combining the joy one feels in reading his poetic ruminations with a catalogue of commentary on the great historical, philosophical, literary works inspired by the Mediterranean."

Il Giornale

Mediterranean has been awarded the Prix Malaparte, the Premio Boccaccio Europeo, the Prix Européen de l'Essai Charles Veillon, and the Prix du Meilleur Livre Étranger.

MEDITERRANEAN

Mediterranean

A Cultural Landscape

PREDRAG MATVEJEVIĆ

Translated by Michael Henry Heim

UNIVERSITY OF CALIFORNIA PRESS   BERKELEY   LOS ANGELES   LONDON

Previously published as Predrag Matvejević,
Mediteranski brevijar. Zagreb: Grafički zavod
Hrvatske, 1987. Predrag Matvejevitch, *Bréviaire
méditerranéen*. Paris: Fayard, 1992. Predrag
Matvejević, *Mediterraneo: Un nuovo breviario*.
Milan: Garzanti, 1993.

Jacket illustration: Detail from *Livre des Marveilles*,
illuminated manuscript, 1300s. Courtesy
Bibliothèque Nationale de France.

University of California Press
Berkeley and Los Angeles, California

University of California Press, Ltd.
London, England

Library of Congress Cataloging-in-Publication Data

Matvejević, Predrag, 1932–
    [Mediteranski brevijar. English]
    Mediterranean : a cultural landscape / Predrag
Matvejević ; translated from the Croatian by
Michael Henry Heim.
        p. cm.
    ISBN 0-520-20738-6 (alk. paper)
    1. Mediterranean Region—Description and
travel. I. Heim, Michael Henry. II. Title.
D973   1999
909'.09822—dc21   98-47186
                                        CIP

Printed in the United States of America
9   8   7   6   5   4   3   2

The paper used in this publication meets the
minimum requirements of American National
Standards for Information Sciences—Permanence
of Paper for Printed Library Materials, ANSI
Z39.48-1984.

CONTENTS

INTRODUCTION :: A PHILOLOGY OF THE SEA

Claudio Magris

In a wonderful passage from the book you are about to read, Predrag Matvejević tells of meeting a Catalonian watchmaker who is battling with an extreme paucity of facts in his attempt to catalogue the largest collection of writings in the ancient world, the famous library destroyed by Caliph Omar. In its combination of rigor and temerity, of scholarly precision and epiphany, Matvejević's richly intelligent and poetic book, a veritable philology of the sea, recalls the Catalonian watchmaker's wild yet methodical undertaking.

The science of the sea encompasses not only the tracing of currents and routes, the chemical analysis of salinity, the study of stratigraphy and of maps of the benthic and the pelagic layers of marine life, its euphotic, oligophotic, and aphotic zones, and the measurement of temperatures and winds but also stories of shipwrecks, myths of galleons gone under and ancient leviathans, the amniotic fluid of humanity and the cradle of civilization, Greek beauty, which like Aphrodite arises perfect from the sea, the great temptation of the soul as told by Musil, the clash between symbols of eternity and conviction, that is, life itself, resplendent in a pure present and the plenitude of its meaning. The *Odyssey*—the greatest *Bildungsroman,* the model novel of personal development, of an individual venturing out into the world and coming home, coming back to himself—is unthinkable without the sea, the Mediterranean, the basis for our history and culture.

A voice from Central Europe, from the continent, the broad Pannonian plains of Croatia, has masterminded a brilliant and totally original book about the Mediterranean, a book that enriches cultural historiography as well as the literature of the sea and a thousand-year-old tradition of treasures as varied as those resting in the briny deep. But Predrag Matvejević is also a man of the coast: born in Mostar, the chief town of Herzegovina and only fifty kilometers from the Adriatic, he was fascinated as a child by rivers and coasts; he wondered why people living along the narrow strip of land lining the sea practice different customs and sing different songs from those only a short distance inland. The poetic curiosity of the child grew and eventually developed into the perceptions of the scholar, critic, and leading European intellectual Matvejević is today; that is, it developed into an unusual "breviary," as he calls the first part of this book, with a form and phenomenology all its own.

What is this book, which in its own discreet way refuses to be pinned down to a genre? Matvejević's *Mediterranean,* as he himself tells us, is not merely an evocation of the historical and cultural space so masterfully, even definitively studied by Braudel, nor of the mythical and lyrical construct celebrated by Camus or Gide; it is more an alluring mixture of portolano, lexicon, and essay-novel resting firmly on absolute fidelity to the facts. Sui generis and autonomous though it be, it is also reminiscent of Michelet's *La Mer,* another brilliant and bizarre book in which, having sounded the depths of the archives for materials about the history of France and its Revolution, the author turned his tireless attention to the depths of the sea, to lighthouses and the geologic strata of coastal lands, to shells and marine flora, to thermal baths and legends about sirens.

Reading Matvejević, I occasionally had the feeling that the narrative voice belonged to the characters, men who have lived by the sea, observing lighthouses and sifting through marine glossaries. But, as Giorgio Bergamini has put it, nowadays even the truest Ulysses is more at home in a sports jacket than a pea jacket, more likely to navigate among bookshelves than lost islands. Today's Ulysses must be well versed in myths lost and a nature in exile; he must explore absence and the loss of true life.

Predrag Matvejević is no seaman, no lighthouse keeper, or perhaps he is both; primarily, however, he is one of the leaders in contemporary intellectual discourse. His bibliography covers a number of wide-ranging topics, and he has taught at several major European universities. His critical approach is based on a Marxism free of orthodoxy and ideological dogma. Many of his works—and in particular *Pour une poétique de l'événement* (Paris, 1979), a masterpiece of critical historiography—deal with the Sartrian concept of *engagement,* commitment, which he gives a highly original interpretation. He thereby enters the international debate on the function and freedom of literature with impeccable credentials. Now perhaps more than ever, intellectuals—Western intellectuals, for the most part—are foundering in fruitless debates over realism or classicism and progress, between Scylla and Charybdis: humanists have sunk into an anachronistic and repressive conservatism, while liberal demands degenerate into vague, impulsive, and regressive repetition, in what Nietzsche calls the "anarchy of atoms."

Writers who give us a means to confront the current impasse are rare. Matvejević is one of them. He uses his cosmopolitan culture and intellectual dexterity as well as his dialectical, proximity/detachment approach to life, things, and history to defend subjectivity without rejecting universality, to oppose totalitarianism without losing sight of the global perspective. He substantiates his ideas time and again in literary studies, papers on ethical and political issues, and in the famous and daring *Open Letters* addressed—during difficult times and not without personal risk—to the mighty of this world in defense of freedom or, rather, freedoms and the victims of power.

While battling Stalinism and totalitarian formulas and concepts in general, Matvejević also unmasked and rejected the opposite and complementary danger currently threatening to corrode all forms of cultural unity, all systems of values: he rejected the particularism and atomism of embitterment. As an expert on Central Europe—that complex, heterogeneous, and sometimes centrifugal mosaic—he warns that "being different is not in itself a value," thus putting us on our guard against the visceral exaltation of our own identity and self-love.

In *Mediterranean: A Cultural Landscape* Matvejević, the interpreter of dialogues between overriding systems, remains true to his ideals and his vocation. All that changes is the register, the key signature: instead of reading only books, as he did in preparation for his former projects, he now reads the world, reality, the gestures and intonations of individuals, the styles of harbors and harbormasters; he records the enigmatic way nature turns into history and arts, the extension of the forms of the coast in the forms of its architecture, the borders described by the cultivation of the olive, the spread of religion and the migrations of eels, stories and whole destinies as they appear in nautical lexicons in extinct languages; he documents the idiom of the waves and wharves, the jargons and argots that change imperceptibly as they move along the coast and through time from one language to another: *chiacchiera, ciacola, čakula* (chatter); *sharq, scirocco, šilok* (sirocco); *neve, nevera, neverin* (snow); *barca, barcón, barcosa, barcutus, bragoč* (boat).

Matvejević's *Mediterranean* thus becomes an epic of compassion for each of the countless fates cradled and buried by the sea, a vast archive or etymological dictionary, if you will. The sea is fathomless and without end, and Matvejević's discourse is leisurely, plumbing the depths through glistening ripples, catching both the surf and the sometimes tragic immensity of the waters. He succeeds in bringing out the grace of the Mediterranean, showing it off to its advantage much like Raffaele La Capria in his wonderful *Armonia perduta*. He injects culture and history directly into its stones, its wrinkled faces, the taste of its wine and oil, the color of its waves. He attempts to encompass everything. Yet even as he conveys the charm of the Mediterranean, he rigorously defines his terms and draws his boundaries. He traces numerous Mediterranean peregrinations, from amber to Sephardic Jewry, from vineyards to riverbeds. Borders that once seemed clear-cut and concentric suddenly lose their contours and start meandering, looking more like isobars or wave crests.

Matvejević deals with many things that need to be described in detail if they are to be properly appreciated: the smell of riggings on the docks and the superstitions they engender, the foam and how it differs from that of other seas, the manifold tonalities of darkness on the sea, the variety and nomenclature of nets, the names of the sea itself and variations on the compass card, the theatrical structure of the fish auction, a comparative lexical and gesticular vocabulary of insults and curses, and the contemplation of the sea as a form of prayer. Citing a Berber dictionary that gives a word designating the shaft of an oar but no word for the oar itself, he draws the appropriate conclusions for the relationship of the Berbers to the sea.

What he says about the voyages of antiquity—namely, that they beg the distinction between history and fiction—applies as well to his *Mediterranean:* when in the magnificent chapter on cartography (which shows how the fortunes of maritime maps coincide with those of their compilers, so bold and imaginative in their search for accuracy), he becomes one of his own characters, meeting and conversing with a retired monk by the name of Irinei, who is writing a life of Saint Simeon Stylites; or when he brings in his own sea voyages and visits to ghost-town ports, or natural and cultural landscapes, or a prayer in the desert, or the mountains of Georgia and their poets.

Mediterranean: A Cultural Landscape tells a story, but a story that brings facts alive and seamlessly grafts culture onto fantasy. This may be the most lively and imaginative literature being written today, in prose, at least. It is infinitely more vigorous and poetic than the novels that tell us how and why Mr. X is happy or unhappy with Mrs. Y.

As the potamologist who in *Danube* expressed great nostalgia for the sea (the Adriatic, in my case), I hereby declare myself fraternally jealous of the thalassologist Matvejević. Much as I rejoice in the fact that the Danube flows into the sea, I regret that the sea in question is Black rather than Mediterranean.

5

ONE :: BREVIARY

Let us begin our tour of the Mediterranean by choosing a point of departure: coast or scene, port or event, cruise or narrative. Eventually the place of embarkation will be less important than the place of destination and what we have seen and how. Sometimes all seas seem one, particularly when the journey is long; sometimes each sea is a different sea.

Let us set out from the Adriatic. Not only is the whole northern coast of the Mediterranean, from Málaga to the Bosporus, more readily accessible from there; the southern coast, from Haifa to Ceuta, has fewer gulfs and ports. I have sailed the islands—first in the Adriatic, then in the Ionian and Aegean—seeking out similarities and differences, comparing Sicily with Corsica, Majorca with Minorca. I have not put in at every port, however; I have spent most of my time at the mouths of rivers. Getting to know the length and breadth of the Mediterranean is no easy task.

We are never certain how far it extends, that is, how much of the coast it occupies and where it ends, on either land or sea. The Greeks thought of it as running east-west from the Phasis in the Caucasus to the Pillars of Hercules, taking for granted its natural border in the north and ignoring it in the south. Ancient sages taught that the Mediterranean extends as far as the olive grows. Such has not been always and everywhere the case, however: certain stretches along the coast are not Mediterranean in climate or are less so than points farther removed. In some places land and sea do not seem to mesh; in others Mediterranean traits penetrate large areas of the mainland and have a vast and varied impact. The Mediterranean is not merely geography.

Ptolemy's world according to the Cosmographia. Ulm, 1482.

Its boundaries are drawn in neither space nor time. There is in fact no way of drawing them: they are neither ethnic nor historical, state nor national; they are like a chalk circle that is constantly traced and erased, that the winds and waves, that obligations and inspirations expand or reduce. The Mediterranean shores have seen not only the silk route but also the crisscrossing of many others: routes of salt and spices, amber and ornaments, oils and perfumes, tools and arms, skills and knowledge, arts and sciences. Hellenic emporia were markets and embassies; Roman roads spread power and civilization; Asian soil provided prophets and religions. Europe was conceived on the Mediterranean.

IT IS DIFFICULT TO EXPLAIN the repeated impulse to piece the Mediterranean mosaic together, to make yet another catalogue of its components, verify the meaning of each and the value of each with respect to the other: Europe, the Maghreb, and the Levant; Judaism, Christianity, and Islam; the Talmud, the Bible, and the Qur'an; Athens and Rome; Jerusalem, Alexandria, Constantinople, and Venice; Greek dialectics, art, and democracy; Roman law, the forum, and the republic; Arab scholarship; Provençal and Catalan poetry; Italy in the Renaissance; Spain in various periods, glorious and inglorious; the Southern Slavs on the Adriatic; and many more. Emphasizing or isolating the dominant, most salient components and treating their relations with only two or three of the others reduces the range and distorts the content of the Mediterranean. Nations and races have conjoined and disjoined here over the centuries; more peoples have lived with one another and clashed with one another here than perhaps anywhere on the planet. Overplaying their similarities and interchanges and underplaying their differences and conflicts is so much bravado. The Mediterranean is not merely history.

MEDITERRANEAN FEATURES do not dovetail completely with other entities; they do not enter into all aspects of the relationships between coast and mainland, North and South, and East or West and South. Many incongruities have marked Mediterranean civilizations, old and new: from the Greek and Roman to the Byzantine, and on to the Italian, French Provençal, Spanish Catalan, Arab (in a number of regions), Croatian (from Dalmatia to Pannonia), Slovenian (from the coast to

the Alps), Serbian and Montenegrin, Macedonian and Bulgarian, Albanian, Romanian, Turk, and most likely others as well, preceding Greco-Roman times, parallel to them, or following them, together and separately. Mediterranean cultures are not merely national cultures.

Solomon's temple according to Hartmann Schedel's reconstruction in Liber Chronicarum. Nuremberg, 1493.

THE MEDITERRANEAN will not abide a scale incommensurate with itself. We do it an injustice by approaching it from a Eurocentric point of view, that is, as an exclusively Latin, Roman, or Romance creation, or from a purely pan-Hellenic, pan-Arab, or Zionist point of view, that is, on the basis of a particularist criterion, be it ethnic, religious, or political. Our image of the Mediterranean has been distorted by fanatic tribunals and biased exegetes, by scholars without convictions and preachers without faith, by official chroniclers and court poets. Churches and states, prelates and kings, legislators ecclesiastical and lay have divided up space and people in every possible manner. Internal links, however, resist all divisions. The Mediterranean is not merely belonging.

MEDITERRANEAN DISCOURSE has suffered from Mediterranean discursiveness: sun and sea, scent and color, sandy beaches and islands of fortune, girls maturing young and widows shrouded in black, ports and ships and *invitations au voyage,* journeys and wrecks and tales thereof, oranges and olives and myrtle, palms and pines and cypresses, pomp and poverty, reality and illusion, life and dreams—such are the commonplaces plaguing the literature, all description and repetition. Mediterranean oratory has served democracy and demagogy, freedom and tyranny; Mediterranean rhetoric has taken over speech and sermon, forum and temple. Its arena ranges far beyond the Areopagus. The Mediterranean is inseparable from its discourse.

IN EVERY PERIOD AND PART of the region we find contradictions. True, there is clarity and form, geometry and logic, law and justice, knowledge and poetics, but there is everything opposed to them as well: holy books of love and reconciliation along with crusades and jihads, the ecumenical spirit and fanatical ostracism, universality and autarchy, agora and labyrinth, *alêtheia* and enigma, Dionysian joy and the labor of Sisyphus, Athens and Sparta, Rome and the barbarians, Orient and Occident, north coast and south coast, Europe and Africa, Christianity and Islam, Catholicism and Orthodoxy, the teachings of the Nazarene and the persecution of the Jews. The Mediterranean made it hard for the Renaissance to overcome the Middle Ages.

MEDITERRANEAN ILLUSIONS are important as well. The peculiarity of the Mediterranean's position and homogeneity of its space make it seem a world in and of itself or the center of the world. Is it a sea surrounded by land or land by a sea? The sun that rises in its skies and shines down upon it seems there for it and it alone; it seems to belong to it. (Cosmographers and geographers of the ancient world incorporated aspects of that illusion into their theories and maps.) The sun's rays give rise to interesting psychological phenomena—some transitory, others per-

Bibliotheca Alexandrina.

fita parte Mareotim lacum, quem alij Ma brum, & ex eo mari nauigatur in urbis pulcherrimū aiunt esse mar spectu insula est Pharos nomine,

uros & doctores ecclesiasticos. Nempe Marcum Euangelistam, Amanum Clementem & Origenem presbyteros, Athanasium episcopum, Didymum,

manent. The openness and transparency of the sky produce mystic states and fear of the other world. The Mediterranean has raised monuments to faith and superstition, magnanimity and vanity.

Mediterranean cities, which experts claim create villages around and for themselves rather than grow out of villages (as cities are wont to do elsewhere), have had virtually everything said about them in terms of polis and politics, ground plans and property registers, structure and style, stones and stonecutters, sculpture and architecture, temples and ceremonies, buildings and institutions, steps and portals, façades and palaces, capitals and castles, squares and fountains, embankments and promenades, streets and street life. Cities by the sea have always had strong laws and strongholds, charters and seals, banners and shields. Cities with ports differ from city-ports, the former building their piers out of necessity, the latter growing up around them by the nature of

Library and light-house in ancient Alexandria. Sebastian Münster, Cosmographia Universale. *Basel, 1559.*

things. In the former they are a means and an afterthought; in the latter, starting point and goal. Some remain mere anchorages, while others turn into stages and worlds of their own. The latter accommodate all things streaming to them from all places, by land and by sea. They are the free ports (all true ports wish to be free), and their wise inhabitants build lazarets and establish quarantines. The Mediterranean gave birth to the first asylums for spirits adrift, torn from their moorings.

The nature of a port is determined by whether it is formed by a river, chosen by the land or hinterland, or willed by the sea itself. The virtue of a port depends on the way the sea is present in it and on the population with access to it. The Atlantic and the Pacific are seas of distance, the Mediterranean a sea of propinquity, the Adriatic a sea of intimacy. Free ports give the greatest sense of the sea's presence: they are not exclusively involved in business, at least not on a grand scale. (Some ports on the Ionian islands long dealt primarily in shells and corals for necklaces.) The belief that sunken cities retain their ports has long been prevalent on the Mediterranean.

ALL PIERS DEFEND THEIR PORTS against the sea (and are thus sometimes called breakwaters), but there are as many types of piers as their are ports. Some grow out of the shore or lean back on it; others are mere piles of stones hauled in from the back of beyond and hurled into the water. The former are good for strolling and idling, the latter only for unloading goods and doing business. The former deserve the name of pier; the latter, especially in large harbors, are mere docks, and as such are avoided by seagulls and most kinds of fish. Piers on which long years of service have left their mark cannot be distinguished from the surrounding rocks. When a pier develops cracks or begins to sag, further consequences are in the offing. Some piers are like elongated ships: they await their ships so patiently that in the end they come to resemble them. Piers encourage old salts to recount their youths with no regrets. On the Mediterranean the flesh ages faster than the spirit.

Thanks to piers there is more to a port than landing, loading, and unloading, more than equipment and services. But the bollards (also called dolphins or mooring posts) testify to the daily grind of arrivals and departures, tyings and untyings, and if there is no boat tied to them, they are surely awaiting one. The age of a pier can be gauged from the

state of its bollards, how much is left of them; and because the word *bollard* can also refer to the mooring post on board ship, the term itself ties vessel to pier. The city returns a bit of what the port has given it, making it richer than it would be on its own. But a port of call can become a port of oblivion. In ports of oblivion women have a particularly high value, and sailors live lives of their own. Ports of oblivion exist outside the Mediterranean as well and do not therefore constitute a distinguishing feature. But while remorse here is as insincere as elsewhere, repentance is perhaps more stringent. Such at least is the case in the Christian parts of the Mediterranean.

Ports and piers determine the ways in which ships approach and berth by offering various aids and contrivances: buoys, winches, cordage, mats, moorings, knots (in styles differing from sea to sea), pilots and harbormasters, charts and portolanos, banners and signals for deck-to-deck, skipper-to-skipper communication. They also tell us about the crews: how they are chosen, what holds them together, how they speak on the high seas and on land. Few people know how much pressure mooring posts can support or how much an anchor weighs. I shall withstand the temptation to speak of smuggling, which can be as enigmatic as the sea itself and is perhaps the most mysterious link between sea and land. Harbor officials have long since given up on it, smugglers being amphibious, equally dexterous on land and sea. Nor shall I speak of theft, which in some cities—and above all in ports— has progressed beyond a skill. Theft is a Mediterranean art form.

Harbormasters regulate relations between port and crew, service and navigation, work and adventure. In ports where the sea is calm and the land amenable, their role and influence are considerable, extending even to architectural configurations. Students of architecture have neglected the stylistic imprint left on ports by harbormasters. Harbormasters are not mere administrators: their sympathies are not with the powers that be or are so only occasionally. They tend to be sticklers for form, though (like so many Mediterraneans) they are not distinguished by their meticulousness. When they are inattentive or indecorous, state-navy and regime-sea relations are upset. Harbormasters are a breed unto themselves, the Mediterranean breed being more eccentric than most.

TALK ABOUT MEDITERRANEANS can be serious or ironic: how they became city dwellers, fishermen, and navigators or how they remained peasants, shepherds, and landlubbers. Mediterraneans feel closer to their cities than to their states or nations; indeed, cities are their states and nations and more. City dwellers—nobles and commoners alike— aspire to a patrician rather than republican order; they communicate more with one another than with the provincials, whom they despise and mock. Mediterraneans assign newcomers the most menial chores in the city, the coarsest in the port.

Coastal dwellers differ in how they relate to the sea: some build their houses along it, others withdraw lest they lose the feel of terra firma beneath their feet; the former gaze upon it, the latter turn their backs. Old salts and johnnies-come-lately speak differently of the sea; those who know it best feel no need to speak of it at all. Some bathe in it; others do not. Some take their hats off to it; others keep them on. The Mediterranean itself salutes its skippers.

ISLANDS ARE SPECIAL PLACES. They may be classified according to such criteria as where they lie in relation to the coast, what type of channel separates them from the mainland, and whether or not one can row or swim across the channel (a measure of the extent to which the sea unites or divides). Islands also differ in the images they project: some seem to be floating or floundering, others look anchored, stonelike, and, though torn-off and incomplete remains of the land mass, quite satisfied with themselves, having escaped in the nick of time and declared their independence; some are in disarray and dissolution, others neat and trim, on the point of establishing an ideal order. Islands take on human characteristics and moods: they too can be solitary, quiet, parched, naked, barren, inscrutable, cursed, and even happy or blissful. They are defined not only by their similarities and differences but also by the company they keep. The ancient classification of the Sporades and the Cyclades in the Aegean Sea offers us two patterns (which certain cenobites appear to have used as models). Similar configurations include the Balearic Islands and the Pityusae or Pine Islands, the Adriatic Islands and the Kornati, the small Elafit Archipelago off Dubrovnik, the Hyères Islands between the Gulf of Lions and the Riviera, the Kerkenna Islands just east of Tunisia, the Lipari Islands in the Tyrrhenian Sea and the Tuscan Archipelago between the Tyrrhenian and Ligurian Seas. Certain long-settled islands—Malta with its knights, Sicily with its royal past, and possibly Corsica—resist generalization. Reefs are notoriously neglected (more than any other form of karst), especially those lacking in hollows and potable water; they are often excluded from recognized archipelagos, thus losing their place in the coastal protocol and forever remaining renegades, anchorites. The crags topping many islands have given rise to all sorts of horror and ghost stories. Mediterraneans lend them more credence than do others.

Islands can be abodes of calm and serenity, contrition and expiation (which is why they accommodate so many monasteries, prisons, and asylums). Yet even the most fortunate of islands (Atlantis, for instance) have disappeared in the sea—ports, cities, and all. One trait most islands share is the anticipation of things to come: even the smallest looks forward to the next boat, to the news it will bring, to some scene, some event. Islanders have more time for waiting than others; waiting marks their time. Certain islands were once used for burying the dead because they were believed to exist outside of time. On the other hand, a glorious past and the vanity ensuing therefrom have led larger and stronger islands to compete with the mainland and measure up to the demands of the present. It is difficult to establish the effects of such phenomena on the Mediterranean.

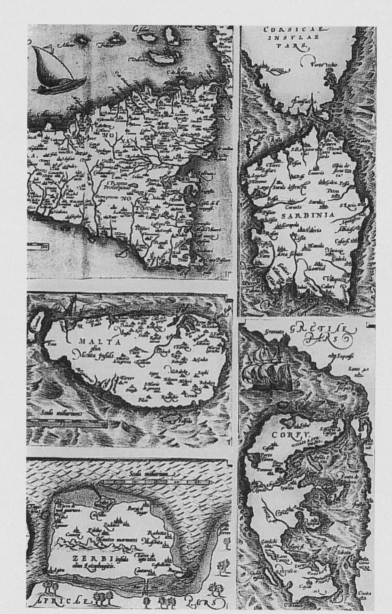

Mediterranean islands. Abraham Ortelius, Theatrum Orbis Terrarum. Antwerp, 1579.

Island dwellers are less frivolous than coast dwellers, perhaps because they are isolated by the sea and therefore left to their own devices: they do not feel they are on terra firma until they have crossed the channel. The way they speak differs from the way their neighbors on shore speak to a greater extent than one might expect from the distance involved; moreover, the linguistic gap has an effect on their relations with the outside world and can make them seem outlandish. Some islands are multilingual, depending on where their inhabitants come from, how long they have stayed, and how much the islands have dispersed or confined them. Be that as it may, islanders tend to accept newcomers more readily than others, perhaps because when they crossed the channel they too were newcomers and because they retain memories of their former selves. Newcomers dream only in the early days; the time for dreams soon passes. They come to view the future as a repetition of the past, the best part of the past. The same may hold for dwellers of coastal areas, though to a lesser extent. Such would seem to be the case through most of the Mediterranean.

The islanders' relation to the sea changes as they move inland. Coastal dwellers feel the change as well. I myself have experienced it when traveling from the sea to Florence, Verona, or Brescia, from Athens to the interior, from Málaga to Madrid, when climbing the Dinaric Alps from the Dalmatian coast or hiking from the sandy shores of Africa to the Sahara, from the ports of Palestine to the Dead Sea. It does not diminish one's predilection for the sea or passion for the Mediterranean.

Island ports lack the aspirations of ports along the mainland's edge, the former serving mostly sailors, the latter serving mostly ships. Island ports and cities are born of different circumstances, though they often imitate their coastal counterparts. They are built by the stronger party, and the sea must yield. They too have their hinterland, but as it is closer, cities and villages share more, are more "insular." Besides, certain coastal cites were themselves originally islands, the channel having been bridged over or filled in, the isthmus broadened or discreetly hidden. The port of ancient Athens began as an island—Piraeus. Practical considerations are not necessarily of the essence: some islands are uncomfortable with their fate, others proud of it. Discomfort and pride are traits often associated with the character of island dwellers as well. They even enable us to trace certain genealogies, both along the coast and farther inland. Islanders the world over have strong characters. Island characteristics are particularly marked on the Mediterranean.

Wherever there are many islands, the land is difficult to rule, a fact islanders do not seem to appreciate or at least do not always turn to their advantage. Islands are less useful for conquering the sea than is generally presumed. There are islandlike areas on the mainland, some with sunken, invisible ports. It is hard to say whether they were true islands back when land and sea were divided up or whether they have yet to become them. In any case, land masses shift on a daily basis, and we can sense the map of tomorrow, for better or for worse. Increased attention is currently being paid to issues of insularity—material and spiritual, genuine and bogus. We must leave such matters to the experts, yet grant them the recognition they deserve. The Mediterranean will take only what suits it.

It is generally assumed that peninsulas are in a better position than islands, that they have an easier time of it. Such generalizations are misleading. Different peninsulas have different ways of being in the sea: of some it laps no more than half the shores, while of others it laps them all; some belong to terra firma, others to larger peninsulas. The three major Mediterranean peninsulas—the Pyrenean, the Apennine, and the Balkan—are not in fact peninsulas in their entirety, yet it is hard to determine where they cease to be them. And why is Tunisia never called a peninsula? The question is perfectly relevant. Peninsulas constituting parts of other peninsulas come close to being islands, yet the same criteria cannot be applied to all of them. There are many deciding factors, the principal one being land rather than sea. In Italy Gargano and Salentina are peninsulas by nature, while Calabria is an island without a sea. The Peloponnese retained all its peninsular qualities even after the Isthmus of Corinth was crossed by a canal, though it acquired a few insular ones into the bargain. Mount Athos, the Holy Mountain (Hagion Oros) of the Greek Church, is an island of the spirit on the Acte Peninsula of Chalcidice in the Aegean. Istria on the Adriatic is island, peninsula, and hinterland all in one. Peljesač (Sabbioncello in Italian) was forced to become an island by girding itself with walls and calling itself Ston. All Mediterranean coasts have similar dualities about them, dualities as moral as they are geographic. Leaving a peninsula is not always easier than leaving an island, because while the desire to leave is more readily realizable, it is also less final. The differences between islands and peninsulas must not be overlooked: the two are everywhere throughout the Mediterranean.

BUOYS BELONG TO BOTH PORT and pier, though at times more to one than the other. Just whose jurisdiction they come under is not clear: harbormasters are not particularly concerned about them. Yet buoys take an active part in the activities of the pier. They can be spotted by the points they mark, the chains that keep them there, the iron rings that hold the rope, the algae and shells that bedeck them, and their bearings inside and outside the port. At one time they were made of wood—ash, oak, or, occasionally, cypress—and smelled accordingly. Later iron took over, though in the sea iron rusts faster than wood rots. Iron buoys, usually painted dark red to protect them and make them more visible, boom like drums when hit by waves, rope, or their own rings, but few people have heard their modest music or even know of its existence. Buoys, like islands, may come undone and drift hither and yon through the Mediterranean or be cast by breakers onto the rocks and smashed to smithereens.

The rope, which is made of hemp (or, in some places, palm or aloe fibers), ingests the odors of sea and port, marine plants and tar, giving the harbor a redolence all its own. Though not particularly sharp or stiff, it leaves grooves and calluses on the bollards and buoy rings. In some places it rubs smooth; in others it twists into tassels the color of gray hair. It has been known to unravel by itself. Be that as it may, it serves long and well, especially in the poorer parts of the Mediterranean.

There is nothing so pounded and trampled in a port as mats, those bundles of hemp and tow protecting the ship's flank from the pier and the pier from the ship's flank and letting out a screech every time the two come in contact. Known to the earliest of seafarers (wooden ships were especially sensitive), they were originally made of straw and are thus called *paillets, paglietti, pajeti,* and the like in various Mediterranean languages (cf. Latin *palea* [chaff]). Mats have their day in port: they come into play only when a ship is putting ashore. When a ship is at sea or at anchor, they are hung out to dry. It is easy to forget that they keep the Mediterranean's ships beautiful and extend the longevity of its piers.

SEAS ALSO HARBOR REMAINS of former seas in their immediate and not so immediate vicinity. (The Mediterranean, for example, has the Pannonian Sea, though there must have been more in Europe's interior.)

The soil in such regions has certain properties—layers of salt, sand, and fossils or the presence of vegetation of a type not normally found at the given longitude and latitude—that bewilder geographers and give rise to all sorts of conjectures. As far as we can tell, former seas had their own islands and possibly ports as well. Some Central European cities have been called Mediterranean in character: Salzburg during its festival, for one, or old Prague—which brings us back to the question of the Mediterranean's borders.

In cities and ports graveyards resemble islands and peninsulas, though graveyards, too, differ more from one another than meets the eye. Some lean more towards the sea, others are more attached to land: sometimes people are inclined to believe that the sea purifies and prevents putrefaction, sometimes that the earth is lighter and more accommodating than the briny deep. The positioning of lesser sanctuaries (basilicas and chapels but also small synagogues and mosques) is somewhat similar. Moreover, cypresses and pines are often planted near places of worship and graveyards either one by one, in isolation, or mixed, in groups. None of this would seem to be arbitrary, though patterns are difficult to establish. Cypresses bring peace and a certain melancholy to their environment, for example, though they are planted in places other than graveyards and churches: they also rise up over the Mediterranean's schools and sacrificial altars.

Talk of graveyards leads naturally to talk of dead languages. The Mediterranean has many, perhaps as many as it has islands. Why some were lost on land and others drowned at sea is a question that cannot be answered exclusively by linguists. Some words belonging to dead languages have survived in other, living languages, yet they are recalcitrant, resistant to penetration, because they lack memory and a sense of belonging. Although collectors of these antiques advance interesting interpretations, most are problematic in that they confuse words with things, trusting that each word vouches for the object or concept it designates and can therefore replace it. However, the collectors do deserve credit for creating archives that have become all but sanctuaries. Nearly every Mediterranean city has at least one such archive, public or private, open or secret, just as each has at least one cemetery. The Mediterranean is a vast archive, an immense grave.

WAVES PLAY AN IMPORTANT ROLE in the dramaturgy of the sea, its scenes and peripeteias. They have many names, varying not only from one gulf to the next but also according to whether we view them from ship or shore and what we expect of them. They combine with adjectives (or, less commonly, other nouns), which are for the most part descriptive: regular or irregular, longitudinal or transversal; they are connected with high tide or low tide, with the surface or the depths; they are solitary, frequent, fortuitous, rolling, choppy, cyclical (experts claim that the cycles of some waves can be measured in terms of geologic periods). What matters most from the deck is their size; their strength; whether they hit flank, bow, or stern; and whether masting, sails, and, especially, sailors can handle them. The distinctions that interest us here are of a different sort: how they break on the shore, how long they last after they have broken in the eyes of their beholders, whether they are the same when they return, how the sound they make differs when they hit sand and when they hit rock, how they sleep when they are tired and barely perceptible. All that remains of the huge waves tapering and dying on the shore is a gurgle or a lap, a splash on the pier or the hull of the boat, buoy, or reef, though this sound can last a long time and is most likely to be audible at night. Even though everyone recognizes it—this gurgle or lap or whatever one calls it—there is disagreement over whether it is a noise or a voice. Stories of waves drowsing in the sea awaiting their day in the sun are quite prevalent among the superstitious, whose numbers along the coasts are legion. Romantic descriptions of waves supply no new data. To speak of waves as a language and shells as its lexicon is to beg the question, though certain recurrent signs and structures cannot be overlooked. The true connections, which have best been sensed by poets (though no more than one or two per generation), bring to mind the ancient Mediterranean alphabets that died out together with their languages.

The Mediterraneans talk less of waves than of winds, perhaps because the latter have a greater effect on their moods and in the end on their discourse. The coasts lend one another their names for winds, readily modifying them or their direction and causing thereby—intentionally at times—certain misapprehensions. On the basis of these names we can trace which regions ruled the sea and its ships. The coasts also alter the forms and meanings of names—out of ignorance at times. On the Adriatic, for instance, we have the *jugo* (south wind, also called the *sirocco* or *scirocco*) and *bura* (north or boreal wind), the *maestral* (which is usually mild and blows from the sea, while on other coasts—under basically the same name, *mistral*—it comes from the land and, as the Provençal saying goes, "tweaks the donkey's tail"), the *levanat* (east wind), and *pulenat* (west wind)—from the Italian *levante* (east) and *ponente* (west)—and a host of others, many of which are likewise adaptations of Italian roots: *garbin* for *garbino, lebić* for *libeccio, tramuntana* for *tramontana,* and *buraca* for *burazza* (which is not to be confused with *burasca,* cf. Italian *burrasca,* French *bourrasque* [squall]), though local and regional names are also common. The classifications used by meteorologists are oversimplified, but practical. Poets, on the other hand, ascribe the various winds masculine and feminine attributes—erotic, divine, demonic, diabolical, life-giving and death-dealing, cajoling and meek—making the head ache and life beautiful, offering inspiration and parodying our aspirations and illusions (unfortunately, the lower genres have horned their way in). Time was when every epic had its tempest: winds were the divinities of the Mediterranean.

Winds' influence on waves has been somewhat overrated, as is plain when a so-called dead sea is set in motion by no visible impetus or cause, of its own volition, the riffles advancing from nowhere and receding thence, with no rhyme or reason. Some winds change as they climb from sea to land or plunge from land to sea; others remain as they were. Instances in which the combination of wind, wave, and rain affects the sea's color are not uncommon. The jugo, for example, makes the sea greenish and slightly misty, while the bura makes it bluer and more transparent. Strong winds from the north reveal the depths and alter our way of thinking about them: they make the sea an entity sui generis, brooking no comparison, bare. Painters have painted it in this state—old Italian and Spanish masters, and the Arabs, who used the colors of the sea on the walls of their mosques to tone down the rigor of Qur'anic adages in stylized script. Similar hues occur in the frescoes and icons of Greek, Romanian, and Slav painters who lived a hermit's existence along the shores of the Mediterranean.

On days when the sea is particularly transparent and its depths most visible, the outlines of uncommon objects, constructions, and wrecks come into sight, and we can almost believe we have discovered a sunken galley with a precious cargo, a palace, the remains of an ancient city. The wavering forms evoke the relics of history, the ruins of destiny. The Mediterranean is a passionate collector.

OCEAN CURRENTS are like vast rivers: they are determined and taciturn, indeterminable and uncontrollable. Unlike rivers, however, they are ignorant of their source or mouth; they know only that they are both somewhere at sea. Nor do they know their exact dimensions or how their waters keep separate from others, their only bed being, once more, the sea itself. Some of them can be observed from the cliffs along the coast, and sailors believe they see them from the highest mast on board. When the sea is at its calmest, they tint the surface in various hues or form huge shoreless gulfs, now lighter, now darker than the surrounding water. The best judges of the nature of a current—how long it is and how long it lasts, what it contains or takes with it—are probably seagulls. Helmsmen must take into account how much resistance is offered by one current, how much support by another. It is impossible to measure how far they extend. Some consider them migrations analogous to migrations of fish, birds, or peoples. Mediterranean currents are not particularly strong, but they are deep. They rarely form whirlpools in their wake, but they do leave their traces, the best known being in the Strait of Messina, between Italy and Sicily; along the Dardanelles, between Europe and Turkey in Asia; and in Evripos, next to Marathon and not far from Thermopylae. In our sea the tides do not do much to stimulate the currents, neither high nor low tide altering the scene of the coast or port or determining the rhythm of day and night; they are not major events. Still, Mediterraneans have spoken much and said little about the relationship between currents and destiny.

WHEN PEOPLE SPEAK OF FOAM—the subject usually comes up in connection with winds and waves—they do so either in general terms or with great bombast. Images such as airiness, futility, infidelity, fury, and even fertility remain images: they do not get at what foam actually is— whether it has volume, whether it is salty, what it is made of, why the sea hurls it onto the land with such determination and in such quantity. But is quantity the word to use in connection with foam? Then there is the distinction between sea foam and coast foam: hard as it is to differentiate them, they are sometimes mutually exclusive. Both are recognized; each has its place. Unlike the Mediterranean, the Dead Sea has no foam.

THE NATURE OF CLOUDS, which likewise comes up in connection with winds and waves, has been needlessly relegated to meteorologists. Meteorologists merely classify and name clouds according to form, appearance, and effect. Clouds figure in literature as well, especially poetry: they float through the sky like cutters on the sea; they rise up o'er the sea (or they press upon the sea) like mantles (or like curtains), now light and fluffy, bringing joy and even bliss, now dark and massive, portending doom. At dawn they cannot be distinguished from the dawn itself; at twilight they are part of the twilight; at night they are night. They seem one thing on board and another on shore: their shape, their number, the direction they take, the phenomena that accompany and follow them. The adept know how to predict the weather from them. Clouds are the subject of confabulation and conflict throughout the Mediterranean.

The weather is also intimately connected with the water itself, and that on both the coast and high seas. The states of the sea cannot be numbered, to say nothing of put into words: days one like the other when the sea does not change, days differing from one another only because the sea has changed, periods of dry or sultry air, of winds and rains, the humidity that comes from the sea, mood swings after a sirocco or a tramontana, periods of paralysis or torpor on stuffy summer afternoons, lively summer evenings along ports and piers (people describing them tend to get carried away). Darkness on the sea changes with time, from first darkness, which descends with more or less alacrity, to pitch darkness, which is darker on sea than on land, dense and humid (particularly when mixed with a sirocco or a bank of clouds), when the depths of the sea join with the depths of night, each heightening the other, when an oar striking the hull of a ship resounds with great intensity, when there is no way to tell what part of the bow is slicing the water, what is standing still and what is moving. (I leave the numerous other effects to my literary colleagues.) The beginnings and ends of darkness are the fisherman's most important calendar. Representations of eclipses recalling the creation or end of the world are legion. Epic poets have compared a certain Mediterranean darkness to the color of wine.

Dawns and twilights have been likened to everything possible, so I shall pass over them in silence. Besides, fishermen and sailors know much more about them: for example, that at daybreak sea and sky are so similar in color as to be scarcely distinguishable. If descriptions of sunsets, of the sun sinking into the sea, resemble one another more than they should, the fault lies rather with the coast than with the Mediterranean itself.

Rain does not fall equally on all the coasts: there is more in the north than in the south; it is more abundant in the west than in the east. Nor does it arrive at the same time or within the same intervals: at Gibraltar it starts falling nearly half a season earlier than at the Dead Sea. Rain did not generally fall on the Holy Land in summer. "Early" rains— manna to the arid soil and parched river beds—came in autumn, but it was not until winter and the winter rains that the basins filled. The ancient Jews thus regarded spring rains as "late." It is hard to overestimate the importance of rain for desert dwellers. Rain falling at the opportune moment is interpreted all along the Canaan coast as a sign of God's mercy; rain falling in a storm or with hail is viewed as a scourge. But rain is the subject of more than prayer; it is the subject of *exercices de style* that lend themselves to parody: droplets running down a face like tears of joy, moisture refreshing the earth, restoring sap and savor to stalk and vine, an inebriating torrent, and so on. Rain is a genuine event in time of drought, particularly on islands, where there are precious few events to begin with. For many Mediterraneans rainwater in cisterns and wells has the taste of unslaked thirsts and a deprived childhood.

Greece and Asia Minor. Abraham Ortelius, Theatrum Orbis Terrarum. Antwerp, 1579.

SOME DAY SOMEONE may classify coasts according to the ways in which they come together with the sea, that is, the places where their relations are stable and complete and where they are fragmentary and haphazard, the stretches where sea and land are at one with each other and where they bristle and always shall, the points where entry and access are possible and where no approach is tolerated. But how can anyone take so many forms and structures, so many groupings of land and vegetation, stone and light, so much resistance and concession and compress it into a system? The rocky headlands and reefy strands, pebbles and sand, straits more or less dangerous, inlets, creeks, and coves, caves and grottoes, fords and capes, cliffs, bluffs, and crags, precipices and promontories—we cannot dismiss them with concrete appellations; they need conceptual amplification, clarification. We need to explain, for example, why in one place masses of stone have remained whole and intact, while in another, though compositionally all but identical, they have fallen to pieces or been turned into detritus; how in one place they are smooth, flat slabs, while in another they have become boulders and crags, rough or blade-sharp. Epochs of prehistory, shifts and fissures in the earth, major rifts, *rapprochements,* and related phenomena, tectonic and architectonic, have left their imprints in the layers of rock. Who can tell how much Mediterranean architecture— the Ionic or the Doric, say, or their predecessors—owes to them? Certain sites—where the rock has completely crumbled or is decaying, where it has been stripped of all vegetation and crust, where its nerves and veins burst out on the surface—are literally dramatic. It is enough to make one a geologist, a calling particularly noble on the Mediterranean.

Equally dramatic are the striking red, mineral-rich rocks between Antibes and Agay in Provence, formations that owe their origins to the massif of the Estérel on the sea and its remains in the sea, and that neither sun nor sand has managed to cleave or corrode. The entire region takes on their color, especially in autumn. There, on a reddish brown reef not far from the mouth of the Siagné called the Cap de Roux, stands a wooden lighthouse guiding fishermen back to land when the mistral starts blustering. There are rocks of this type along the coasts of Catalonia, Anatolia, and Syria and on Sicily, Patmos, and Malta. Nor should we forget the massive *faraglioni,* as the Italians call them—isolated crags jutting white and gray out of the sea off Capri. Along the southern coast of the Mediterranean, where the desert has invaded the land or sunk into the sea, rocks of curious composition and said to be meteorites emerge unexpectedly from the sand.

Many people have written in memoirs of picking up pebbles, weighing them in their hand, and using them to draw pictures in the sand. Some see this as mere child's play, but adults do it as often as children. There must be more to it. Ancient sages and poets have celebrated the role of the Mediterranean in grinding pebbles smooth and sand fine.

MUCH TALK, EFFUSIVE AND CAPTIOUS, has been given over to gulfs large and small, more or less open, symmetrical and ageometrical, hospitable and antisocial. There is no need to describe them. They exhibit a kind of vanity, connected perhaps to island vanity: gulfs often try to pass themselves off as seas. Moreover, they do acquire sea status—and not only in local atlases. Witness the Ligurian Sea, the Tyrrhenian Sea, the Alboranian Sea, the Sea of Marmara, and the Sea of Azov. The Adriatic was once called the Golfo di Venezia. On the opposite shore, however, the Gulf of Sidra (the Syrtis Major of ancient times) has remained a gulf. There are other such cases, the deciding factor being which side happens to have the upper hand, not the Mediterranean as a whole.

Sea caves (caverns or grottoes, the exploration of which is carried out by a special subfield of geology) are said to differ from caves inland. All I know about them is that some are easily accessible, others offer a certain resistance; some present few risks, others are chambers of horrors. Some one can enter only by diving, or bending one's head (if one is in a boat), or waiting for the sea to go down. Each has—or appears to have—a hue of its own: azure, deep blue, and green. Light in caves, when there is any, seems to be flowing. Although the general assumption is that caves are free from both waves and wind, such is not always the case. Some have shadows, others have none. I have never seen coral in a cave. Each has its own echo. Fish look different in caves. Mediterraneans tell all sorts of stories and dream all sorts of dreams about them.

I have toured, one might even say reconnoitered, the caves on the island of Crete, which would clearly not be what it is without them. I recall their walls, their shadows, their silences; I recall names like Ida, Melidoni, Sendoni, Diktaion, Eleithia, Agia. They are more enigmatic than their counterparts on other Mediterranean islands. The time it took to form them! Some must be as old as the Mediterranean itself.

Wells share a number of features with caves and have a number of designations, depending on how deep they are and what kind of water they provide: spring water, rain water, or water on the brackish side. Certain cities and coastal areas are known for their wells and wellheads; some are even named after them. Wells that give spring water have been acclaimed from time immemorial but have served varying functions over time: they are places of refuge, retreat, and destination, places of good news yet also of torture (what is more agonizing than thirst hard by a well?). The baptismal font is a type of well, bringing freshness into the basilica during times of heat and religious fervor. There is a folk belief that the inside of a well contains or conserves the whole truth, a belief sometimes shared by the educated. In poorer regions—parts of the Adriatic and several Greek islands, for example—a well with a chiseled or otherwise decorated stone opening may be called a fountain. Similarly, modest mooring posts are called columns in a part of Dalmatia. Such cases derive more from humility than hyperbole and are thus deserving of mention: a poetics of humility has yet to be formulated on the Mediterranean.

LIGHTHOUSES ARE ANOTHER important Mediterranean institution, and one too important to be left entirely to the coastal or port authorities. They are usually classified by age, size, type of construction, and location, that is, the points or islands on which they stand. Also significant are such factors as the manner in which the sea surrounds them, their distance from one another, their relationship to the nearest ports and whether they themselves intend to become the sites of ports, and, finally, whose way they are lighting (faintly, fitfully, mournfully, as the sentimental clichés would have it) and on what course. Lighthouses occupy a place of honor on large-scale nautical maps; nor are they ignored in the memoirs of the shipwrecked. Mediterraneans are not known for their gratitude (though when they do thank, they make many promises and believe in them), and lighthouse crews, whose members are more monks than sailors, expect none, yet pictures dedicated to them may be found in the houses of people who have lost their dear ones at sea: the *ex voto* stems from popular pagan beliefs and results in untold shrines along the Mediterranean.

Lighthouses share certain features—not to be pooh-poohed by en-

Jerusalem. Georg Braun and Hans Hogenberg, Civitates Orbis Terrarum. *Antwerp, between 1572 and 1618.*

lightened laymen—with monasteries. A number of monasteries and convents overlook the sea; there are also many on islands. In Greece they are called meteors; in Antioch and Cappadocia they have other names. From Libya to Syria, in Upper and Lower Egypt, and in Palestine, the most important ones (I have visited a few and shall have something to say about them later) were once situated near the sea at the edge of the desert, where prayer and a view of the open sea come together. Few can speak impartially about the monastic orders and religious communities and the differences between them along the eastern and western shores of the Mediterranean. Monasteries may be classified on the basis of the number of valuable objects, holy and secular, in their treasuries, halls, cloisters, and chapter houses: early editions, evangelistaries, manuscripts, transcriptions, chronicles, medical treatises, illuminations, embroidered vestments (the embroidery being more important than the vestment), objects in gold and silver (the artistry being more valuable than the raw material), chalices, icons, and incomparably sublime liturgical chants. These treasures more than anything distinguish Mediterranean monasteries from others. In some regions (on the east coast of the Adriatic, which I know best; on the Aegean, which I have tried to know better; and in two or three spots in Spain and Italy) monasteries have a limpid, almost pellucid look about them, though they are closer to abomination and sin than most. The Mediterranean is constant temptation, an earthly sea.

FISHERMEN OFTEN have faces furrowed by the wind, sun, rains, and waves, even as they are depicted on picture postcards and in mass-market paintings. What is rarely shown are hands hardened by salt and nets, ropes and oars. True fishermen curse, but do not steal; they lose their tempers and quarrel (over bad weather, a bad catch, or bad workers), but do not fight like, say, dockers or common peasants. When arguments break out among them (as they do over to or from which side to cast the net or when and how to haul it in), they never reach the intensity of arguments over who owns what land. The sea is easier to divide than the land because it is harder to own. And there is no catch that does not recall an earlier one, one the fisherman himself has experienced or heard tell of. Fishing is nothing new on the Mediterranean.

No MEDITERRANEAN INVENTORY would be complete without seagulls and estuaries. Of all the birds accompanying ships on their rounds, seagulls are by far the most mentioned. But seagulls are less alike than they appear at first glance: the more they move inland from the mouth of a river and lose touch with the sea, the more varied they become, some trailing boats for no reason, others remaining practical and voracious; some hovering near the mast like normal birds, others staying below like fellow travelers. Some people toss them leftover food, marveling at their strong digestive systems, others admire the way they glide through the air; some people wonder where they are headed, others how they get there. Few people notice how they make contact with the water: with the tips of their wings or with their bodies, breast first. Sailors sometimes judge ports by the way the seagulls greet them. The connection between crew and gull is one of the oldest secrets (if it is my place to bring up secrets) of the sea and in particular of the Mediterranean, where it is the oldest bar none.

OF THE SEA AND ALL that goes with it—its various states; the reflections of sky, sun, and clouds in it; the colors its bed takes on and the stones, sand, and algae along that bed; the dark and translucent patches on the coast; then farther out, the transitions between morning sea and evening sea, day sea and night sea, today's sea and the sea eternal (to which any number of terms might be added)—all Mediterraneans have something to say, something they deem of the utmost importance.

It has often been claimed that winds, waves, and currents (about which I have not said enough, though they are present by implication throughout) and their interactions, permanent and contingent, affect the behavior of both individuals and communities. Yet in many instances they do not. They do not help to explain, for instance, why Mediterranean lands, which boast of giving birth to democracy, so often feel the need (or the illusion of the need) for strong, autocratic rule. As for the hypothesis that Mediterranean navigators transported the dialectic of laxity and force, anarchy and tyranny to Latin America, where they expanded to fill the dimensions and nature of the continent, no one has been able to prove it.

Differences between the coasts are also hard to explain. The Apen-

nine side of the Adriatic, for instance, gradually rises, while the Balkan side gradually falls; the former was laid bare by winds coming from the northeast across the open sea (which popular belief regards as a kind of revenge on the part of the insulted and the injured), while the latter took refuge inland and begat a number of inlets and islands. Dalmatia was thickly wooded at one time, but the Venetians' practical bent took care of that, and the Slavs' impractical bent has kept the trees from growing back. The conflict between practicality and impracticality runs the length and breadth of the Mediterranean.

THE LAND TOO DIFFERS from one region to another. Nor does it look the same when we view it from the sea and when we view it on the shore: the reddish soil among the rocks, the gray or ashlike soil that appears to be made of rock (while at points it is more or less sand, whence the name "white earth" on some Adriatic islands), the black soil, rare and highly valued in these parts, and finally plain, ordinary brown dirt, the kind that exists all over Europe, Asia Minor, and a part of Africa. The vegetation veils or unveils, dresses or denudes the land and its character, changing backdrops from one occasion to the next,

A bird's-eye view of Venice. Matthäus Merian, Italiae Nov-Antiquae. *Frankfurt am Main, 1640.*

depending on how much the rock has disintegrated under the burning sun and how much the water and moisture coming from the sea have furthered the process. Thus even the land is the creation of the sea, the Mediterranean.

On the African side, soil surrenders to sand as it recedes from the sea. In Morocco and Algeria red soil, more or less fertile, predominates on the borders of a steppe. In Tunisia black soil shows up here and there at oases and on high land. Farther east, in Libya and a part of Egypt and Palestine, pure sand and sandy soil generally alternate, the latter being yellower than the rocky soil in the northern Mediterranean regions—unless a fata morgana is at work here. Closer to the Near East, in Lebanon and Syria, the white and yellow-gray plains shade more and more into true brown and—here and there—black soil. At least this is how they appear to someone lacking an intimate acquaintance with the regions (an acquaintance not easy to come by). The soil in southern Spain most resembles African soil, which would suggest that the continents split later there than elsewhere, though my impression may just as well derive from such historical and cultural memories as Spain's conflicts with Africa, the Carthaginian incursions, the Arab conquests, battles with the Saracens and Moors, and perhaps a literary work or two dealing with the subject and capable of creating illusions even about the soil. The Apennines and parts of the Balkans share certain geologic and geographic traits, but their histories differ significantly. The black soil in the Ukrainian plains, known as *chernozyom* in Russian, differs more from its Mediterranean counterpart than the Black Sea from our sea. It may thus be more for the land than for the water that many do not consider it part of the Mediterranean.

I HAVE LISTENED TO PEOPLE living on both the north and south coasts of the Mediterranean speak of sea smells. I have taken careful notes. One point I have heard everywhere is that sea smells differ not only from place to place—in the depths and on the surface—but also from moment to moment—at dawn and at dusk. They differ when the sea is calm and when it is agitated; when it evaporates in the heat and the wind or when it is soaked in rain and humidity; when it rolls across the pebbles or breaks on the rocks; when it is whipped by the tramontana or rocked by the sirocco. The smells of the sea (this too I have heard everywhere) combine with the smells of the pines and their resins and the smells of other trees, plants, and grasses. We associate smells with specific places along the shore: the spot where the waves have ripped the grass up from the sea bed and exposed it to the sun or where the seaweed has dried on the reefs; how the sea smells in port or along a pier, on a boat or ship, in the bailing bucket or the hold, in puddles from a wave or a storm. Many people believe that the inside of a shell or the scales of a fish preserve the smell of the depths; they say that the sea that floods a salt marsh differs in smell from the sea that chafes palms and nostrils, the sea that emanates from nets laid out to dry differs in smell from the sea that imbues the ropes tied to buoys and anchors. The sea smells different (as we learn from descriptions of meetings and farewells) when we approach it and when we move away. There are certain maritime conditions that militate against the generalization of smells. I shall report only one: the moment the desert wind begins to blow, the coast loses its marine fragrance. The Atlantic Ocean (I have checked it in Morocco, near Tangier) stands up to the desert wind with its waves; the Mediterranean, one might say, gives in.

THE MOST DIFFICULT SUBJECT to broach in connection with the Mediterranean is the subject of the Mediterraneans. They speak of themselves one way in private and another way in public. It is even difficult to list the objects characterizing their everyday existence, the foods they consume, the tools they use, and the special terms they have developed for them to list them for one region, to say nothing of the entire area: sea salt and olive oil, dried figs and salted herring, wine red and white, full strength and watered down, vinegar, the demijohn that replaced the amphora, the vat, the stone bowl, the wine barrel and wine cellar, caskets and trunks, ropes, fish traps such as pots and boulters, the caïque, the trabaccolo and the lampboat, the lateen and other skiffs and schooners, the goat, the ass, the mule, and the rat (the ship's rat and the household variety), brine and marinade, coconut and aubergine, grills and frying pans of various proportions, pasta, salsa, brodetto and bouillabaisse, fritella and frittata, the substantial mid-morning marenda, macaroni and macaronic literature, chitchat and confabulation, fishing and the lore of fishfolk, the fishmonger's, the bottega and the osteria, rolling shutters on shop windows, lampions and lanterns strung along embankments, terraces in life and terraces in literature, loggias and pergolas in provincial paintings, portals and porticoes, balconies and gal-

leries, cocklofts and attics perched on houses or praised in ribald dit-
ties, piazzas and pizzas (one never knows what is going to pop into
one's head when one starts making lists), flower-, herb-, and kitchen-
gardens, guitars and serenades, lethargy and dolce far niente, deck-
chairs and terry towels, siesta and festa, denunciation and imprecation,
bocce and boules, tresette and briscola, various maestri and middlemen,
ciceroni and charlatans, caulkers and balkers, grandees and magnificoes
from everywhere and nowhere, lechers from Split, eccentrics from
Dubrovnik, pilgrims and commodores, hooligans, rapscallions, and gut-
tersnipes, thespians and pimps, brides of Christ and ladies of the night,
apostles and con men, in other words, *tutti quanti.*

Such lists can be compiled in endless, more or less arbitrary varieties
for each particular coast and language. Certain things can be said only
in the local dialect, which may differ substantially from dialects spoken inland; indeed, even a ship's crew that has sailed together over long
periods of time develops a dialect of its own. My list includes a number of Dalmatian words with their characteristic admixture of Italian—
more specifically, Venetian—borrowings. There are similar combina-
tions of Provençal and French, of Catalan and Castilian (and, within
Catalan, of the language used on the Balearic Islands and the language
of Barcelona or Valencia), of the Arabic used by fishermen and the
Arabic of the *jabal,* of colloquial Arabic and the official language of
Malta, and, lastly—in Greece, where it is most dramatic and where it
probably all began—of what is called *katharevusa* and the demotic or
popular language of the port. As a result, the coast has developed a
diglossia composed of the local (Mediterranean) and national (which
is more or less equivalent to mainland) variants. Each complements the
other, the standard language sometimes taking on features of the dialect and the dialect sometimes taking on features (though not necessarily the finest) of the standard language. The authors of Greek and
Roman comedy observed this Mediterranean phenomenon and made
skillful use of it in their dialogue.

*Constantinople
in an anonymous
sepia. Bibliothèque
Nationale, Paris.
Sixteenth century.*

O. *La Mesquee de Rustan bassa*

P. *Le prison*

41

Breviary

I do not know to what extent languages east of ours have borrowed terms from our languages (though I do not see how they could do otherwise); I do know that many—with much the same Mediterranean flavor as the words just enumerated—have reached my language from Turkish and, to a lesser extent, Arabic: words like *avlija* (courtyard), *česma* and *šadrvan* (fountain), *sokak* (a narrow street), *mehana* (tavern) and *mahala* (district), *sofa* and *divan* (couch), *eglen* (chat) and *eglen-beglen* (chitchat), *džezva* (uncovered metal receptacle with a long handle for making Turkish coffee) and *sofra* (round table at which one eats while sitting on mats), *istilah* (lethargy) and *rahatluk* (satisfaction), *merak* (pleasure) and *merhamet* (pity), *sevdah* (amorous passion), and *teferič* (outing). I could add many more. On the Levant end, the traits generally thought of as Mediterranean run all the way to Persia, whence many doubtless came. It is the most open space on the Mediterranean and the path along which the prophecies made their way to us, the place where the sun first rises and darkness first falls.

42

Breviary

IT IS NO EASY TASK TO FIND the words for actions simultaneously majestic and ordinary, holy and profane, actions like baking bread of various shapes, sizes, ingredients, and tastes, drying fish and meat (prosciutto in particular), building barrels and decanting wine, harvesting olives and extracting their oil according to formulas so time-honored that they may even have the blessing of an apocryphal gospel or two. The Mediterranean has its guides to fasting and humility, its handbooks of expiation and chastisement, its treatises on sins capital and venial, its recipes for simple fare and orgies, its compendia of love and lust. I will not list them here. Some are considered major works of genius, others disgracefully opportunistic. All are integral parts of Mediterranean culture.

Even if each has its place in the Mediterranean atlas, however, they cannot be measured by blanket criteria. Some questions only charlatans, eccentrics, or fools (the Mediterranean vocabulary being rich in synonyms for them all) dare to answer. I especially honor those who have devoted their lives with great passion—and, on occasion, great folly—to solving the prodigious mysteries of our sea, starting with the Phoenicians or Punics and moving on to the Etruscans, Colchidians, and Copts, Illyrians or Thracians and Albanians, the Maltese, Celts, Iberians, and Celtiberians, the Galicians and Basques, the Veneti and the Venetians, the Liburnians, the Wallachians, and others, including the South Slavs, the Croats, and Dalmatians in particular. In Alexandria I met a Catalonian, a watchmaker by trade, whose goal in life was to gather the scant data available and compile a catalogue of the devastated library, the largest in antiquity. He considered his native language doomed to extinction and hoped his efforts in another domain would help to make up for the loss. Southern eccentrics differ from their northern counterparts, and not only for reasons of climate: the Mediterranean's psychic climate is also distinctive.

Mediterraneans tend to confront the primary, basic, life-and-death questions in childhood. Their answers are sometimes childish even in old age. I have heard them, especially the self-taught among them, spin endless theories about their sea and its sources, about the birth and death of languages, about the origins of their people and how they are related to the surrounding peoples, and about their forefathers, exclusive or common: the Goths and Ostrogoths, the Veneti, the Sorabs, the Illyrians or Thracians, the Trojans, the Montenegrins, the paleo-Danubians, the proto-Iranians, et al. Some of these theses and hypotheses—and the way they are set forth or defended—are ludicrous; others give food for thought. They include the tides, the position of the moon on the mainland and on the islands, the differences between mainland and island sleepwalkers, the morning and evening star (Venus) and the north or polar star (Polaris) and their courses and influences, the signs of the zodiac and calendars of all sorts (many Mediterraneans go in for horoscopes), defunct alphabets and manuscripts using them, places where manuscripts have been found or may yet be found, former seas and their remains, the causes and effects of yellow or red rains and the winds that blow them across the sea from the African coast, the types of mist on the sea's surface at various times of the day and year, their provenance, density, and degree of transparency, carnivals and brothels and their functions in everyday life, catacombs and their role in politics, dog days and their influence on the powers that be, earthquakes and their history in the Mediterranean basin, the hair shirts worn by Greek monks and Russian penitents in Orthodox monasteries, the genres of ancient Arab music and the instruments that played them, hourglasses and degrees of patience, hidden, nameless coves and the names given them by people who use them as hideaways, country houses—*villae rusticae*—from antiquity to the Renaissance and what has remained of them, subterranean rivers running through the karst and their tribu-

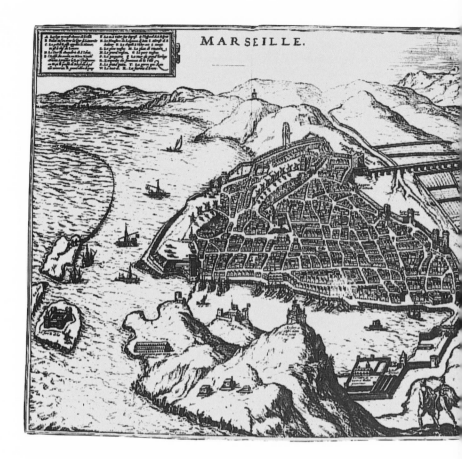

Marseille.
Georg Braun and
Hans Hogenberg,
Civitates Orbis
Terrarum. *Ant-*
werp, between
1572 and 1618.

taries, eels and the paths they take away from and back to Mediterranean waters (they apparently swim upstream all the way to the source
of a river and return, thus completing the Mediterranean circle), swal-
lows and their song or cry in Ischia, near Sorrento, on Korčula, or in
La Valletta, the flora and fauna in coastal and inland caves, snakes, snake
catchers, and snake-poison cures, fireplaces, chimneys, and various
types of smoke. I have limited myself to categories I have heard repeatedly, up and down the coasts, at hole-in-the-wall drinking estab-
lishments in ports or on the outskirts of town, in castles on the Split
riviera, in Fos-sur-Mer not far from Marseille, along Las Ramblas in
Barcelona, in the suks in Málaga, Haifa, Sfax, Smyrna, and Salonika. I

RAN CITTA DEL CAIRO
LEVANTE

Old Cairo. Fr. Vincenzo Coronelli, Memorie storico-geografiche. *Late seventeenth century, reproduced by Giuseppe Ballino, 1569.*

have transcribed only a fraction of the notebooks with "Mediterranean" on the cover.

Some of the theses and hypotheses (I clearly have trouble defining them) take the form of questions, others of answers. Why do so many of the coastal dwellers turn their backs on the sea? Is the northern border of the Mediterranean the point beyond which the Sephardi do not go, and, if so, why do they refuse to move outside the Mediterranean area? What has Islam given the Arabs, what has it taken of what they had before, and what remains of what they had then? Are the Venetians descendants of a Slav tribe from along the Vistula? Which Greek islands under Venetian rule switched to Italian as a written language, and which kept Greek? Were the prisons on Patmos and Samos worse than the prisons in the rest of the Greek archipelago? What distinguishes the ghettoes in Venice and Naples from the ghettoes in Split and Dubrovnik? Did the island of Susak (which the Italians call Sansego), with its vast layers of sand, break off from the mouth of the Po and float more than eighty nautical miles to the south? Or did some subterranean river drag the huge pyramid along and deposit it on the high seas? (Old maps show that the Istros, a branch of the Danube, was believed to have its mouth there.) Or did the winds simply waft the sandy mantle from the Sahara to the Adriatic? (Science has yet to provide an answer.) Does the name of the Srakana Islands (the Greater and the Lesser) come from the ethonym Saracene and thus imply that the Arabs came all the way up to the Istrian Peninsula and the Kvarner? How did the sheep paths through Spain—the *cañadas, cordeles, veredas*—come about? What is the connection between the sea and the memory of the sheep paths? Did spaghetti really originate in China, and, if so, what did the original look like, and who brought it to the Apennines? Where were the pirates' nests on the Adriatic? Where did they build their boats, and how did they equip them? Where at the mouth of the Neretva was the city named Drijeva? Who founded the ancient theater on the island of Hvar, and what did its early repertory consist of? What is the design behind the pines of Rome, and how do easterly and westerly winds affect their music? What did the captains from the Gulf of Kotor—from Perast in particular—give to the navy of Tsarist Russia? Did the Turkish Empire fall because it failed to turn adequately to the sea? Did the South Slavs and the Greeks save European civilization from the Turks? What quarrels divided Monaco and Nice, and what quarrels within Nice itself divided the French and Provençal factions and the Franco-Provençal and Italian factions? Why was the Île-de-France so antagonistic to the Midi? Some of these questions branch out to spawn new ones. Why do women wear such heavy clothing so tightly buttoned in so warm a climate, and why are the cuts so severe, the colors so somber? Why do women hide their hair in fine plaits and parts of their faces with kerchiefs or veils? Why in some regions do men cover not only their heads but also their foreheads and shoulders with berets, hats, or keffiyeh, while in others with the same climate they expose heads, foreheads, and shoulders blithely to the sun? Are people who believe in God and pray to Him more divided by their various faiths and prayers than people who do not believe or pray? How do Mediterraneans look at other seas and coasts? (This is a question that concerns me more than most, because I refer most often here to the Adriatic and may therefore be generalizing on the basis of what is in fact specific to one area.) Do sailors have themselves tattooed on all seas and shores? Why are mockers and jeerers in coastal towns so merciless? Are there natural pearls in our sea? Why shouldn't there be? And finally, can anyone who has never smelled the hold of a ship, or unwashed barrels in a wine cellar, or rancid olive oil, or tar in a shipyard, or raw fish gone bad in a port speak with authority of the Mediterranean? Or write of it? None of these questions comes off the top of my head, and hard as they are to categorize, the people who asked them provided a certain classification of their own in their figures of speech and finger, face, and elbow gestures—none of which appears in any Mediterranean glossary.

MEDITERRANEAN CURSES differ from mainland curses. Some peoples—the modern Greeks, the Turks, the South Slavs—use curses to perform or, rather, portray lascivious acts with gods, saints, or relatives; others—the Italians, the Spanish, the Catalans, the Provençals, and other assorted Catholics—couple the same gods, saints, and relatives (of both sexes) with animals like the dog (or bitch), the pig (or sow), the goat (or nanny), and the ass (or she-ass) in any number of variations. Both categories feature the procreative organs and their functions modified by adjectives scatological, coprological, or sacred. But Mediterranean fervor will out, and not only hell-and-brimstone blasphemies but even the milder curses of the folk often drag in larger sections of the body; in comparison, the Latin *digitus impudicus* and Greek *katapygon* represent a kind of diminutive.

The conviction or, rather, impression that the Mediterranean sky is more open and transparent than others (the astronomers of antiquity tended to uphold it as did certain geographers) may have contributed to the immediate, no-holds-barred character of the curses. The Old Testament meted out severe punishments for the sins and transgressions of the blasphemer. Jews were supposed to tear the clothes from their backs in his presence. I am not acquainted with Arab curses (am I right in thinking that the Arabs hide their curses as they hide their women?), but I presume they exist, and in forms no blander than ours. During the dog days, when the hot winds blow, troubling the spirit and draining the body, when even the sea does not know where to turn, certain words become hard, immoderate, fierce, and those who pronounce them repent after the fact. The sins of those who curse immoderately are assumed and atoned for by martyrs, hermits, and dervishes, of which God has willed the Mediterranean the lion's share.

WEIGHTS AND MEASURES vary from coast to coast, more so perhaps on Mediterranean coasts. They have, moreover, varied over time, adapting to circumstances and conventions and accepting regulation by

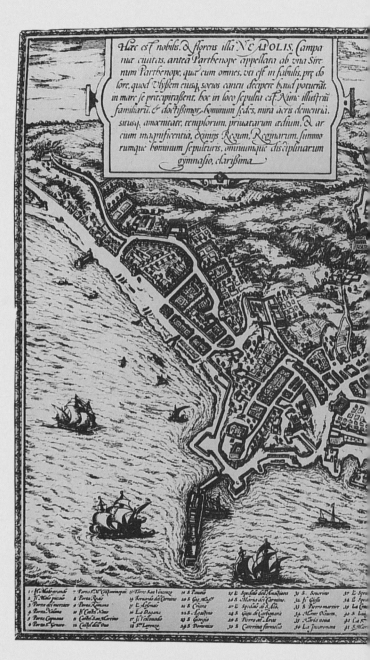

Naples. Georg Braun and Hans Hogenberg, Civitates Orbis Terrarum. *Antwerp, between 1572 and 1618.*

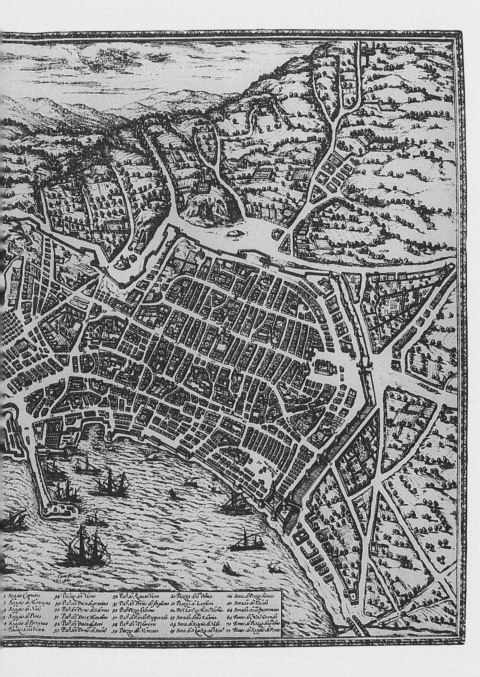

49

Breviary

church and trade, law and scholarship. The statutes of Mediterranean towns set standards not only for weighing and measuring but also for punishing those who violated them, weights and measures being intimately connected with order and progress, power and the state. Clever rulers grasped the connection immediately, and their profiles remained longest in copper, silver, or gold coinage. Weights and measures are an integral part of numismatics: coins are measured by size and weight. The saying that money isn't everything may well have been coined to console the Mediterranean masses.

The history of weights and measures has left traces visible to this day. Biblical measures were abandoned by the early Christians. Rome used Greek measures as a model, yet did not accept them indiscriminately. Venice used measures of Greek, Roman, and native provenance. The Turks measured everything according to their own bushel, so to speak, and the Arabs devised measures completely different from those of their African neighbors. In Spain traditional rivalries held sway even after the reconquista forced out the Arabs and expelled the Jews: there were times when standards on Majorca and Minorca differed more than standards in Naples or Palermo, Marseille or Avignon. The Slavs gave up their pagan system of measures after settling along the Mediterranean, though they kept their system of weights. In Italy it was long difficult to find two cities with the same system of weights and measures, even in the same region. (Not surprisingly, islanders like the British are less than receptive to the Mediterranean system of meters and grams.) The days of marketplaces with areas set aside for the verification of weights and measures (which was financed by special taxes and accomplished by special scales and containers hollowed out of stone for given volumes of oil, salt, or grain) are gone forever. Regions that still respect the natural, approximate folk ways of measuring—a skin of wine or oil, a load of wood, a fistful of salt, a sack of flour, a pinch of pepper—that is, regions that still respect the scruples of propriety, are few and far between. Common weights make for common authorities. The links between speech and measures on the Mediterranean cannot be explained by the links between mainland and sea.

EVERY PORT—NEAR ITS PIER, where there is easy access to the quay and to roads leading inland and where the harbormaster and his services tend to be located—has its warehouses as old as the port and pier themselves. I like to speculate on the wares they have housed and how those wares entered and left their rusty gates, the freight on the ships sailing in and out, from the most varied points of embarkation to the most varied destinations, piled and waiting, orderly or not, and I wonder, when I walk or sail past them, what use the warehouses are put to now, whether they have any purpose left to serve, and what, if anything, their stone walls (generally blind) conceal. Some will change function if not form, others will be abandoned or destroyed. A person in desperate straits may take refuge in them, but most give them a wide berth. A person born near a pier may look upon them with nostalgia, but most find them unsettling. They remind us that Mediterranean ports and markets too have their youth and old age.

THE LOCATIONS of Mediterranean marketplaces are commensurate with those of major institutions such as the town hall and the fortress, the place of worship and the place of eternal rest. Politics and trade meet in the marketplace, meet as friends and as enemies. Thus it was in the Greek agora; thus it was in the Roman forum. Few rulers have been able to purge the marketplace of political gatherings. In ancient Egypt women went to market with their husbands. The Athenians looked upon shopping as men's work. The ancients advised young men to avoid all places frequented by promiscuous women. In predecadent Rome only women slaves circulated freely in the marketplace, and in Islamic countries women covered their faces more there than elsewhere. Equality of sexes was never the rule in the Mediterranean marketplace.

Our descriptions of early marketplaces come from the chronicles, which record their location in the city and their design. Throughout the Levant there were special stands for fragrances like myrrh, cinnamon, thyme, labdanum, and cassia. They spread so pungent and persistent an aroma that many believed it would never stop. At various points they seem to be spreading it still. The use of scents in spices, sacrifices, and carnal love may have caused marketplaces to flourish more in the east than in the west. The bazaar has its origins in Persia, the word coming to us from Persian via Turkish and Italian. The word *suq* is of Semitic origin and was spread by the Arabs throughout their sphere of influence. The Spanish and Portuguese picked it up and took it overseas with them. The paths of the market overlap with the paths of faith, and conflicts arise when they part. In Mediterranean marketplaces what is bought and sold is sometimes less important than the buying and selling—trade for trade's sake.

MARKETS WERE USUALLY CONNECTED with saltworks. Every city or island, every port had to have its saltworks to be independent: salt proved the commodity easiest to exchange for grain and meat in inland commerce as it was needed by both farmers and cattle breeders. Travelers kept salt in their bags, families kept it in sacks, communities in warehouses. Food was salted on long journeys to prevent it from spoiling. Because wise men maintained that white salt should be saved for black days, it became an emblem of wisdom. Legislators saw to its purity and equitable distribution; priests required that it be honored and used it in their blessings; doctors prescribed it as a medicine; friends offered it to one another with bread; enemies threw it in one another's eyes; poets sang the praises of sacred salt, divine salt, and, when particularly inspired, even called the sea as such by its name: the ship plows the salt, that is, the Mediterranean.

Saltworks resemble one another all over our sea: on Paros, Pag, Salina (which is part of the Lipari Islands and is called thus after its saltworks, *salina* meaning just that in Italian), and many other islands, Malta, for example (the Knights of Malta long held the monopoly on salt), Ibiza (which is known as the island of salt), the Kerkenna Islands, the Gulfs of Alicante and Tarragona, Smyrna, Santa Eufemia, Salerno (which folk etymology connects with the word for salt, *sale,* in Italian), in Libya and Syria, to the far reaches of the Bulgarian and Albanian Balkans, in the Montenegrin towns of Bar and Ulcinj, on peninsulas like Istria (Sečovje and Piran on the coast of Slovenia) or Pelješac, near the walls of old Ston. The layout is as old as the hills and as simple: a space on the coast allowing the water to enter and remain stagnant, ringed by dikes and embankments and crisscrossed by drainage channels that create a kind of field. It uses ordinary tools like toothless rakes, buckets, pumps, scoops, shovels, tarpaulins, sacks, wheelbarrows, and clogs. The energy comes from the sun, assisted by the wind, but the one and only raw material is the sea. People employed in saltworks are considered either sailors or farmers. They are in fact both: they must keep track of the weather and the wind on the sea; they work from one harvest to the next and speak of harvests and crops as if dealing with wheat

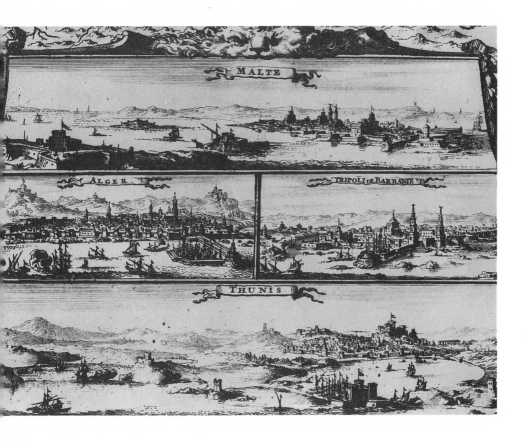

or vines, which may explain the connection between salt and bread and wine; they know from experience when to start, how long to expose the harvest to the sun, how to keep it sheltered, and how to preserve it; they are usually silent when they work, and we have little information about their speech; they are exposed to many perils, often have trouble with their feet, hands, and eyes, and therefore need the protection afforded them by Saint Bartholomew, their patron saint, whose birthday, 24 August, just after the Feast of the Assumption, is celebrated throughout the Mediterranean.

Malta, Algiers, Tripoli, and Tunis. Romeyn de Hooghe (called Hogius).

TOOLS FOR MAKING OIL are as modest as tools for making salt: a press (for which dialects show a particularly rich stock of terms), an olive mill, sieves with mesh both fine and coarse, funnels of various sizes, containers made of earthenware, wood, or glass (for the numerous decantings that oil, like wine, requires), and a storage area where the containers will be cool and sheltered. There are still regions where donkeys turn the mill wheel, in Morocco and Tunisia, for example, and on the coast of Asia Minor, but even in Europe, especially on islands faithful to the past like Crete and Rhodes, Sardinia, Jerba, Alboran, Lampedusa in the Pelagian Islands, Šipan in the Elafit Islands, Formentera in the Balearic Islands, Panaria in the Lipari Islands. Olives are ground into oil, wheat is ground into flour: fat and lean are one on the Mediterranean.

Making oil is not only a trade, it is a tradition; the olive is not only a fruit, it is a holy object. Many books have expounded the significance of the olive branch in the beak of the dove announcing the end of the flood or Christ's prayer in the olive grove called Gethsemane, the olive tree in the valley of Eleusis or on the peak of Mount Sinai. Religions have used oil in their rites—in extreme unction, for example—at the end of life and in the hope of life eternal; it has burned in menorahs and in Alexandria's lighthouse; it has served to cure the body and pretty the face; it has been rubbed into the muscles of athletes and the thighs of hetaeras; it has been transported from coast to coast in amphoras, urns, and barrels, in barques and galleons, and from the coast inland in all sorts of receptacles, including skins and gourds. Preserving olives takes a good deal of effort. At one time they were soaked in the sea. Maintaining the purity of the oil by removing the marc, which is like removing the dregs from wine, is a great art. Straining is not enough. The desire for a pure, unadulterated product is such that procedures bordering on alchemy come into play. (It is not by chance that alchemy originated on these shores.) Oil can also be obtained from flax, castor beans, and almonds, from myrtle and palm, from thyme and angelica, from various animals, fishes, and fruits, but oil from the olive has always been the most important. Gazing on the places where olive trees grow, we can only ask how so dry and austere a soil can produce so rich and aromatic a nectar. Does it come only from the earth? Does the sea play no part? I refuse to believe the assertion that the olive is not native to the area, that like the fig and the vine it was brought here in ancient times, that it has not been Mediterranean forever.

MANY OTHER CRAFTS, though disappearing, are still alive in the Mediterranean memory: stonecutting and stonecarving (without which there would be no great structures, no fortresses to protect the independent spirit, no aqueducts to water the parched throat), road paving, lime- and cement-making. Of viticulture and viticulturists much has been written—and with much glee. But also worthy of mention are the craftsmen who in their altarlike, stone-covered shelters make sulfate solutions in strange copper vessels. More sweat has been shed clearing slopes for vines than was shed building the pyramids. A stone wall is a monument to a strong will; the leaf of a vine is a symbol of virginity; a bunch of grapes is a sign of well being. Wherever there are vineyards and wine, there is civility and artistry, lunacy and poetry. No one knows the thirst for wine better than the sailors who transported it (along with oil, salt, and spices) from coast to coast in amphoras, barrels, and demijohns. The folk has often had to mix its wine with water. Roman soldiers, whom fate routinely sent to foreign parts, pined for the wines of Latium, Umbria, and Campania. The Greeks have always prized wine from their islands. They claim that the first vine was planted on Crete, where the ecumenical word *oinos* was accordingly first pronounced. There is no way of proving the claim, however: vines predate history on the Mediterranean.

Nor should we neglect the cooper's trade, for how could seamen face their bouts with solitude, temptation, and danger without casks? (And barrelmaking has much in common with shipbuilding.) The sea shares many such trades with the mainland, as does the coast with the hinterland. Hard-and-fast divisions are misleading when it comes to activities like building roads and ports, weaving nets and sails, or making ornaments of glass and coral that look like fruits of the sea and the land. There are many reasons to spend time in the workshops of the Mediterranean's shipbuilders, caulkers, ropemakers, netmakers, or spongemakers: without knowing their works and days, their rites and customs, we can never come to know the Mediterranean, what it was and is.

PEOPLES HAVE COME DOWN to the Mediterranean coast from inland with no experience of the sea, acquiring knowledge of its ways from the people they found there and passing it on to the people who came after them. Each of them thus either learned from someone or considered

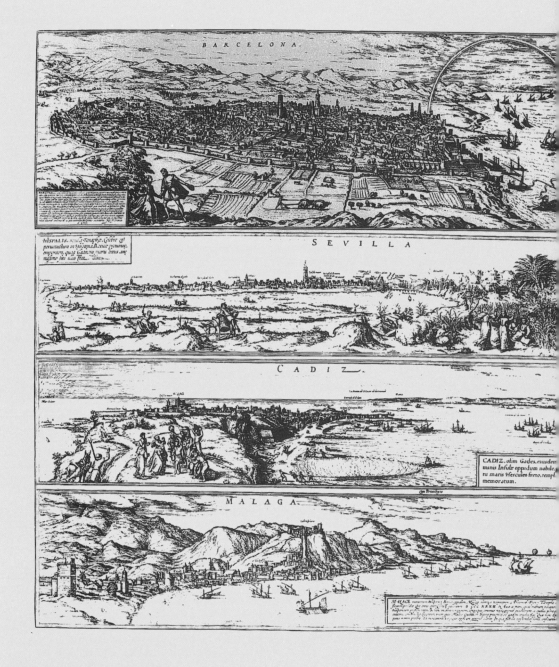

BARCELONA.

SEVILLA

CADIZ.

MALAGA.

HISPALIS, *vulgo Sevilla, Gætæ & provincialum in Hispania, sive provinciæ, emporium, quod Gades mare totius amplissimo his usus fuit. Olim...*

CADIZ, olim Gades, eiusdem nominis Insulæ oppidum nobile, tu maris Herculis freto, templ. memoratum.

themselves someone's teacher, a Mediterranean relationship that has survived a long time.

Although Mediterranean artisans connected with the sea and maritime trades share many traits and even tools, none have so much in common as shipbuilders. The names and shapes of ships, their origins and uses have filled numerous tomes, old and new, and I have neither the intention nor the ability to compete with them. History has left us with fewer shipbuilders than builders per se. All we have to go on are traces (themselves history) of vessels from the early galleys—biremes and triremes, all sails and oars—to the steamships and finally motorized ships that announced a new age; of vessels made of acacia and sycamore and vessels made of papyrus (papyrus being only the first in a long line of links between sailing and writing); and of the ways in which the firm cedar of Lebanon was bent, the mighty oak or elm trimmed, the larch hauled in from colder climes, the beech, pine, or mulberry turned into floorboards and planking, the cypress into masts and the ash or maple into oars. The exhibits we find in naval museums, be they modest or ambitious, show us how trees were selected during the most propitious seasons ("between the two Madonnas," as the saying went in Dalmatia—that is, between the feast days of Mary of Carmel and the Assumption in mid-summer—or in the dead of winter, when the sap is lowest), how long the trunk had to soak or "steep" in the sea (for as long as a few years) and dry in the sun, how it was rubbed with oil or petroleum and hewn into timber to be "burnt" and thus made supple enough to bend like bows. Shipbuilding required a myriad of professionals, from the men who hewed the wood into larger and smaller pieces to the men who caulked it, entrepreneurs and overseers, sawyers and planers, tinkers, blacksmiths (who often came from inland, where there was more metal and hence more experience

Breviary

Barcelona, Seville, Cádiz, and Malaga. Georg Braun and Hans Hogenberg, Civitates Orbis Terrarum. *Antwerp, between 1572 and 1618.*

in working it), weavers, ropemakers, painters, and tarrers. Even lesser shipyards, like those active until recently in Greece, southern Italy, along the shores of Anatolia, and at various points from Antibes to Algeciras and Cádiz, from Morocco to Beirut, from Bar to the Gulf of Trieste, used dozens of tools whose very names have fallen into desuetude. Assiduous linguists have compiled long lists of the Italo-Slav terms for them, words like (and I shall give a sampling of them here if only to save them from oblivion): *šega, šegun,* and *šaraman* (planes that shave more thickly or less); *trapan* and *lime, rašpe* and *raškete* (files and rasps); *škarpeli, lita, aše* or *ašete, ašuni,* and *tesla* (chisels and adzes); *mlati, mace,* and *macole* (hammers); *kantiri, kavaleti,* and *tajaferi* (stands and trestles); *brokve* (jugs) of various sizes; *špinjeli, skošuri,* and *škvari* (measures and levels); and finally words for the tar or pitch—*pegula* (from the Italian *pegola*) and *paklina* or *pakal* (reflecting the Slav root for "hell")—poured by the caulker, boiling hot and darker than the depths of the Mediterranean.

THE SMELL OF TAR has always been the giveaway to the location of the nearest shipyard. Tar is made of spruce or pine so old that no sap flows when it is cut. The trunk is then burned until nothing remains but a thick, dark mass, from which all the rot is later removed. Building even the most modest vessel is unthinkable without tar. (I am speaking of organic tar only, not the mineral tar used in road building.) Tar preserves the boards from water and heat, closes cracks, and prevents decay. It also serves to coat ropes, especially thick ones, and barrels. Tallow or wax is occasionally added to tone it down a bit. It hardens easily and needs to be melted periodically. It will do so when heated, and is then combined with skeins of tow and introduced into the ribbing of the keel as if it were a medicine. It gives off a strong and strongly smelling flame when melting and leaves a dry, light coal after burning. It has been used to treat skin ailments and the gout as well as certain diseases sailors tend to contract in Mediterranean ports.

Hemp too requires careful treatment. Like wood it is soaked or heated to release resin and oil; like salt it is sifted and dried in the sun. Then it must be scoured and beaten like a sponge and combed to cleanse and smooth its fibers so they may be braided into rope or woven into sails. (Anything that cannot be removed remains as coarse, shapeless tow.) It is usually rinsed in fresh water so as not to poison saltwater fish. Its stalk contains oils and intoxicants that were known to antiquity: Herodotus recorded seeing the Scythians high on hemp on the shores of the Euxine, or Black, Sea. Sailors are known to stand at the ropes and take long whiffs, all but lapping them up and probably dreaming of home. The best hemp in the Apennines used to grow in Piedmont; it was sought all over the northern Mediterranean. Egyptian hemp, similar to bulrushes, was prized on the southern shores. Istrian hemp has a solid reputation along the Adriatic, and Marseille has its rue Canebière (Hemp Street). Hemp will grow in cooler climates as well, but it is not the same there. It is occasionally replaced by agave and aloe fibers, but they have not succeeded in supplanting it: Mediterranean sailors will not countenance it.

IF ANY PART OF THE MEDITERRANEAN GEAR can be considered symbolic, it is the net. Its form depends not only on the modesty or grandiosity of our intentions but also on the fish we wish to catch, the boat or ship from which we cast it and to which we haul it, the time of day or night we use it, and whether we are out at sea or hugging the coast, that is, engaged in deep-water or shallow-water fishing. All these factors will influence the form of the mesh and its heft, the thickness of the upper and lower ropes, the size of the cork floats, the weight of the lead along the bottom, the dimensions of the sack in the center, the extent of the "wings" on the sides, and so forth. The implements used for weaving nets are the same on all coasts: a needle made of light wood (like ash) or, in modern times, of copper or other metals; a bobbin, likewise of wood or metal, for determining the size of the spaces or interstices; and a penknife or a pair of scissors for thread cutting. Winding the thread around the finger (or bobbin, which often takes its place) in such a way that each loop makes a potential trap takes a great deal of skill. Not surprisingly, there are many names for nets, sometimes even for one and the same type in one and the same port. Nets differ according to whether they are hauled on board with a windlass or (to the great detriment of the fingers, shoulders, and back) by hand, but both types are imbued with a solution of spruce, tamarisk, or pine bark, pine needles, and leaves, and require constant care. Seeing them rise out of the deep, we do not think of the enormous amount of work that goes into washing them (removing the scales, mire, and marine vegetation), spreading them out to dry, patching them when they tear, and packing them in their trunks so the mice cannot get at them. Besides, piers do not always have room for drying stands, so the nets may need to be carried quite far. The stands, constructed of wooden rods or dried grapevines stuck into the ground or propped up by stones, allow the nets to bask in the sun, take their ease, so to say, after the oft-forgotten role they have performed on board. There, spread beneath the crow's nest, they serve to catch sailors who might otherwise fall into the sea during rough weather when, squalls and vertigo notwithstanding, they climb the masts and untangle the sails from the yardarms. Much history has remained in the nets of the Mediterranean.

Net fishing has not completely supplanted rod fishing (or boulter, harpoon, or trap fishing for that matter). The proper bait (lure, troll, fly, decoy) is all-important, and choosing it is an art in itself, one that depends as much on the appetite of the fishermen as on the appetite of the fish. It is an art honed to perfection on the older shores of the Mediterranean. Not all Mediterranean shores are of equal age.

THE WEAVING OF ROPES and nets is inextricably bound to the tying of knots. Like the former, the latter has been known since antiquity. (The speed of a ship used to be measured by counting knots on a rope, whence the term—still current—*knot.*) We have a wealth of guides to tying knots but a dearth of theoretical knowledge on the subject. Every knot (bow, loop, noose, hitch) may in theory be untied, yet no Mediterranean language is without its tales of womenfolk tying knots their sailor and fisherman husbands were unable to undo.

The names given to knots can be quite telling. We have, for example, the fisherman's knot, the midshipman's knot, and the monk's knot; we have male knots and female knots, soft knots and hard; we have Florentine knots and Flemish knots, each coast exhibiting its own geographic variants. We also have a number of knots named after the way they are tied: the figure-of-eight knot, the lanyard knot, the tassel knot, the pincer knot, the turban knot, the crown knot, and so on. Along the east coast of the Adriatic the word for knot is *grop,* a borrowing from the Italian *groppo* but also close to the Slav root for grave, *grob,* which gives folk etymology a chance to turn tying the knot into something quite sinister. In the town of Calvi on Corsica, sometimes called the "isle of beauty," I visited a ropemaker who was said to know more about knots—how to make them, how to use them, where they come from—than anyone in the world; it was from him I learned what I have reported here. The island's wicked tongues—and no Mediterranean island is without them—nicknamed him Turiddù, which apparently caused him great suffering and led him to retreat even more into his work.

THE STABILITY OF THE SHIP was the responsibility of the ballast master, who was always the last to arrive on the scene. Placing the ballast in such a way that it might be easily supplemented, moved, or removed required a great deal of hard-to-come-by experience. The makers of figureheads were also important, their sole task being to carve monsters and dragons, saints and sirens, grandees and their escutcheons for the ship's prow. Figureheads were sometimes—on the island of Hvar, for instance—called "beasts" and served as a kind of amulet: during great tempests, sailors would cover them with a sail or tarpaulin to protect them from the winds and waves. Pirates kept them hidden from their enemies and victims alike. (It is hard to draw the line between maritime architecture and maritime lore.) In Škrip, on the island of Brač, you can find the figurehead of a polacre called the *Buon Viandante,* which sank in mysterious circumstances (the figurehead was the only part of the ship retrieved). The beautiful nude on the prow of the Trogirian galleon, *La Donna,* caused a scandal when it passed through the Turkish fleet during the Battle of Lepanto; and when it recently disappeared from the museum at Trogir, there were those who claimed it had been abducted rather than stolen. Such tales are legion, but they vanish like the nautical nomenclature I have cited, like the very languages in which they are told. Let us therefore remember all ships setting sail and all ships putting into port, who sees them off and who awaits their return, why they appear on the horizon and why they disappear. The history of Mediterranean welcomes and farewells belongs to world literature.

ALL SEA VOYAGES have several beginnings and several ends; they are never complete (especially when a book or ship's log prolongs them). We first sail in the smallest of craft, along the coast, under the surveillance of somebody who knows more than we do and whom we obey and imitate. Then we move on to oars, sails, and the like, to risks great and

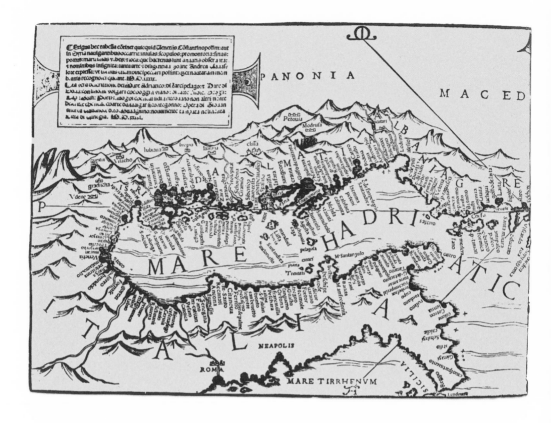

The Adriatic Sea (the first printed nautical map). Giovanni Andrea Vavassori. Venice, 1539.

small, until at last, on our own or at that somebody's prompting, we set off on our first true voyage. It may be on a ship that happened to be in port or that we have long been awaiting, with gear that happened to come our way or that we had long been gathering. This is how all the great explorers began. Some leave forever, others return. There are voyages that make us look at the world in a new way, voyages that make us look at our past in a new way, and voyages that provide a beginning and end to the story of the Mediterranean.

SWIMMING IS A NECESSITY and an art. Swimming does not vary much from sea to sea, though differences do obtain. Unlearned motions—hand, foot, and body motions—are perhaps everywhere the same;

learned motions—learned so we can deal with waves and currents, the deep sea and the open sea—tend to differ. Body position changes according to the situation: now our face skims the water, now it ducks into it or lifts above it—the higher the head, the lower the body. The way we swim betrays our point of departure: coast, island, or estuary. The best swimmers are not necessarily born near the sea, but they always yearn to be near it. People who live on islands generally have their own way of swimming. People who live on rivers remain proud of their rivers even as they swim in the sea. The greatest difference between swimmers, however, is between those who swim out of need and those who swim for pleasure (though this is not the place to examine the ramifications of the latter). Much has been written about the benefits of swimming: the various strokes as ways of embracing the sea, the interpenetration of body and sea, the illusion that the sea belongs to us gradually becoming reality. Not all Mediterraneans are equally enamored of swimming, the elderly swimming less than the young, and women often being discouraged from entering the water.

Underwater swimming takes a great deal more effort than surface swimming, and it comes from a deeper impetus. Yet the possibilities are limited, the true depths being off limits. Swimming and rowing, on the other hand, have much in common: hands and feet were the first oars, and today's oars still resemble them. Being press-ganged to row in a galley was the worst fate on the sea, and the sea's indifference compounded the rowers' despair. Galley slaves envied even shipwrecks. Swimmers, divers, and rowers—the Mediterranean rewards and penalizes them in equal measure, whether they love the sea or fear it.

A SHIP THAT SINKS, truly and definitively sinks, does so in silence or in bedlam. Because we do not know how most sinkings come about, they are difficult to classify. All that can be said for certain is that some ships end in oblivion, at the bottom of the sea, while others we think we remember. The latter interrupt our story, the former conclude it. Not all sinkings are sudden or fortuitous; some are perfectly ordinary and even expected. The Mediterranean used to rise and fall, but for some time now it has apparently wanted only to fall.

Occasionally, when the sea is calmer and more limpid than usual, a wreck is sighted and recognized as such. Occasionally the breakers send it crashing against the reefs or cast it onto the shore, over the beach.

And because it may still have its cargo, it elicits much curiosity and cupidity, anxiety and misapprehension. The coastal dwellers want to take it over, the harbormasters to clear it away. Wrecks are admonitions to navigators and adventures to scholars. The first things a sunken ship loses are its sails, masts, and rudder. The hull remains. Inside we often find amphoras of various sizes, because olive and myrtle oil and wine were so commonly transported by ship. Once, when I was young, I dived down to an ancient galley that had sunk in a storm near the town of Pernat, off the island of Cres, in the Gulf of Kvarner. The town has turned its cargo into a small museum. By choosing to go down with their ships, Mediterranean captains turned wrecks into graves.

Wrecks lie on their sides, that is, on their keels, with bow or stern jutting straight up, depending on the nature of the disaster that caused them to go under and the contour of the terrain that has accommodated them. In time they become part of the floor itself. Fish swim in and out as they would do through chinks in a cave, shells stick to them as they would to a rock, and all kinds of marine vegetation wrap around them. Sand and mud preserve some lineaments even as salt and rust corrode others. Wrecks seem to glitter in the sun; in the moonlight they appear to be sailing; in the dark they take on the shape of rocks. They figure quite often in literature, and I have heard many oral accounts of them, the saddest on the island of Elba. The Mediterranean's past is scattered with wrecks.

CERTAIN RITES OR CUSTOMS have to be taken into account while the ship is in dry dock, as they require special equipment. Burial at sea, for instance, differs from burial on land. When voyages were long and corpse preservation time short, the body was wrapped in a sail, wound round with rope, and dropped from the deck. An edge of the sail was sewn through the dead man's nose and a weight attached to his legs (a rock that had been part of the ballast, a slab of metal, or occasionally a cannonball) to make him sink straight down as befits a sailor. Several symbolic drops of oil were sprinkled after him. If there happened to be an island in the vicinity and the crew decided to bury the body in the mainland manner, an oar was thrust into the ground next to the cross. All deaths were duly recorded in the log, a fact of note for writers on the subject. Also of note: until recently you could meet sailors in any Mediterranean port who remembered these rites.

QUAY, PORT, PIER, OR DECK, central square or marketplace, shipyard or fish shop, fountain or lighthouse, church, monastery, or cemetery, the sea itself—they can all become open-air stages, backdrops for all kinds of roles, trivial and fateful, all kinds of rituals, quotidian and eternal. The centuries teem with these scenes and events. They are the past and present of the Mediterranean, the history of the Mediterranean theater.

Bringing sponges up from the sea is a spectacular profession. Sponges tend to meld into its depths, its rocks and vegetation. Were we to seek a parable here, it would soon emerge. Sponges are hunted as fish and plucked as plants. Both naturalists and gatherers have long wondered whether sponges are animal or vegetable. They do not move; they let the sea stream through them, cleanse them. They have the whole sea at their disposal, one might say, and all the time in the world. They have been known from time immemorial: the oldest frescoes discovered on Crete—they look like stage sets—show sponges. Sponges are used in hygiene and medicine (certain genera have iodine in their skeletons), in the potter's workshop and the classroom. Because they are also used for erasing blackboards, they are thought of as an aid to forgetting. They are perhaps better exploited on the Mediterranean than on other seas.

The sponging season is rather brief, as is the professional life of the gatherer. The tools of his trade long remained unchanged. He would dive to the floor of the sea with the aid of a rock tied to a rope, stab the sponge clusters with a harpoon or spear like a warrior, grab them with his hands and twist like a wrestler (the most theatrical part of the process, though rarely witnessed by an audience), then toss them into a bag, which was also tied to a rope. The catch was then squeezed together in another bag, strained, and beaten with sticks and battledores, like grain being threshed. Sometimes it was put through a press, as are olives or grapes. It was then rinsed with sea water and spread out in the sun, as are figs. The longer the sponges drank up the sun, the lighter and more valuable they became. Sponge gatherers were less respected than coral gatherers, even though their job was no less onerous. There was no animosity among them, however. The name a sponge received on one coast tended to stick to it on another. Names like Turkish jug (or cup), Levantine rose, Tunisian or barbarian star have no trace of scorn or invective attached to them. Yet the craft clearly had its problems. In this exceptional case linguists would do well to look at the correlation between scientific appellations for sponges and, say, classical wives and rivers: Geodia, Tethya, Calyx, Cliona, Chondrosia, Axinella, and so on. The men who gave them such names must have suffered greatly. There are those who have compared the Mediterranean to a vast sponge that has absorbed all knowledge.

Coral gatherers (who are sometimes called coral hunters, which again points to the ambiguity of their nature) used a tool whose Dalmatian name, *inžegn*, reflects its Venetian origins (cf. *ingegno*). It consisted of a wooden cross with long tassels made of hemp or tattered nets and was cast from shore to catch on a reef and tear off pieces of red (as on the Adriatic island of Zlarin), purple, or even black coral. It thus differed substantially from the sponge gatherers' tools. Both trades expanded considerably at the turn of the century when the grape phylloxera devastated vineyards, depriving vintagers of their daily bread and forcing them to seek salvation in the depths of the sea. Down they went, bound to their rocks like suicides, to seek a living. It would be too cruel to call such scenes theatrical. There were not enough sponges or coral to go around, and many gatherers left the Mediterranean for the Americas, North and South.

No one writes about the Mediterranean or sails it without personal involvement. The city where I was born is located fifty kilometers from the Adriatic. Thanks to its location and the river that runs through it, it has taken on certain Mediterranean traits. Slightly farther upstream, the Mediterranean traits disperse and the mainland takes over.

I am particularly interested in Mediterranean rivers and borders and the connections between them. I cannot explain why at some points the coastal area is so narrow and ends so abruptly and major transformations occur at so short a stretch from the sea. Cross a mountain and the bond with the sea is broken: land turns into hinterland and grows coarser, harder of access; people practice different customs, sing different songs (Balkan *gange,* for example), play different games (stone throwing or number guessing), thus appearing alien to their maritime neighbors; indeed, the latter call the former *Vlasi,* that is, Vlachs or Wallachians literally, but in the Balkans the name reserved for "the other" (non-Slavs when used by Slavs, Catholics and Muslims when used by the Orthodox, etc.). In other areas, analogous obstacles notwithstanding, there is still a Mediterranean element molding land, customs, and people. People the sea has in one way or another distanced from itself are prone to doubt their origins. Stone may play a part here as well: there are more rocks (or sand, on the southern shore) in these regions than there is soil. The world of karst is a world all its own, a world too exposed to the sun to be conventional or anything but vulnerable. Opening only at the coast, it is an emblem of the Mediterranean, a context for myth, a proscenium for classical tragedy.

Mediterranean rivers flow down to the sea in their own ways: some are quite ceremonious, even smug about doing their duty, others seem caught off guard and flow along abashed, confused; there are those that are haughty and resolute and those that are timid or resigned; there are those that do not care to mix their waters with the waters of others and those that are only too eager to take part in affairs of the sea, set up an alliance with it. Nor does the sea accept them all uniformly or the coast suffer them to leave it in one and the same way. Some rivers tend to linger by the sea, forcing it to yield some of its territory; others plunge deep into the karst to emerge either at the coast itself or in the cold springs at rock bottom. Estuaries are of a dual nature: they let the river flow into the sea, and they let the sea make its way inland. The riddle of their reciprocity makes itself felt here and there in their deltas. When swimmers from nearby rivers swim in the Mediterranean, they claim they can recognize the water of their rivers in it.

I have frequented the beds and streams of numerous Mediterranean rivers; I have bathed in them; I have smelled the vegetation along their banks, comparing it with that of their upper and lower basins. Mouths of rivers are characterized by various kinds of reeds (cattails, bulrush, sedge). Large rivers have a special type of reed that flourishes where fresh and salt water come together. I have in mind rivers like the Ebro, the Rhône, the Po, the Neretva, the Menderes, the Orontes, the Don, and especially the Nile, where reeds are possibly more imposing than anywhere in the world. (Nor should believers in the Scriptures forget that papyrus is a variety of river reed.) Conifers have different aromas near a river and farther away. They can do without water for long periods, their sap growing thicker, their bark harder. Smells tell a great deal about regions along the Mediterranean: what conifers they support, how they lie, whether they line river banks or the coast.

WHERE THE OLIVE LEAVES OFF, the fig takes over, thereby extending the confines of the Mediterranean. According to a proverb from Herzegovina, the south ends "where the fig grows not and the ass brays not." Carob and almond trees accompany the fig until the first cold tributary. Whether oranges and lemons continue to grow beyond the mouth of one or another river depends on the soil: citrus is not native to the region. Grasses grow farther, all the way to the mountains: they are tougher and have been here forever. Some fragrant bushes—lavender and rosemary, for instance—disappear early. Oleander, agave, and even the sinewy maquis vanish one after the other, wind-resistant though they are. (It is hard to believe that agave has not grown here from time immemorial, that it had to be imported. Five centuries have passed since it was brought from the New World to the Spanish coast, taking root in the poor soil that preserves it and that it preserves, that keeps it from rolling away along the precipitous cliffs. Only after sprouting its flowers on stems several meters tall topped by yellow calyx cups and, exhausted from the effort, wilting down to the roots, does it show that it comes from an ecosystem more savage and uncivilized than the Mediterranean's.) The pomegranate perseveres (it has grown here forever), but farther north it turns sour and wilder and takes on new names. Sage loses its zest and medicinal properties, and it too finds new names. Of tamarisk and myrtle all that remains are the names, of palms and dates the memory, of capers and fennel scarcely the taste and again a variety of names. Onions and garlic change their composition, smell, and nomenclature as they move away from the sea. Tomatoes are redder by the sea. (Who would believe that they too were once brought here from other shores!) Gorse, also called furze and whin, is much devoted to the south, deriving its yellow hue and characteristic aroma from the driest of earth, perhaps even from bedrock. (The various names may be ascribed not only to the demands of botany but also to the laws specific to semantics.) The laurel tree is full and vigorous in the south; its leaves curl and shrivel as it moves north. The laurel wreath represents glory even where the laurel tree has never grown. The grapevine adapts by changing position and genus, but loses its biblical attributes, save along three or four blessed rivers that crisscross the mainland. Finding a mandrake is no easy task: there are very few left along the coast. I was taken to one by some sailors from Kotor. It was near a stream called Ljuta (Raging) that was near a lake named after Aesculapius, just above Konvale on the border of the Republic of Dubrovnik (also known as the Republic of Ragusa) and Montenegro, the boundary between the Catholic and Orthodox Mediterranean.

To those of us who grew up on the banks of a river, every genuinely southern river represents a kind of sea. We have no trouble following its Mediterranean element upstream. I have followed the Rhône to Lyon, though when I went on in the direction of Lake Leman, the Lake of Geneva, I kept losing track of it. The Po flows all the way to the Alps, though with occasional interruptions as well. I am not sure how far the Arno flows, perhaps to the very source of the Tuscan dialect. Follow the Tiber upstream or down and you enter history. Climb the Nile and you reach the Aswan miracles. The Ebro opens the way to Aragon and Navarre; the Guadalquivir is to a large extent Mediterranean (though it flows into the Atlantic), as is, to a lesser extent, the Tagus. I have spent some time on the Jordan River, which we see through the Scriptures (as we see the Dead Sea into which it flows), never wondering how its waters, near Jericho, manage to cross the deepest valley on earth and quench the thirst of the surrounding peoples or how worthy of the great Mediterranean baptism its waters remained at the onset of its rebirth.

Every country has its hydrographic map. Mediterranean breezes waft along the Vardar all the way to Skopje and beyond (they are felt as far as Lake Ohrid), along the Isonzo all the way to the Julian Alps; they accompany the Neretva through Mostar (the city where I was born) all the way to Bosnia, crossing Lake Scutari and following the Morača all the way to Montenegro. Then there are the many minor rivers with Mediterranean features in their backwaters: the Bojana, the Mirna, the Dragonja; the Zrmanja, the Krka, the Žrnovica; the Cetina and the Poljici with their tiny republic at the foot of the Mosor; and many other tributaries and their principalities. Most rivers on the Italian side of the Adriatic, except the Po and the Adige in the North, would seem to originate on the Apennine Peninsula, rivers mellifluous of name and meager of water like the Rhône, the Lamone, the Savio, the Pescara, the Biferno, the Ofanto, and several others on the way down to the Gulf of Tartano. Balkan rivers thus rise from the hinterland, the mainland, the nature of their ties with the Mediterranean being diverse and often quite tenuous.

Greece is not crossed by rivers of particular magnitude, except perhaps the Vardar, which the Greeks call Axios and share with today's Macedonia. Without its capricious flux, the Gulf of Salonika and Salonika itself would scarcely be what they are. On the same Aegean side of the peninsula there are several rivers smaller than the Axios: the Aliakmonas, the Peneios, the Sperkheios, and the Kefisos. I give the names as I heard them. On the Ionian side I recall the Thyamis, the Arakhthos, the Akheloos, and the Mornos. They serve to differentiate Aegean from Ionian Greece. The situation may look different in the Peloponnese, with the Pyrrhos, the Peneios (as distinct from the aforementioned river with the same name in the north), the Eurotas in the Gulf of Lakonia, and the Alfeios, but in fact they are more streams than rivers. Their tributaries are so ephemeral as to be mysterious: they cannot possibly manage to survive the arid summers with so little water unless they maintain a deeper connection with the hinterland. Hence the ancients' great concern with underground waterways: the Periphlegeton in flames, the Acheron in pain and tribulation, the Styx "a most grievous malediction," the Cocytus "a cry and a lament." Nor did the more noble of the surface rivers care to mix with waters beneath their station: the Titarisios meeting the waves of the Peneios flowed over them "like oil." Greece has always been open to the water, winning on the sea and losing on the mainland. It was the mainland that finally did her in: rivers alone cannot save a Mediterranean country.

Greek rivers on the Aegean side differ from their Turkish counterparts, at least from those I have seen—the Bakir, the Menderes, the Gediz—which clearly show they come from a different shore and a different hinterland. The continents having long since separated, the rivers have long since severed contact. But an enormous surplus of water flows through the Bosporus and the Dardanelles in one immense current brought to the Black Sea by the Danube and the ancient Russian rivers. I have spent some time traveling around the estuaries of the Don, the Dniestr, and especially the Dniepr (on the banks of which Kievan Rus was converted to Christianity). Their waters differ from the corresponding Mediterranean waters, though less, along the coast at least, than is commonly thought. A Ukrainian from Odessa once told me that the Danube in Belgrade or Novi Sad reminded him of the Black Sea and that he considered himself a Mediterranean: "Ex Ponto." Waters flowing from the mainland do more than preserve the water level, and the Black Sea is in the end inseparable from the Mediterranean, despite the strait keeping them apart.

I AM NOT SUFFICIENTLY FAMILIAR with the rivers of northern Africa. Everyone knows the Nile, but scores of other rivers remain in the back-

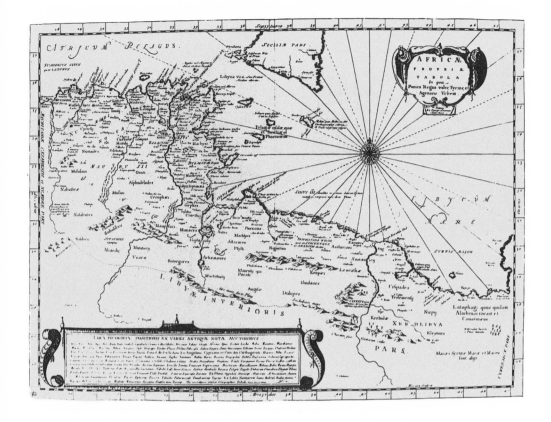

ground, rivers that survive the heat in unusual beds, in sand or near it, and sometimes only underground, at great depths, away from the sun. I have followed several that go down to the sea: the Mejerda in Tunisia, which emerges near Carthage; the Chéliff in Algeria, which breaks off several times in its upper reaches until it is reinforced by tributaries between Médéa and Mascara; and the Moulouya in Morocco, which debouches in the vicinity of Melilla not far from the Cape of Three Forks. These three more fortunate rivers satisfy the common desires of the regions through which they flow: they are green along deep stretches and in whirlpools, they have rock and pebble beds, and they are capable of resisting sand and desert and the sun of Africa, the most blazing and cruel on the Mediterranean.

Africa, according to writings of ancient authors. Padua, 1697.

The experience of sand is rarely acquired by devotees of the sea. I have never acquired it. Many speak of the similarities between the desert and the open sea, between dunes and waves, winds and destinies. A number of Arab poets have devoted their talents to the subject. But where sea and desert meet, the sea loses part of its character, at least the Mediterranean does.

Passing from sandy regions to landscapes of milder aridity, vegetation changes, comes to life. Mediterranean plants begin to appear along the borders of the Great Plateaux on the slopes of the Tell. I recognize the jujube (*al-sidra*), rue (*al-fayhal*), lavender (*al-khuzama*), a heather that is brighter here, sage (which the Arabs call *al-kuwaysa* and *al-meriema* on the coast and inland), and broom (*al-wazal*), and myrtle (*al-rayhan*), along with several that exude a thick, sticky, milk-like juice when snapped, but whose names I was unable to discover. Mediterranean plants extend farther south, across the African ranges, than north into the European hinterland.

Even this far from the sea there are major fountainheads, but only a part of their water ends up in riverbeds. People do not want the water to flow into rivers, because then it will empty into the sea; they would rather keep it for themselves. There are several ancient cities named after these sources—Tlemtsen, for instance, which comes from an ancient Hamitic dialect. They are particularly important along dry routes. Sahara means "poor land," and their water is truly a source of riches, a source of life and faith in life eternal: it saves the body and cleanses the spirit. Water is more highly valued than along the northern coast. Nor should we forget that for people on the southern coast of the Mediterranean, we are the north.

We can never be well versed in Mediterranean rivers unless we are familiar with the winds that blow in their vicinity, with the corridors in which they mix sea systems and land systems, with the people who live along their banks and at their estuaries. Rivers receive the same rains as coasts only up to a point, after which they share them with the hinterland. It is difficult to authenticate or refute the conviction, widespread among lowland dwellers, that rains can be distinguished on the basis of their origins, that there are rains only recently freed of their Mediterranean salt and rains extracted by the Mediterranean sun from its lean soil.

No one can know all the peoples living along the Mediterranean; they do not know one another well. In some cases we cannot even pinpoint what the word *people* means: city or country, nation or state, one or the other, or the two together. My goal is not to rewrite histories others have written or search for a past others have found; I wish merely to portray the presence of these peoples on the sea or, rather, their relationship to the sea insofar as it can be derived from history or the past. The sequence I adhere to depends on many factors, personal and otherwise; it does not imply privilege or primacy. Some peoples deserve more attention than they have received, nor can I give all the attention they deserve: there are stretches of the Mediterranean coast I have not visited.

History provides evidence of peoples that made their way to the Mediterranean and remained and of peoples that disappeared or mingled and merged with others: the Pelasgians, the Illyrians, the Liburnians, the Siculians or Sardinians, and, along the Black Sea, the Scythians and the Khazars. The Cretans and the Philistines are known to have been peoples of the sea, though the shore from which they set sail is not known. The Etruscans prepared the Roman Empire to go to sea by teaching them everything they knew about it. The Phoenicians and their descendants, the Punics, are also worthy of mention here. Not only were these Semites adept at navigating great distances, they left behind important vestiges of themselves. Though completely lacking in imperialist designs, they built ports capable of standing up to empires. Besides Tyre and Sidon, they are responsible for Carthage (Kart Hadesht means "new city" in Punic), Tiphsah, Leptis, and Cádiz. Many have noted their enterprising nature. Let me stress here that they had the oldest and most reliable nautical maps in the ancient world and that they engraved them on copper plates. The fame accompanying them on their journeys through the Mediterranean and beyond is more durable than bronze.

Peoples of the sea recorded in the earliest annals tended to be enemies of the Jews. Even before arriving in Canaan, the Jews clashed with the seagoing Philistines, who gave Palestine its name. The Jews called the Mediterranean the Philistine Sea (but also the Large Sea).

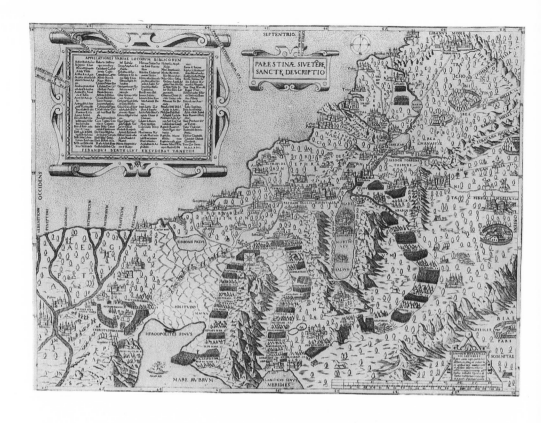

Within the map the following labels are visible: SEPTENTRIO; PALESTINÆ SIVE TERRÆ SANCTÆ DESCRIPTIO; APPELLATIONES VARIAE LOCORVM BIBLICORVM; FERNANDVS BERTELLVS EXCVDEBAT VENETIIS; OCCIDENS; ORIENS; SIRBONIS PALVS; SOLITVDO; HEROOPOLITES SINVS; MARE RVBRVM; ELANITICVS SINVS MERIDIES.

Description of Palestine, the Holy Land. Fernando Bertelli. Venice, 1563.

The Dead Sea, which gave them an easier time, they called the Salty or Bitter Sea and the Desert Sea. What is usually called the Sea of Galilee in the Gospels (though it also appears as the Sea of Tiberias and the Lake of Gennesaret) is in fact a freshwater lake below sea level that derives most of its inflow from the Jordan River. The confusion of sea and lake may stem from its size or simply from the fact that the distinction was not deemed important at the time. The Sea of Galilee was used more often for fishing than the Large, or Philistine, Sea. King Solomon had his ships built at Ezion-geber on the Red Sea, which was considered more important than the Mediterranean. Moses led the chosen people across a sea that parted for him: they walked across its bed. Jonah the Prophet swam, not sailed, into the whale's belly: his name in Hebrew means dove, not gull. The ancient Jews were farmers, bound to the land; they were forced by circumstance to become nomads. With no shores of their own they were unable to build ships, nor did they become helmsmen on the ships of others. They were led into exile by rabbis, not captains, and were less attracted by new worlds than by a desire to return to the world from which they had been expelled. From the outset they set their sights back on the transparent Mediterranean sky. Under that sky they had come to know their one and only God; under that sky they had received His first messages. They thus tried to avoid the north, to remain as close as possible to the south, never forgetting, always longing for the land in the desert and on the water between the Dead Sea and the Mediterranean.

We do not know what maritime experience the Arabs had before coming to the Mediterranean. The eastern and western seas had long been separate and gave rise to different types of ships, ships of different material and design. The Arabs did not call their sea the Mediterranean or Middle Land Sea as did the Greeks and Romans; they called it the Syrian or Rumelian Sea. Their sea was the one that washed the Arab peninsula, which they called their own island (Jazirat al-Arab) and which was and remains the heart of the nation, the focal point of its faith, the mainstay of its memory. They did not sail to other seas from the Mediterranean because it was itself another sea for them, and they wanted to prove themselves equal to their peers on it. They did not venture into the Atlantic, as did their Iberian rivals, but into the Arabian Sea to the south of them, which forms part of the Indian Ocean. Perhaps acquiring ascendancy over two seas is beyond the strength of a single state, of a single nation's warriors and sailors. Only an island people may succeed in such a venture: surrounded by water, it does not know whence comes salvation. In this, Mediterranean islands do not differ from islands elsewhere.

The Arabs do not comprise a unified people: for long periods they were more side by side than together. Nor do they share a vision of the sea: people who move about cannot have the same relationship to the sea as people who live permanently on its shores—nomads and sedentary peoples have different horizons. Moreover, the Arab shores themselves are too broad to ensure unity among the populace, and the hinterland has little inclination to provide aid or support. As a result, there are enormous differences between coast and continent, Sahel and Sahara, sea people and oasis people, *tell* people and *jabal* people. The aridity of the soil focuses energy on irrigation rather than navigation. Deserts are as hard to conquer as seas—and as exhausting. The Arabs create beautiful gardens, but their ports are wanting. The triangular sail they invented for their ships proved insufficient to assure them dominion over the Mediterranean or enable them to move beyond it to other, more distant seas.

Little is known of the Copts and their connection to the sea. Their Egyptian predecessors were more concerned with the Nile and its delta than with the Mediterranean, and history has ascribed few feats of navigation to them. Ancient travelers record that the word for sea in the land of the Pharaohs was *iam*. The Copts preserved the term into the nineteenth century and in some places into the twentieth, though pronouncing it with a darker vowel: *iom* or *eiom*. More than their phonetics has its dark side: the sea had no room for them; they were attacked from the water, then from the land. They adopted a new faith and tried to give it their stamp; it was proclaimed heretical. They built churches rather than ships, monasteries rather than ports (sometimes on the water, more often on the edge of the desert); they did not sail, they prayed. Some of the Mediterranean's greatest and most humble anchorites—Saint Anthony, Saint Pachomius, Saint Macarius—have Coptic roots.

The Berbers too were chased from coast to plateau, mountain, and desert, but parts of their dialects remained in the inlets and on the islands. Early travelogues report that the Berbers feared the sea more than the Arabs, yet they preserved their own words for ship, sail, and helm. They also have their own word for sea, *ilel,* and for fruit of the palm, *tegla,* but they were not—nor could they have been—a seafaring people. They have no native word for oar, though they have one for oar handle: they rowed the galleys of other peoples, Christian and Muslim. Some became pirates known for their cruelty, though they were also cruelly treated. The space that fell to them (and the space their bedouins shared with others) was less than rewarding. We do not know how far the ancient predecessors of the Berbers spread, whether they headed towards the Atlantic, made it all the way to Britain, Ireland, and Scotland, or set down roots there. Not all Mediterranean peoples managed to become Mediterranean.

From time to time—and from Morocco to Libya, from Egypt to Sinai and Syria—I have run into bedouins. I have tasted their thick, rich camel's milk; I have heard them tell their stories in their difficult dialects. Yet I have never come to know them, know where they are going and why or even whether they are coming or going. Do they belong to a nation? Are they seeking a national identity? Do they need one? Is their country the place they leave from or the place they set out for? Or is it everything in between? Is their state the desert, its borders the horizons? They have never been attracted to the sea. Yet they pitch their tents like sails among the dunes; oases are their ports, caravans their fleets. Whatever traces they leave on the shores of the Mediterranean are erased by wind and sand.

The Turks came from the depths of Asia, crossing river after river in their boats and bringing us the word we use for boat, *čamac.* Yet they had no feeling for the sea and had to borrow a word for it, *derya,* from the Persians. (Their native word, *deniz,* refers to all waters, fresh or salty.) They were more successful on land: they were horsemen, not shipbuilders. We do not know to what extent they differed among themselves when they arrived or whether their differences influenced where they settled, near or far from the sea, but they have always been more warriors than sailors, more farmers than fishermen. They have consecrated the olive and the fig and sung their praises; they have cultivated the vine, the pomegranate, and the almond on their Mediterranean slopes.

Asia Minor is more continent than peninsula. At many points its outlets to the sea are narrow or blocked. Cliffs turn coastal land into hinterland. The northern coast is plagued by winds and frost; the southern and western coasts are sometimes sunny, sometimes not. A number of cities near the sea were destroyed before the Turkish conquest. Such antiquities as survived remained in the hands of the original settlers. As for the Turks, torn between past and present, imperial glory and the fall of the empire, they are themselves amazed at the harmony that once united them and the dissension that eventually rent them asunder. They did not make good use of the sea. Along the border with Europe, Rumelia, they have always been more Balkan than Mediterranean.

Syria and Lebanon I have seen only in passing. Syria is an Arab country, but its past and population are mixed. The Ansaria Mountains cut it off from the sea. Of the three rivers emptying into the Syrian Sea (which, as I have mentioned, is the Arab name for the Mediterranean) only one, the Orontes, which the natives call the Nahr al-Asi, provides an entry into the interior. The hinterland begins immediately after the mountain range, and both coast and hinterland border on the desert,

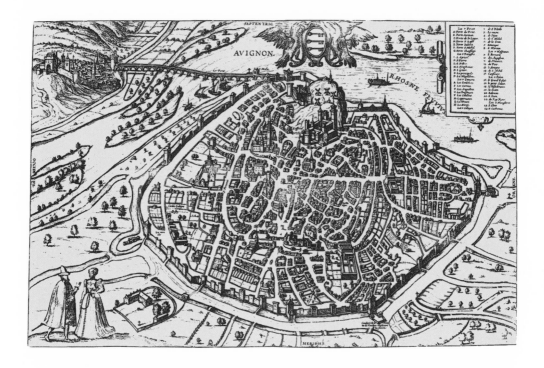

*Description of the
Turkish Empire.*
Abraham Ortelius,
Theatrum Or-
bis Terrarum.
Antwerp, 1579.

which has greater contact with each of them than each has with the
other. Everything that is not desert breathes antiquity: the road from
Antioch to Aleppo (Halab) across Lebanon, the ruins of Beirut (many
Mediterranean cities, the finest among them, were similarly razed in
the past), the workshops of Damascus (where the sharpest of sabers
and the softest of cloths were once made). The desert is reminiscent
of nothing and breathes nothing but itself. The sea loses its smell when
it comes into contact with it. I have stood at the mouth of the Orontes
among reeds as large as the Nile's; I have stood on the sites of the Tell
Kalakh and the Tell Kazel, where archeologists are still seeking a sunken
port presumably called Simyrra. The attitudes of people on the coastal
plains and the nearby mountains, people of the sea and of the desert,
differ as greatly in the Mediterranean region as they do in analogous
regions elsewhere.

We all look to Greece and think of her as our own. But Greece is not always as we think of her. Greece is not all sea, as many imagine; she has her mountains, snow-covered mountains, as well. The sea laps her shores and moves inland, but to various degrees and in various ways. The geography is as it was: the islands—the Cyclades and Sporades—are in place, the Ionian and Aegean Seas likewise; the sky is as blue as always. Yet the past does not return; history refuses to repeat itself. Greece and Magna Graecia have long since separated, as have Hellas and Byzantium; Byzantium and the Eastern Empire may never have come together in the first place. The ruptures are profound, the losses great, each requiring the loser to take stock. The Greeks have constantly pondered over whether to move on or start from scratch. The fate of the Mediterranean often parallels the fate of Greece.

Many important things have had Greek names—old, new, and ecumenical—but belonged to other nations, and names cannot take the place of things. Non-Greeks have interpreted the Greek past better than Greeks. Greeks have been relegated to serving the foreigners who come to pay homage to their country. The foreigners admire the Greek past and either ignore the Greek present or confound the two. Greeks themselves have sought their identity more in the past than in the present. Many leave the country, dissatisfied, and many who stay behind complain. Nostalgia is truly a Greek word. It transforms great feats into the memory of same; it replaces personalities and events with their histories. Glory has been preempted by words. The Greek language has preserved memory, history, and glory while itself changing radically. Yet who can imagine the past without Greece? The very question derives from Greek tradition, which poses all the important questions, Mediterranean or not.

Italy has two Mediterranean coasts, east and west. It is thus divided by the sea, but in ways different from countries with an internal or external sea. At various times one side of the Apennines has fared better than the other, and Italians make a clear distinction between the upper and lower seas (*mare superum* and *mare inferum*), that is, the Adriatic to the east and the Ligurian and Tyrrhenian (demarcated by Corsica) to the west. The south was once more open and more powerful than the north (the north having been long in becoming Mediterranean), and their rapprochement has been due more to the narrow land mass than to the broad sea. A divided peninsula was unable to accumulate the ways and means for the arduous voyage to the New World.

It consoled its vanity with the idea of its past—and hence of itself—as a bastion of world culture. The Mediterranean nourishes all manner of illusions.

Italy is more open to the sea than other Mediterranean countries. The ancient Romans were not a seafaring nation, though they were able to keep their waters safe and supply them with ports. The Apennines are simultaneously an island and a peninsula. There are more or less independent gulfs on either side. The entire Adriatic was once the Gulf of Venice. Although the cities along the coast resemble states and long dealt with one another as foreign powers, Italy accomplished what no other nation was able to accomplish in the modern age: it reanimated both itself and the world around it. The result was now exhilarating, now exhausting. In happier times Italy combined trade, navigation, handicrafts, construction, manufacturing, and art with great productivity and creativity; in less favorable times, when parts of the country were out to get the better of the whole, internecine wars proved more disastrous than attacks from without, pride among the principalities fostered disunity, institutional inertia impeded progress. Italy was often at one with Rome, but as often did without her. Self-satisfaction receded as others succeeded: others invented printing, others built sounder, safer ships, others discovered America. Columbus did not set sail from his native Genoa under the aegis of the city fathers or the Holy See; he set sail from Palos under the aegis of the Spanish monarchs who had unified Spain. The Latin sail was for plowing the Mediterranean, not the Atlantic.

Italians seem to attract more generalities than do other Mediterranean peoples: they have an explosive, southern temperament, swinging back and forth between joy and sorrow, farce and fury. But no nation embodies all Mediterranean idiosyncrasies.

So much has been said, so much written about the beauties of Italy that many see what they have been told to see rather than what is before their eyes. They fail to distinguish either past or present from abstract notions of same, imagine conflicts between Rome and the provinces and rivalries between Venice and Genoa, Naples and Palermo, Florence and Siena, and find an inferno, purgatory, and paradise in every nook and cranny, Guelphs and Ghibellines, Montagues and Capulets in every city, the mafia and the camorra in every commercial enterprise, the Medicis and Borgias in every palace, and an array of saints

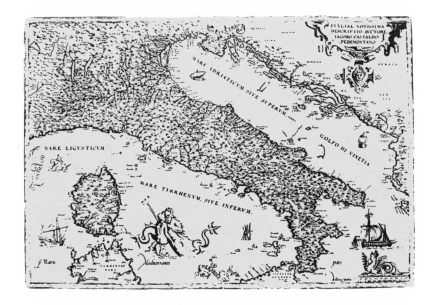

Giacomo Gastaldi (Jacobo Castaldo), "Italiae novissima descriptio," from Abraham Ortelius, Theatrum Orbis Terrarum. Antwerp, 1570.

and prelates in every chapel. "Don't discover the Mediterranean for us," know-it-all visitors may expect to hear.

The Iberian Peninsula is actually less a peninsula than the extension or the tail end of the continent (or, rarely, both at once). Its interior is not at all Mediterranean, while its edges are, though to varying degrees. The Spaniards do not comprise a single people, but Spain is their common home. The Pyrenees have contributed more to keeping them together than the will of the populace. Various pasts have merged into a single past, histories combined with histories; various parts of the country have had to conquer the whole country. Spain has proved that such things can happen on the Mediterranean and shown the price they exact.

The peninsula divides two major bodies of water, creating different horizons, suggesting different missions. The Mediterranean did not have great perspectives for Iberia: its Apennine rivals had sailed it earlier, were better connected, and had better coasts. The Atlantic was long a great unknown and deemed perilous, and it was there the Iberians (the sixteenth century viewed Spain and Portugal as one) decided

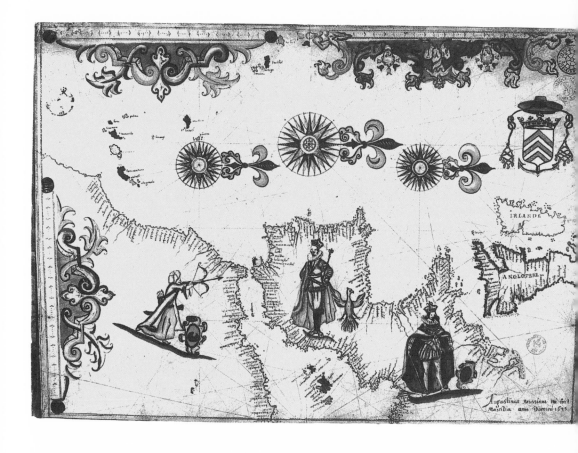

France, Spain, and Northern Africa. Augustin Roussin, Atlas provençal de la Méditerranée. *1633.*

to seek their salvation. In effect, Spain transferred a part of itself to the other end of the world. The split took a great toll: Spaniards proved better *conquistadores* than *conservadores*. Having lost their Latinity in the neo-Latin world, they weakened an already tenuous link with the Mediterranean.

I have stalked the soil of Spain more than I have plowed its waters. I found the differences between Castile, Catalonia, Galicia, and the Basque provinces both greater and less than do the people I spoke to about them. Iberia has its own Levant: Catalonia and Occitania. Though side by side, one belongs to Spain, the other to France, neither of which made much of our sea. I have spent more time in Catalonia than in other parts of Spain. The only way to understand it is to see it as undergoing a long process of recovery. Barcelona is its center. Valencia is closer to Castile, and the Balearic Islands are not quite sure where they stand (islanders in general care little about such matters). The coastal area has a plethora of terms for *llanuras* (plains): *huertas, vegas, planas, marismas, marinas*. It is easier to understand what each designates than why there should be so many of them. Some coastal dwellers would like to create a more positive attitude towards the sea. They have derogatory names for their inland compatriots. (I believe I heard the word *churros* in Valencia, but I may have misconstrued it.) Castilians use both genders for the sea: *el mar* and *la mar*. Linguists (and in Spain everyone is somewhat of a linguist) would have us believe that Spanish speakers express their relationship to the sea in the choice of gender they make, though in a country flanked by the Mediterranean and the Atlantic there are certain to be other factors involved.

France is also flanked by two major bodies of water, but is only partly maritime with respect to both. It is oriented more towards the continent than towards either coast, Mediterranean or Atlantic. Provence in the south is divided into upper and lower regions—the former less, the latter more Mediterranean. Both are part of Languedoc, which has its own upper and lower regions. Roussillon belongs to both Languedoc and Catalonia. The delta of the Rhône has two main branches, with the island of La Camargue in the middle. The hinterland is near, yet far: in the adjacent mountains life differs significantly from life on the coast. Even the language is full of differences: only the mistral and the sea seem to have the same name everywhere. The southern slopes of the Alps are called the Maritime Alps. I am certain they were named by people unfamiliar with the Mediterranean: the Provençals are a southern, not a seafaring people.

The Riviera (Côte d'Azur) and the Gulf of Lions (Sinus Gallicus) were settled prior to Roman times. The coastal towns, which came into being before the Middle Ages, have never attained their true potential. The border of the Kingdom and the Empire passed through the region. The south was ruled by the monarch of the north, the feudal lords having presented him with Provence as a kind of dowry. He had a port called Dead Waters (Aigues-Mortes) built in the estuary of the Rhône, but it was of poor quality, linked with the sea by means of a time- and silt-clogged canal. Neither the Monarchy nor the Republic was particularly interested in the Mediterranean, and the Empire had

Avignon. Georg Braun and Hans Hogenberg, Civitates Orbis Terrarum. *Antwerp, between 1572 and 1618.*

no time for it. The great seaman of Albi set sail from Brest on his *Astrolabe* and *Boussole,* the fleur-de-lis flying from the masts. He may have frightened the neighboring potentates a bit when he reached Toulon or Marseille, but never enough to make France a maritime power on the Mediterranean.

The Balkan Peninsula, like its Iberian and even Apennine analogues, is not entirely Mediterranean. Dalmatia is Mediterranean, but the eastern coast of the Adriatic is not entirely Dalmatian. It includes the Slovenian littoral and the Gulf of Trieste to the north and the Bay of Kotor in Montenegro to the south. Historically speaking, there have been narrow and broad Dalmatias, upper and lower Dalmatias, and red and white Dalmatias, depending on whether the region was under the Croatian crown or under foreign rule, especially the Lion of Venice. At first it was mostly hinterland, but it eventually expanded along the coast to stretch from the Raša River in Istria to the Mat in Albania; at another point it was reduced to a cluster of towns along the central coast; at yet another it engulfed a vast amount of surrounding territory. Early Ptolemaic maps show it encompassing parts of Illyricum, Liburnia, or Bosnia. The Republic of Dubrovnik was not part of Dalmatia until it lost its independence to Napoleon in the Illyrian provinces. At that point Dubrovnik turned into something quite different. The Kvarner Gulf was and has remained outside Dalmatia. The same holds for its islands: the islanders are not considered Dalmatians. National borders did not exist in the distant past; state borders have fluctuated through the centuries. Periods during which the coast and hinterland of the eastern Adriatic were under the same ruler and laws have been few and far between. And while many assume the entire coast to be Dalmatian, those more familiar with the region limit Dalmatia proper to the area between the mouth of the Neretva and Zrmanja in the south to the walls of the old seaport of Senj in the north (whence a piratelike band of anti-Turk renegades known as *uskoci* terrorized the Mediterranean in the sixteenth and seventeenth centuries).

Most of the eastern Adriatic is Croatian. It differs, however, from the Croatian interior, cut off as it is by mountains from the Pannonian plain, by dialect from Zagreb and Varaždin, and by customs from Slavonia. Although the Southern Slavs arrived in the Balkans overland, a small part of their tribes adapted to the sea and settled along its shores. With few exceptions their maritime exploits have remained within the bounds of the Adriatic, and when they sailed the Mediterranean or other seas they were more likely to do so under foreign flags than under their own.

Speaking of one's own people is no easy task: fulfilling the expectations of others is impossible, especially on Mediterranean shores, and praising one's own lowers one in the estimation of others. Yet speak I must, because the world knows little about the Mediterranean's South Slavs—even their neighbors on the Adriatic—and because we ourselves have done little to remedy the situation. We have reiterated ad nauseum the extent to which the Mediterranean has marked the land we inhabit. It is a crossroads between East and West: the meeting place of Latin and Byzantine culture and the scene of the major schism within Christianity, the boundary between the Holy Roman and Ottoman Empires and a battlefield for Christianity and Islam. Our culture has developed in a symbiosis with Mediterranean cultures as a "third component" among such oppositions as east/west, north/south, land/sea,

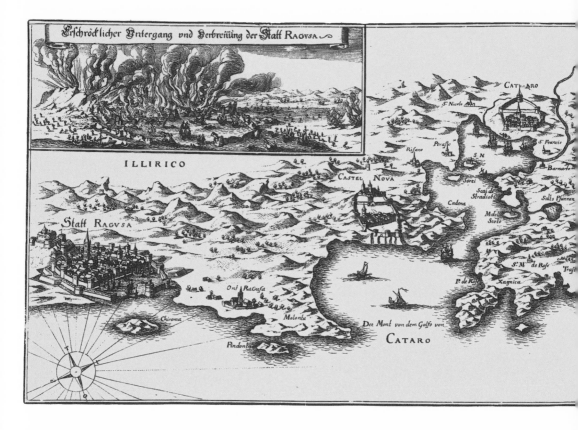

Erschröcklicher Untergang vnd Verbreñüng der Statt RAGVSA

ILLIRICO

CATARO

S: Nicolo

Perasto

Risano

S. N

Storzi

Scai de Stradioti

Cadena

CASTEL NOVA

Statt RAGVSA

Ont. RaGusa

Chiroma

Molonta

Pindonta

S: Francis

Barnato

Salts Pfannen

Mdei Scoto

S: M de Rose

Traste

P. de Rose

Xagnica

Der Mont von dem Golfo von

CATARO

Dubrovnik before and after the great earthquake and fire of 1667, including the Gulf of Kotor. Theatrum Europaeum, *vol. 10. Frankfurt am Main, 1677.*

Balkan/European, and others more homegrown. (I shall return to them in the Glossary section.) Like everyone, we ask ourselves what we are, individually and as a whole. The answers—peoples on the edge of the European continent, inhabitants of the Balkans, Slavs on the Adriatic, the first Third World country in Europe, the first European country in the Third World—are not mutually exclusive: the Mediterranean does not determine where we belong.

Albanians would appear to be longtime inhabitants of the Balkans. No one has been able to establish whether their ancestors were the Illyrians or the Thracians. (National origins are especially difficult to establish when they are a bone of contention.) The Tosks in the south are closer to the sea than the Ghegs in the north, the latter tending to be mountain dwellers, and here too coastal dwellers tend to mock mountain dwellers whenever the opportunity arises. Their dialects differ significantly and, as so often happens, each has tried to impose its speech on the other. Having belonged to various communities, they have accumulated a hodgepodge of traditions and customs. Moreover, they move constantly between the sea and the mountains, livestock breeders and nomads turning into farmers and fishermen and their view of the world varying accordingly. As pagans they converted to Christianity, and as Christians to Islam, though a significant minority has remained either Catholic or Eastern Orthodox. Their vocabulary for boating and sailing comes from their neighbors, though they use native terms for planting and grazing. Separate as they are, however, they retain a common past. The Albanians call the sea *det*: they are apparently the only Mediterraneans to use it.

THE SHORES OF THE BLACK SEA are usually excluded from the purview of the Mediterranean as if they had no relationship to it. Wishing to see for myself whether such was the case, I visited those shores accessible to me. I had no adventures along the Bulgarian coast, the edge of the continent. Inland there is a rugged mountain range, once called by geographers the Balkan Atlas or the *catena mundi*. Inhabitants of the region are known as "Balkaneers." The major roads skirt the mountains, the Roman roads avoided them altogether. Bulgarian rivers have had a hard time furrowing their beds. The Maritsa, the Struma, and the Mesta empty into the Aegean (I saw them only in passing), the Mandra and Kamchia into the Black Sea. The waters of the latter have earned the epithet "devilish" at various points along their downstream race to the Bosporus. The Danube ports of Vidin, Lom, and Ruse used to be more important than the Black Sea ports of Burgas and Varna. Burgas has a Mediterranean flavor that Varna lacks. In the south, between coastal towns bearing the names Pomorie and Primorsko (derived from the Slav root meaning "sea") and Cape Maslen (derived from the Slav root meaning "olive"), there are such typically Mediterranean crops as almonds, rosemary, and mild tobacco.

The space now occupied by the Romanians has been home to many peoples. They have left their traces in ancient Dacia, Moesia, and Thrace, in Greek colonies, Roman provinces, and Byzantine themes. The earlier settlers intermarried with the new arrivals, creating a language that is basically Romance but incorporates a number of Greek words along the coast, Slav words in the plains, and Hungarian words in the mountains. Historians report that the mysterious Scythians, Khazars, Avars, Cumans, and Pechenegs as well as people with even more arcane names made their way across this part of the Balkans. They were followed by the Romanians or Aromanians, the Vlachs, the Tzintzars, and the Chiches, who drove their flocks all the way to Istria. The Black Sea does not temper the Romanian winter, and the Romanian steppe begins in Muntenia, not far from the coast. A longing for the south is clear in the expression "to promise the sea with salt" (*a promite marea cu sarea*), meaning "to promise the moon" and perhaps more if it is true that people of the continent tend to be more reticent with their promises than Mediterraneans. Olives are an integral part of Romanian cuisine, though the word they use, *măslină,* is of Slav origin. Until recently there were any number of Greeks, Turks, and Russian and Ukrainian Old Believers to be found fishing off the Romanian coast, more than Romanians, in fact, who prefer the Danube. They built ships on the Danube in a town called Calafat founded in the fourteenth century by Genoese shipbuilders whose workmen (calfats) gave the town its name, but they borrowed their word for fishing net, *mreajă,* from the Slavs. The Danube delta, which breaks up into endless streams and channels, inlets, shallows, islands, whirlpools, questions without answers, and riddles without solutions, keeps the local population in its thrall. Even I had trouble tearing myself away and exchanging it for a duller Mediterranean shore.

Odessa is where my father's family comes from, and I have been there several times. It is a truly southern city and has an Adriatic twin in Split, whose Bačvice Beach is reminiscent of Odessa's Arcadia. Jews tended to feel safer in Odessa than elsewhere, more so than in Kiev or Lvov, and it had a thriving Greek population until the beginning of the century. In other words, like its Mediterranean counterparts, Odessa was a cosmopolitan city.

The nearby seaport of Kherson was once called Taurid; the Kerch Peninsula, which separates the Sea of Azov from the Black Sea, was called the Cimmerian Bosporus. In summer the sea is warm here. It is fed by the rivers of the continent; they flow currentlike towards the Dardanelles. The Black Sea is less salty than the Sea of Marmara and sustains both saltwater and freshwater fish. Olives, figs, and grapes thrive on the lee side of the Crimean mountains. Vines from the island of

Madeira were transplanted here in the nineteenth century, and a fine Crimean Madeira is produced from the grapes. Feodosia still has a Greek feel to it. Simferopol as well. The church choirs are not to be missed. I have not been to Sochi, but I hear it has palms that, like those on the Adriatic coast, survive the winter. Koktebel has beaches with the most unusual pebbles. I hope some day to sail the coast of Georgia. I have been to Georgia, I have sampled its dry wines, juicy figs, and sweet almonds, but I have never experienced its sea. Georgian poets (whom I have read in an unusually fine translation by a Russian poet) love the sun and coastal towns like Sukhumi and Kobuleti. In nearby Colchis the Argonauts sought the Golden Fleece, and its shores have lured the more intrepid among Mediterranean sailors ever since.

The Black Sea is known for its fishermen, but its sailors lack the chance to shine that comes from sailing to other shores. The songs sung by wandering Ukrainian bards (*kobzari*) rarely mention sailing: there is a fear of waves. The state giving orders from the north, then and now, has never felt at home in the south. Is not the southern and northern sea we call Black in fact one with the Mediterranean?

I CANNOT HELP WONDERING how the history of each people whose link to the sea I have tried to represent has been influenced by that link. It would provide a way of determining how Mediterranean a given people is (though I am not sure the entire region lends itself to such a hierarchy).

THE DISCOVERY OF THE NEW WORLD and new maritime routes was not the sole cause of the Mediterranean's decline. What with Spain and her losses, the Arabs and their defeats, Christianity and its divisive schism, the Jews and their exodus, Italy and her internal lacerations, Croatia and her disjointedness, the Greeks, Albanians, Romanians, and South Slavs and their clashes with the Ottoman Empire, and the Turks and their eventual fall, by the time modernity made its appearance in Europe much of the Mediterranean was spent. It was as if an eclipse (the metaphor comes from the chroniclers of the times) had darkened the very Mediterranean skies where the light of the Renaissance had once glittered.

The Mediterranean was late in facing up to modernity and long in responding to its challenges. It remained true to its own traditions and encumbered by their respectable but out-dated legacy. Secularization came hard to the Mediterranean: the Enlightenment was not congenial to the superstition, intolerance, and obscurantism that continued to reign there; Islam refused to revise its reading of the Qur'an. The industrial revolution passed over the cities of the Mediterranean, discouraged by their inertia. The courts became mere decoration, rule by ostracism banished democracy, tyrants occupied thrones. Myths congealed into mythology, history into historicism. For these reasons and others yet to be sorted out, modernity hesitated to drop anchor in the ports—east, west, north, and south—of the Mediterranean.

Nations wage war; navies wage battles. Naval battles are the cruelest part of Mediterranean history. They are waged by people who believe they are resolving the fates of bodies of land and water, not the conflicts of states and governments. They may be categorized in any number of ways: according to what remains in the deep and what comes back to the surface, for example, or how much is lost to oblivion and how much lodged in memory. History has been kind to naval battles: it has writ them large. The memory of the battle between the Greeks and the Persians at Salamis survived the fall of Hellas. The Greek historians claim that the Persians believed they could subdue the sea by whipping it, which only goes to show that experience of one sea is inapplicable to another. The Romans waged equally brutal battles with the Carthaginians on land and sea, yet the sea battles did not make their captains as famous as the land battles made their commanders. The battle between Neretva pirate ships and Venetian galleys at Cape Mika was fateful for the Adriatic. Were the Neretvians true pirates, or did the winning side, the Venetians, merely label them as such? The Battle of Lepanto between the Holy League under the papal flag and the Turks under the half moon, the most important naval battle of the Renaissance, had major consequences for Europe and Asia Minor. History books usually speak of Don John of Austria, and the Ottoman Ali Pasha, and admirals such as Doria or Barbarigo, Horuk or Hairedin Barbarossa, but for literature what matters more is that without Lepanto a certain Spaniard, whose left hand was maimed during the fray and who was later held prisoner for five years in North Africa, might never have written his magnificent novel about the knight of the sorrowful countenance from La Mancha. Perhaps Muhammad II, also known as Al Fatih, was indeed dissuaded from running his sword

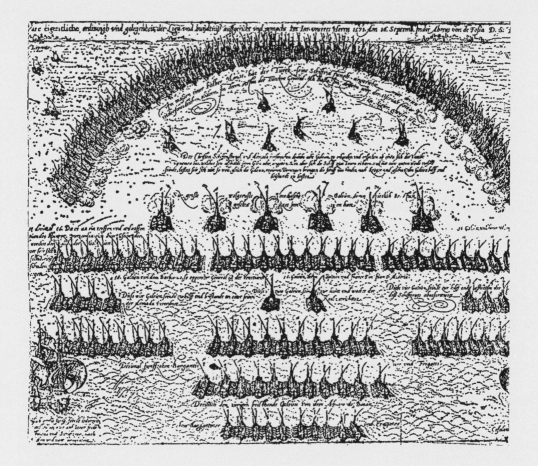

*Disposition of
ships before the
battle of Lepanto.
Copperplate etching
by Martin Kolunić
of Šibenik. Venice,
1572.*

through an admiral who had just lost a battle when a wise counselor reminded him that Allah had entrusted the land to the faithful and left the sea to the giaours. The Battle of Trafalgar, perhaps the most fabled naval battle of all, was won by the better sailors of the bigger sea: the Mediterranean had lost its primacy by then, having clung too long to oars and ignored the new, broader sails.

The South Slavs—the Dalmatian Croats in particular—make much of their role in the war between Austria and Italy in the battle off the island of Vis (Lissa in Italian). Although the enemies lost 643 sailors and the Austro-Dalmatians only 38, for decades thereafter there was nary a Dalmatian who had not sacrificed a relative—distant cousins at first, then grandparents on either or both sides—to the glorious battle. In other words, events like these find a place not only in history books but in people's memories, which is why I bring them up here. (History also has things to say about the fleet of the early Croatian kings, though much has drowned in Mediterranean history.)

In most naval battles—certainly the fiercest and grandest of them—the ships assaulted the sea and the crew members one another. The Mediterranean is no milder than other, larger seas, but for a long time only relatively frail craft tended to embark on it. The wealth of the distant Indies came too late and spread over too many destinations. The literature on the subject is enormous and instructive. It comes from both writers and sailors. The Mediterranean has maintained its primacy in words, but lost it in everything else.

EVERYWHERE THE EYE CAN SEE—from vista to vista, event to event—there are stories about the sea and the coast, the islands and isolation, the body and incarceration, about winds, rivers, and estuaries, about ourselves: the eternal rituals of rise and fall, departure and return, grandiloquence and parody, palingenesis and palimpsest, circlemaking and circlebreaking. The moment we try to penetrate these oppositions, they become eschatology or prosody, yet I do not see how we can avoid them. Putting them into words may represent the Mediterranean's greatest achievement. Setting sail for distant seas and distant continents, the great seafarers have imitated their Mediterranean forebears by keeping minute records of their travels. The ship's log and travelogue are among the earliest genres of literature, the earliest branches of science.

Without the *Iliad*, the *Odyssey*, or the *Anabasis*, the *Aeneid*, the *Divine Comedy*, *Os Lusíadas*, and *Ulysses* would be unthinkable. The Mediterranean is awaiting a new masterpiece dealing with man and the sea.

DENIZENS OF THE NORTH often identify our sea with the South. Something attracts them to it even when they remain perfectly loyal to their homelands. It is more than a need for warm sun and strong light. It may be what has been called "faith in the South." Anyone, regardless of place of birth or residence, can become a Mediterranean. Mediterraneanity is acquired, not inherited; it is a decision, not a privilege. Some even say there are fewer and fewer true Mediterraneans on the Mediterranean. Being Mediterranean entails more than history or geography, tradition or memory, birthright or belief. The Mediterranean is destiny.

93

Breviary

We do not discover the sea ourselves, nor do we view it exclusively through our own eyes. We see it as others have seen it—in the pictures they draw, the stories they tell. We cognize and recognize it simultaneously. We are familiar with seas we have never laid eyes on or bathed in. No view of the Mediterranean is completely autonomous, nor are the descriptions in my breviary all mine.

We prefer older to newer maps, just as we picture ships of olden times more readily than modern ones. Old maps have lost their sharp edges; their colors have faded; they resemble memory. We scan them for seas that are still as they were or seas that have changed; we carry on voyages begun long ago or initiate new ones; we hug the coasts we know or discover the unknown. They bring back the old issues of sea and land: the forms they take, their interaction, and ways to represent them; they bring together knowledge and experience: space and the conception of space, world and world view. They cannot be made without money and power: they require the strong navy and strong state that once prevailed along the Mediterranean.

Sailing along the Adriatic coast from inlet to inlet, island to island, I thought maps were unnecessary; sailing through the Aegean and Ionian Seas on vessels with names like *Hydra* and *Dodekanesos,* I learned how essential they are. (I have not sailed other seas extensively and have never sailed the ocean.) The *Hydra* took its name from the island where it was berthed. Its first mate, a native of Salonika typical of the wise and capable individuals who have always peopled those shores, had two passions besides the sea: Ladino, which was the language of his ancestors

Stein a. A.   O. Szöny   Alt-Ofen

Pettau   Zara   Skardona

Gubbio   Ancona Urbisaglia Ascoli   Potenza Fermo
               Bevagnia Spoleto *pr. Somma*   Androdoco
Civita Vecchia Bagni di Ferrata   Baccano   Narnia *pr. Città*
            Chiaruccia Bagni di Stigliano   Narni

Hr. Bagla   Bu Shater

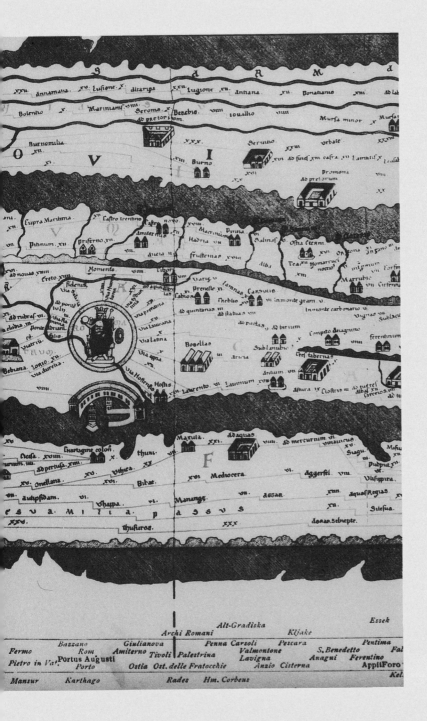

Fragment representing a guide to the streets of Rome from third- and fourth-century sources in the Tabula Peutingeriana. Nationalbibliothek, Vienna.

and which he wanted to make the lingua franca of the Mediterranean, and early maps, about which he knew more than anyone I have ever met. During my two voyages with him—one in the spring, the other in the winter—he taught me most of what I know about maps (certain passages in this section contain more of his words than mine), though I had perused and even studied atlases and albums in various countries before and continued to do so after meeting him. It was like making voyages of a different sort. I would stop in places that had once been ports and locate them on the maps, comparing what was left with what had been, places like Salona, Aquileia, and Adria (Hadria) on the Adriatic; Sybaris on the Gulf of Tarentum and Lilybaeum (Marsala) in Sicily; Phocaea (I have normalized the spelling because the graphemes of the Phoenician originals can be rather shaky) on the Aegean; two Caesareas—one on the African coast, the other on the coast of Asia Minor—and two Ptolemaïses, one in Libya, the other in Phoenicia; the fine piers on Crete near Lasea that are mentioned in the Acts of the Apostles; Tarsus in Cilicia, known for Cleopatra's gate; the biblical Tarshish, known for its ships (though its precise location in the Mediterranean is not known); Apolonia and Berenice on one and the other sides of the Cyrenaica Peninsula; Heraclea and Feodosia in the Crimea (which I reached by land); Dor, south of Carmel; Apsaros, of which only the tiny Osor on the isthmus connecting the islands of Cres and Lošinj (where I have spent a good deal of time) remains; Gorgippia and Germanossa along the strait leading to Lake Meotid, as the Sea of Azov was once called; Cimmerius, or Kimmerion, on the sea itself; the ancient town of Himera on the coast of Sicily; and finally Kithira (Cythera, Cerigo) on the southernmost of the Ionian islands, itself called Kithira. Many ports have changed names, as have the seas they served; others have completely disappeared. If their history has not yet been written, it will never be. As for the maps, I have no intention of going over their history or detailing the scholarship behind them: they can reveal only the wrinkles of the Mediterranean, not its face.

MAPS HAVE EXISTED from time immemorial, though we do not know what the earliest ones looked like. We know they were annotated by logographers (in matters of winds and currents, islands and reefs, potable water, navigational traps, and the like), but the annotations have not been preserved. Herodotus observed bronze plates displaying "all seas and all rivers" during his peregrinations through the Levant, but the Phoenician seafarers refused to let him examine them: maps were strategic and had to be kept secret. The Greeks called them *pinaks,* a word that designated writing tablets in general, but also astrological tables, catalogues of authors, and so on. Hecataeus of Miletus (the same lovers of commonplaces who add the epithet "the father of history" to the name of Herodotus label Hecataeus "the father of geography") called maps "periods of earth," while Apollonius of Rhodes in his *Argonauts* calls them *kyrbeis,* tablets put together in the form of pyramids and used to record laws, wills, and the Homeric epics. Such is the context of the earliest maps in the history of the Mediterranean.

The notions of journey and voyage are so close as to be sometimes interchangeable, though seafarers tend to distinguish them more than others. Greek tradition carefully differentiates between *anabasis* (going up from the coast, overland journey) and *periplous* (circumnavigation, sea voyage), while *periêgesis* denotes travel on both land and sea or its description. The ancients set down the contours of terrestrial and maritime space on a number of surfaces: clay tablets, bronze, stone, wood, parchment or papyrus, mosaics, cloth, rugs and tapestries, coins, walls, and altars. The choice of material depended not only on the way the sea was depicted but also on the place its image had in the general scheme of things. When Solomon built his magnificent temple to Yahweh in Jerusalem, he ordered the sea to be cast in bronze in the form of a circle thirty ells in diameter and five ells high with three figures of bulls supporting it. The Holy Scriptures passed this image on to Christians throughout the Mediterranean region.

Anaximander of Miletus gave form to the *oikumenê* (the inhabited world), and Eratosthenes of Cyrene indicated *sphragides* (rings) on it, the equivalent of seven meridians and seven parallels. The main meridian ran through the island of Rhodes, which was known as a seat of astronomical observation. Eratosthenes' lines of longitude and latitude, measured in stadia and orgia, were reviewed by Hipparchus (whom Pliny with some justification calls Hipparchus of Rhodes, though he was originally from Nicaea). It was Hipparchus who transferred the spheres to the planispheres. The peripatetic Dicaearchus from Sicily divided the world with a "diaphragm," a main parallel of latitude, running from today's Gibraltar through the Strait of Messina and the Peloponnese and on to Lycia and Cilicia in Asia Minor; it was eventually accepted as fact by geographers. Then there is the eccentric Aristarchus

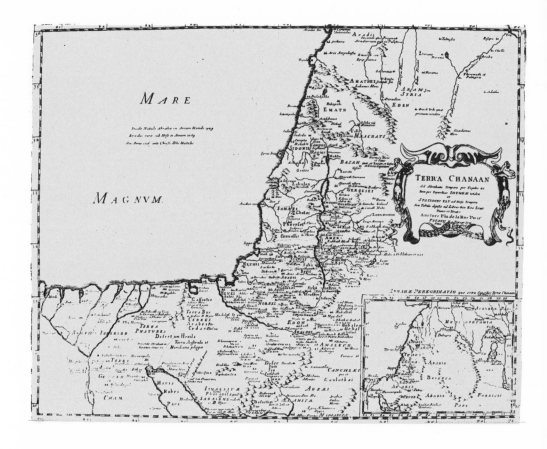

Abraham's journey to Canaan, according to the Old Testament. Philippe de la Rue. Padua, 1669.

of Samos who, back in the first half of the third century before Christ, challenged the Old World and prefigured the New by proclaiming in a fit of inspiration that the earth spins around the sun and not the sun around the earth. The dichotomy between the geography of the scholar and the geography of the mariner pertained from the outset, conditioned as it was by opposing outlooks on the sea. Only the Mediterranean's greatest cartographers earned the trust of the mariners, and only the Mediterranean's most skillful mariners enjoyed the respect of the scholars.

The instruments they both used are reminiscent of figures: the gnomon for finding the sun's meridian altitude, the astrolabe and alemna for taking angular measurements from the surface of the sea to the celestial bodies, the quadrant or sextant for determining position and distance, the organon for choosing straight or curved (*orthodromos* or *loxodromos*) orbits. They sailed without compasses, trusting in vague signs or good fortune and in the belief that Apollo's temple, or the site of the Delphic oracle with its sacred navel-stone (the *omphalos,* which Pausanias the wanderer had seen "sculpted in white marble"), was the center of the earth, or setting their sights on Rhodes or Jerusalem or Mecca. Such were the conceptions of land and sea on the maps and in the memories of the Mediterraneans.

PERIPLI REMAIN TRAVELOGUES or stories even when history validates and scholarship corroborates them. The pharaoh Necho (or Neco—his name has several spellings), who ruled at the turn of the seventh century into the sixth, sent Phoenician mariners to circumnavigate the coast of Africa after realizing he had sacrificed thousands of slaves in a vain attempt to dig through the isthmus separating his two seas. The Phoenicians set sail from Eritrea and returned three years later through the Pillars of Hercules and along the Mediterranean to the northern coast of Egypt. Scylax of Caria (Scylax Caryadensis, as he is called in Latin sources) set sail twenty-five centuries ago in the service of the emperor of Persia, plowing the southern and eastern seas all the way to India, and his successor, known as Pseudo-Scylax, passed through the "Euxine" and "Hadriatic" Seas (providing valuable, if less than reliable, information about the latter). Hanno the Carthaginian sailed through the Strait of Gibraltar (we do not know what the Punics called it) approximately five centuries before the Christian era with "sixty fifty-oared ships" and "thirty thousand men and women" and headed for the south of Africa, where he discovered a number of islands—including Kerne, which is still unknown—observed lotus eaters (lotophagi) and cannibals (anthropophagi), gorillas and torrents of fire spouting from a volcano whose name is also unknown, and heard the tam-tam reverberating from the cliffs along the shore. A Phoenician named Pitheas from the ancient Greek colony of Massilia passed through the same strait in the fourth century before Christ, but headed north (where the Carthaginian Himilkom, en route to the Cassiterides, had been before him), circumnavigated Britain and Ireland, probably seeking amber and tin, and gazed upon the Ultima Thule from the North Sea. The Swedish geologist and explorer Nils Adolf Erik Nordenskjöld depicts many other great early circumnavigations in his *Periplus,* which dates from the end of the nineteenth century and remains to this day the best work on the subject. Having been told of voyages from the Mediterranean's infancy in our own infancy and having plotted them on our first maps, we first saw the sea through their eyes.

PERHAPS THE REASON sea routes of the past are so difficult to establish is that they are so easily confused with the stories about them. The maps on which they figure may thus be wishful thinking, the annotations counterfeit. Pitheas has been vilified by many historians and geographers: Strabo refused to believe that Pitheas had found a place where "the Tropic of Cancer becomes the Arctic Circle" and "the land is such that one can neither tread nor sail it," and Polybius regarded Pitheas' voyages as so many fabrications. (There is a boundary, the sages claimed, between the probable and the improbable or, as we might put it today, between tropes of history and of narrative; the periplus overstepped the boundary and belonged more to the realm of fantastic exploits.) He was, however, taken at his word by Hecataeus and Eratosthenes, who probably shared his view of the earth; by Herodotus and Pliny, who were more than historians; and, last but not least, by Aristotle himself. The account of Hanno's voyage was carved in Punic on a votive stone in the temple to Moloch in the center of Carthage. Although the stone was lost when the temple was destroyed, the inscription had been translated into Greek and survived. What did not survive in any Mediterranean archive was the map the practical Carthaginians must have made to guide him.

Islands are not merely closed-off space; they can also serve to close space off. Early maps show such to be the case with the Ultima Thule in the north, the Insulae Fortunatae in the west, the large island of Taprobana (Ceylon) in the east, and the austral zone in the south. Diodorus Siculus transcribes a fragment from a lost work by Euhemerus of Messene that places the island of Pankaia at the end of the world. The *oikumenê* too is portrayed as a huge island. Mediterranean writers describe a number of fortunate islands as yet unvisited by mariners and uncharted by geographers. I retain mellifluous names like Achilles Tatius, Iamblichus of Syria, Xenophon of Ephesus, Heliodorus, and Juba the Younger more easily than others, though there are many others perhaps equally important and prolific. Once better known than they are now, they eventually became the victims of many a geographer's irony: no islands of the sort exist in any sea or on any map. Literary criticism may thus be said to have had its origins in geographic and cartographic criticism. We owe its existence to islands. The more critics are praised, the fewer praiseworthy critics there are—along the Mediterranean, at least.

The Scriptures contain a number of travel descriptions that were respected by cartographers and used by them for their maps. For all its prophetic discourse, the Old Testament includes the following Mediterranean travelogue: "And the Israelites departed from Rameses on the fifteenth day of the first month. . . . And from Pi-hahiroth they passed through the midst of the sea into the wilderness, and went three day's journey in the wilderness of Etham, and pitched in Marah. And they removed from Marah, and came unto Elim; and in Elim were twelve fountains of water and threescore and ten palm tress; and they pitched there. . . . And they came unto the Valley of Eshcol, and cut down from thence a branch with one cluster of grapes, and they bore it between two upon a staff; and they brought of the pomegranates, and of the figs. . . . Manna was like the coriander seed, white. We remember the fish, which we did eat in Egypt freely; the cucumbers, and the melons, and the leeks, and the onions, and the garlic." This type of text came to be a model for both maps and travel descriptions of the Mediterranean.

THE MEDITERRANEAN is more than the sea and its coasts, as I—and many before me—have pointed out. The Greeks neglected overland routes and paid dearly for it: it kept them from moving beyond antiquity. The Romans conquered more seas than the Greeks and did so thanks to their roads. Roman maps were road maps, "itineraries." Vegetius Renatus, the prime expert on Roman military might, divided them into *itineraria adnotata* (or *itineraria scripta*) and *itineraria picta*. They were uniform and practical. The Romans were more concerned with space and distance than form and ornamentation. They gave their maps banal names: *tabulae* or *mensae*. (Names help us to establish the order of things.) The long parchment scroll known as the Tabula Peutingeriana, which is probably based on a model from the reign of Caracalla, represents the Imperium from the Atlantic to Asia Minor. It indicates roads only, the sea being designated by two gray-green or, occasionally, nearly brown, earthlike zones. One is the Adriatic, the other the Mediterranean.

Roman roads were connected with the sea: the via Ostiensis and the via Portuensis descended straight into the port of the eternal city, Ostia; the via Appia led south, the via Aurelia west, the via Flaminia north, and the via Valeria and via Salaria (which the Sabines used for transporting salt) to the Adriatic; the via Severiana followed the Tyrrhenian coast; the via Iulia Augusta linked the Apennine Peninsula to Provence and Catalonia; the via Flavia led to Istria and Dalmatia and had lesser known extensions for the Gulf of Kotor, Montenegro, and Albania; and the famous via Ignatia was built with the ambition of bringing Rome closer to Greece. On the Iberian Peninsula the Argentea, the Maxima, and the Augusta ran across vertiginous bridges and mountain passes. Forty thousand miles of banked and paved roads stretched along the northern rim of Africa through the desert *limes* from Syrtis Major to Syria, from Tripoli in Libya to Tripoli in Lebanon, from the Marmarica to the "Sea of Reeds." The roads in Palestine and Asia Minor also hugged the sea (*via maris*), providing overland connections between ports like Sidon and Tir, Byblos, Beirut, and Antioch on the Orontes, Miletus, Ephesus, Smyrna, and even the Bosporus (which, as is clear from the Tabula Peutingeriana, could be reached by the forenamed via Ignatia). The port of Aquileia, which after being ravaged by barbarians sank into marshland, was at one time crossed by five major roads, including the "amber way," the pride of the Adriatic. Trajan's legionnaires succeeded in penetrating the stone "caldron" at the Iron Gates on the Danube and thus made their back way to the sea. The feat is recorded in the Tabula Traiana, carved in stone above the river bank and visible to this day. Apollodorus of Damascus immortalized Trajan's career as emperor in the monumental reliefs he designed for the column in the Forum of Trajan, thus turning the anabasis into a map of sorts, and Agrippa ordered the borders of the Imperium, which by his time had stretched far beyond the Mediterranean, to be carved on an oval marble plaque near the Forum: the whole world seemed to be aspiring to mapdom.

CHRISTIANITY DID NOT promote navigation. The Old Testament was not partial to "peoples of the sea": they tended to clash, as we have seen, with the chosen people. The prophets threatened sinners with

europa & affrica   De. Aſiaᶓ

Oriens

MARE

ASIA
Sem

Septentrio

Mare magnum ſiue

EVROPA   AFRICA
Iafeth   Cham

Meridies

Occidens

giones·quarū breuiter nomina et ſitus
a paradiſo ¶Paradiſus eſt locus in or

T-O Christian
world map.
Isidore of Seville,
Etymologiae.
Augsburg, 1472.

sea monsters like the Leviathan and Rahab. Daniel dreams that "four great beasts came up from the sea," and Saint John the Apostle in the Apocalypse sees "a beast rise up out of the sea, having seven heads and ten horns." Homer the pagan also portrays the horrors of the sea, though without neglecting its beauty: besides soulless sirens, he gives us nereids, that is, sea nymphs. Christianity was not interested in nymphlike delights. Medieval Christian geographers in the western Mediterranean did not know Ptolemy.

Joshua in the Old Testament called upon the sun to stand still above Gideon so as to give him time to bring his attack on the Amorites to a victorious conclusion. "And the sun stood still." In other words, it ceased to move over the face of the earth, considered flat at the time. The prophet's feat would have to be transformed into metaphor for exegetes (who are not always fond of metaphor) to allow that the earth was in fact doing the moving. (*E pur si muove,* as Galileo put it: It *does* move.) Saint Augustine used his authority to question the existence of the antipodes, proclaiming them "an absurdity not to be believed." The church fathers put their faith in the T-O map, which depicts the *T* as the Mediterranean between three continents and the *O* as the "sea of oceans" surrounding the earth's surface. Following the Scriptures, it shows Jerusalem as the center of the world, with Gog and Magog, which Ezekiel the prophet damned as the epitome of evil, on the eastern rim. Symbolic significance was attributed to the letters, some considering the *T* to stand for Theos and the *O* for Okeanos, others, more secularly inclined, seeing them as an abbreviation for Terrarum Orbis. In lay terminology (or the terminology of humanism) it was called Sallust's map because it served to illustrate the Roman historian's description of the African campaign and the crossing of the African Sea. Several variants were made to conform to church doctrine: the "Commentary to the Apocalypse" that Beatus of Liebana presented at the Abbey of Saint-Sever follows the *Etymologiae* of Father Isidore of Seville, placing the east along with Jerusalem at the top; the map in Hereford Cathedral has a picture of the Last Judgment above the surface of the sea; and the huge parchment at the Ebstorf Monastery shows a *T* in the form of a crucifix and the name of our sea as Mare Strictum. Until the Renaissance, in fact, maps tended to play down the size of the Mediterranean and depict it in pale hues, the only exception being manuscript miniatures, which used brighter paint for both sky and water. But miniatures were not a genre equal to the task of encompassing the Mediterranean and altering Christianity's view of it.

There is a certain duality in the Christian position: on the one hand we have Saint Augustine, born at Thagaste on the ill-favored Numidian coast and not at all taken with the sea, and on the other Saint Jerome, born in Stridon, a town that has completely disappeared (though we know it was in Illyria, possibly between Split and Šibenik); we have John the Apostle, who suffered under Domitian in the quarries on the island of Patmos, and the Apostle Paul, who survived a tempest on the Adriatic and a shipwreck off Malta on the way from the Holy Land to the Eternal City. The Faith did not renounce the sea, even in the parts of the Mediterranean where it was at its most rigorous.

EARLY IN HIS *GEOGRAPHY* Ptolemy stresses the importance of "the history of travel and the information gleaned from travelers scrupulous in their exploration of foreign parts." Many are the books written by or dedicated to the travelers who trod and sailed the known world during the medieval and early modern periods from the shores of the Mediterranean to the Far East and beyond, many the accounts of their discoveries and adventures, of their persons and often eccentric personalities. Their names evoke admiration and doubt, enthusiasm and scorn.

Description of
the apostle Paul's
journey, according to
the New Testament.
Abraham Ortelius.
Padua, 1697.

Among the first is a man named Cosmas (and nicknamed the Indo-mariner—Indicopleustes—in Byzantium), who began as an adventurer merchant and ended as a monk on Mount Sinai, and who created a map of the world in accordance with the tabernacle of Saint Paul. Then—though my chronology is far from strict—we have Father Rubriquis, or Rubruck; Odorico da Pordenone; Giovanni da Pian del Carine; Bartolomeo di Cremona, whose journeys deserve mention if only because they were so arduous; the French physician Jehan de Mandeville; Presbyter John, whom legend has placed on the throne of "the three Indias"; Ciriaco di Ancona, merchant and humanist, who copied manuscripts and sketched ancient monuments; Fra Maringoli of the order of the Frati Minori or Minorites; Rabbi Benjamin of Tudela, who traveled throughout the Jewish diaspora, caring for it as he could; Varthema Lodovico, a.k.a. Barthema Luiz, who was both Italian and Portuguese and—depending on the circumstances—either Christian or Muslim; and the legendary Brendan, Irish saint and sailor, who probably reached the waters of the Mediterranean.

Travelers vary as greatly as the travels they undertake: some go straight or circle, others criss and cross; some have a specific destination in mind, others have no goal other than the desire to discover the unknown or themselves; some return to where they started, others move on, seeking new and different people or places. (Odysseus makes his way back to Ithaca, while Aeneas never goes home; the *Odyssey* thus finds closure, while the *Aeneid* remains incomplete.) There are lone travelers and travelers with whole caravans of escort and equipment; travelers stimulated by an inner drive or sense of vocation and travelers forced onto the road by circumstance; travelers who talk and write about what they observe and travelers who observe for the sake of observation and for the joy of it. Little is known of the thoughts and feelings that dwell in travelers who spend days, weeks, even months on a ship watching only and always a sea calm or tempestuous, blue or gray. Nor shall we ever learn about the travelers who, God only knows whence and how, brought the seeds and cuttings for olives, grapes, figs, and agave from their distant homelands to the Mediterranean.

The history of travel and the history of mapmaking are inextricably intertwined. Columbus prepared for his voyage by reading Ptolemy's *Geography*, the *Imago Mundi* of Cardinal Petrus de Aliaca (Pierre d'Ailly), and Marco Polo. (Among the many travelers who set forth from the Mediterranean to explore distant shores, Marco Polo might be singled out for having, as one scholar writes, "left static time for space." Soon after he described the archipelago of Zipango—Japan— in the Far East, it started appearing on maps in various vernacular forms: Zinpangu, Cipango, Zapango, etc.) Dante sent Odysseus through the Pillars of Hercules "to a world without people on the far side of the sun"—and this before Columbus; in other words, the imagination set sail for the New World nearly two centuries before the Spanish car- avels, when the ocean came to be seen as more than an extension of the Mediterranean.

Saint Louis, king of France, was surprised when on his voyage to the Crusades (along the coast of Sardinia, near Cagliari—historians have located the precise spot) he was shown a map that clearly distinguished sea and coasts. As the Middle Ages waned, sea captains began using not only compasses but also a new type of marine or nautical map (*carta de marear, carta nautica, roteiro, routier*) for which the generic name was portolano. Routes became clearer, distances more easily discernible, leg- ends more graphic in the new atlases of Luxor and Catalonia and the map of Pisa, in the portolanos of Pietro Visconti of Genoa, the Pizigano brothers of Venice, Angelino Dulcerto of the Balearic Islands, and oth- ers. This was also the period when wind roses made their appearance. The first were from Majorca. They came in various colors and were shaped like stars with eight—and, later, more—points. Things were quite different on the southern shores of the Mediterranean.

EVEN WITHOUT MAPS, the Arabs sailed up and down the coasts, con- quering the sea and making inroads on the land. They went from east to west, from Mashrek to the Maghreb, the direction of the Jewish di- aspora, Christian evangelism, and various campaigns or migrations from the Near and Far East (there is no clear-cut boundary between mili- tary campaigns and the migrations of peoples, the barbaric campaigns that annihilated a number of Mediterranean seaports having been eu- phemistically called migrations). All these peoples followed the sun, which fact may have made them more successful than most. The Arab conquerors took Ifriquia and Iskanderia and crossed to the northern coast, where they came to know Aristotle and Ptolemy before us, de- spite the fire that destroyed the library at Alexandria. Ptolemy's *Geog- raphy* was translated into Arabic from both the Greek and the Syrian before it made its way into the European vernaculars. His *Great Syn-*

tax became the celebrated *Almagest.* The Arab geographer al-Mas'udi knew the maps of the Greek geographer Marinus of Tyrus, which Ptolemy himself had studied. Al-Battani accepted Ptolemy's views; al-Khwarazmi developed them; al-Biruni went so far as to presage Galileo. On the Mediterranean, knowledge of geography traveled from east to west and from south to north.

How much the Arabs knew about seas and navigation in their native realm is unclear, but they learned fast after entering the Mediterranean, subduing the Byzantine navy at Cape Phoenix, threatening Genoa and Venice, and seizing the Spanish and Catalan coasts. The instruments that helped them to do so they partly invented or improved and partly adopted or appropriated. They had their own astrolabe (which they called *asturlab, astrulab,* or, using native terms, *kamal* and *safihah*). The alidade, which had been perfected by Archimedes in Syracuse, enabled them to determine their position with respect to the stars and the sun. Al-Hawkandi constructed a sextant, which he called *suds al-fakhri.* The root of azimuth, a word all European languages have adopted, is the Arab *samt* (way, directory); it is likewise the root of *zenith.* Venice borrowed the word *arsenale* (dock) from the Arabs for its famous building on the lagoon. The word *darsena,* the section of the port of Genoa near the old shipyard, is of the same origin, as is the *vieille darse,* built by Henry IV at Toulon. There are four *dársenas* in the old port of Barcelona, the most attractive being the *dársena de San Beltrán.* (I spent much time there. It is near the former harbor headquarters and the impressive monument to Columbus.) The spread of the Arabic word for tar throughout the region (*al-qatran* in Arabic, *catrame* in Italian, *katran* in Croatian) implies that the Arabs made early and extensive use of the material in shipbuilding. Furthermore, all Mediterranean navies adopted the Arabic word *amir* for admiral. The word *cipher* comes from the Arabic *sifr* (zero), and, more important, Arabic numerals replaced Roman numerals. We do not know whether the Arabs had the compass before other Mediterranean mariners like the famous Amalfians (they called it *da'ira* [circle]), but when Vasco da Gama moored on the east coast of Africa, he chose the Arab Ahmed Ibn Magid to take the helm for his voyage to India. Clearly he was more than equal in skill to the Spanish and Portuguese explorers of the time. Ibn Khaldun noted that while the coasts of the Rumelian Sea had been duly charted, the Atlantic coasts had not. The Arabic words for map were *al-sahifa* (the term used by Ibn Khaldun), *al-sura, tarsim,* *daftar,* the Greek borrowing *kharita,* and the Latin borrowing *tawla.* The very fact that they had so many words is telling and confirms the significance of their role on the Mediterranean.

Arab travelers proved particularly helpful to cartographers. They tended to journey by land rather than by sea, preferring foot travel to the sail. The faithful prayed five times a day—three of which occurred on the road—and each time they turned in the direction of Mecca, east if they were in the west and west if they were in the east, trying to gauge their distance from and position relative to the Kaaba. The well-developed sense of geography their prayers entailed was reflected in their maps. Religious tradition accounts for much Arabic travel: the journey of the first Muslims to Abyssinia, various campaigns, the migration from Mecca to Yathrib—that is, the Hegira to Medina in 622, the year in which the Islam calendar begins—and the hadj, the pilgrimage to the Kaaba. There are many words for voyage in the Qur'an, as there are in Arabic in general. They include *sayr, tariq, sabil,* and *safar* (which comes from the same root as the word *Sephardim,* referring to the Spanish Jews, that is, a traveling people). According to ancient Arabic inscriptions, navigation (*milaha*) is more often understood as part of a journey than as an independent concept. The word *rihla* refers both to a journey and to its description. Such descriptions constitute a genre that flourished more than any and served scholarship—geography and cartography—as well as literature. It was capacious enough to include almanacs, calendars, grammars, zodiacs, horoscopes, the occasional map, and all sorts of accounts connected with peregrinations through the Mediterranean and beyond.

The space conquered by the Arabs was not easy to cross, yet their travelers ventured beyond it. Those who went the farthest were Ibn Jubair, a native of Valencia, and Ibn Battuta, a native of Tangier, a city that like Cádiz and Lisbon lies on the Atlantic coast yet is to a large extent Mediterranean in character. Retelling an Arabic *rihla* is no easy task. Here is how Ibn Battuta describes the lighthouse and city gates in the port of Alexandria: "Bab al-Sidra or the Gate of the Wild Jujube, Bab al-Rashid or the Gate of the Just, Bab al-Bahr or the Gate of the Sea, and Bab al-Akhdar or the Green Gate, which is open on Fridays to give the population a chance to visit the cemetery. Iskandaria shines like a precious stone. It transmits its radiance to the West.

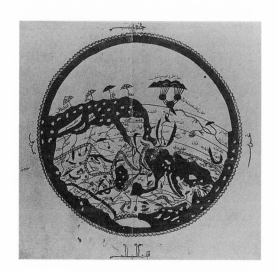

Circular world map. The south is above, the north below. The Mediterranean is on the right in the form of an elephant. Al-Idrisi. Sicily, twelfth century.

112

Maps

It combines all the splendors of East and West." Such is the calligraphic inscription adorning the wall of an ancient Mediterranean city (which has in fact retained little that is ancient).

Interpreters of Arabic tradition make much of the distinction between internal and external travel. They thus differentiate between Ibn Battuta's voyage around the world and the Sufic voyage of Ibn Arabi, who, departing from his native Murcia on the coast of Spain, journeyed into himself in search of Allah, a light (*nur*) stronger than the light shining on his native land. God's ways come together with the ways of the world much as sea and desert come together; indeed, the prophets speak of the sea of the desert. A sura in the Qur'an teaches that those who travel through the world "understand with their hearts what needs to be understood." Without such travelers, there would have been no Arabic maps, which in their day were the best the Mediterranean had to offer.

Yet even they had to make concessions. The Qur'an recognizes two seas separated by a barrier; "seven seas" occurs only in metaphors. According to the Book, "the sun moves within set limits" and Allah "spread" the earth and "made it even." Hence there are no antipodes, and Arabic maps, like their early Christian counterparts, display only a single side of the earth. But the Prophet welcomed ships on the sea:

He encouraged His people to eat of its fruits and use what they could to adorn themselves; He urged them to conquer the sea, stating several times in the *hadith* that a victory at sea is worth ten on land. And for victories at sea, for conquering the Mediterranean, naval maps were a necessity.

Arab cartographers placed south above north, as befit their view of the world, and placed the main meridian at Mecca, as their faith required. They showed Yajuj and Majuj (the biblical Gog and Magog) on their maps, again for reasons of faith, but did not show sea monsters, because the Qur'an does not mention them. The Arabs had excellent cartographers, but I cannot examine all of them here. The most famous, al-Idrisi, had two nicknames: the Sicilian (al-Saqalli), from the island where he did his work, and the Cordovan (al-Qurtubi), from the city where he gained his fame. (He was born near Gibraltar, in Ceuta, which the Arabs call Sabta). Under the aegis of the Norman king Roger II, in twelfth-century Palermo, he made maps "for the diversion of those who would travel the world." (So reads the subtitle of his celebrated *Kitab*.) He illustrated his *invitations au voyage* with what he called "gardens of delight." They are the most exquisite Arabic gardens I know. He fashioned a huge map, three and a half meters long by one and a half meters wide, out of silver. It was known as Roger's Tabula. It soon broke. Al-Idrisi was at home in several cultures: he was acquainted with Greek and Latin sources and sources from the Near East. He borrowed Ptolemy's teachings on climate, according each climate its own color. In the Mediterranean, the "fourth climate" in his categorization, the dominant colors are green, blue (for the sea), yellow (for the desert), and very light to very dark red (for the sunrises and sunsets over the sea and the desert). The Atlantic is dark: the Arabs call it the Dark Sea (Bahr al-Zulumat). Al-Idris's maps are not so much practical as beautiful. They have no equal in medieval Mediterranean art and were influential in the Christian *art mudéjar* of the period.

While promoting traffic along the Mediterranean coasts, the Arabs did not pretend to rule the waves, and the duality of their position proved uncomfortable even when they were at the peak of their power. Later, disunited, weakened by the reconquista, and finally defeated by Ottoman forces, they lost their preeminence in mapmaking as well, and their maps came to convey a sense of nostalgia vis-à-vis the Mediterranean.

Sinbad the Sailor sought his fortune in other climes during the seven voyages he made from Baghdad and the Gulf of Oman to the islands

of earthly paradise in the Indian Ocean. But since on such voyages all seas are one or each is unique, there is no telling but that Sinbad called at one or another of the Mediterranean ports Ibn Battuta described so well.

Arab cartographers are famed for knowing many things. Al-Muqaddasi's map of Syria and Palestine shows Sayda, which is all that remains of Sidon, and Sur, which is all that remains of Tyre; it shows Latakia in the place where Laodicea was once situated. During the ninth century after the Hegira (the sixteenth century, according to the Christian calendar), in the Tunisian city of Sfax, al-Sharfi made a valiant attempt to revive the Arabic tradition of mapmaking. One of his most striking maps (which I saw in a camel-skin copy) shows the Kaaba in the center of the world. The story of Arabic cartography, which in the style of Oriental tales is perhaps overburdened with detail, contains valuable lessons for the entire Mediterranean region.

ON THE EVE OF DISCOVERY of the New World, geographers finally discovered the Old. They discovered it on Ptolemaic maps. At the beginning of the fifteenth century a Byzantine envoy by the name of Manuel Chrysoloras (I give his name in the form in which it most frequently appeared in Europe) visited Rome and Florence on a mission from the court of the Palaeologi, who wished to make Europe aware of the threat coming from the East. Chrysoloras, who counted geography among his interests, brought a manuscript of Ptolemy's *Geography* from Constantinople, a manuscript with twenty-seven maps and seven climates. He started translating it into Latin, but was hampered by illness, and his disciple Jacopus Angelus eventually completed the work. In Paris there is a portrait showing him book in hand, with a broad forehead, tired eyes, and signs of illness on his face. He died of tuberculosis in Konstanz in 1415. People who knew him say he had

The Kaaba in the center of the world. Al-Sharfi, cartographical school of Sfax. Tunisia, sixteenth century.

an extraordinary memory and was a fine speaker. (He spoke with equal passion about Plato and Ptolemy.) Little is known of the young Angelus, though his relationship with Chrysoloras has given rise to speculation. Since Angelus dedicated his translation to Pope Alexander V, he must have completed it in approximately 1410. The Pope absolved him of his sins and blessed him. A patron by the name of Palla Strozzi is said to have taken a copy of the *Geography* to Florence before Chrysoloras. In any case, cartography often served as a backdrop on the Mediterranean.

The translation of Ptolemy's *Geography* bearing the Pope's blessing circulated throughout the capitals of Europe in numerous manuscripts and, after Gutenberg's invention, in printed form, gradually acquiring various accretions, emendations, and *tabulae modernae*. Many scholars took part. The theologian and geographer Cardinal Nicholas of Cusa (whose lay name was Nikolaus Krebs) supplemented the topography of Central Europe, which he saw as closely related to, even dependent on, the Mediterranean, a view that has once more become timely in deliberations about peoples and borders in the area.

The maps Chrysoloras brought from Constantinople were not painted (they are presumed to be copies made by an obscure Alexandrian artisan by the name of Agathodaimon), and color had to be added. The Cinquecento introduced the genre of the *veduta,* or panorama, in which the sea acquired greater prominence and color greater force. The same applied to maps. Moreover, issues of projection had a direct bearing on the new concern with perspective. Mapmakers and painters began working together: Albrecht Dürer collaborated on an edition of Ptolemy; Martin de Vos helped to publish Ortelius's *Theatrum Orbis Terrarum;* Hans Holbein the Younger worked for a number of mapmakers; Andrea Mantegna painted a map on a wall (later destroyed) of the ducal palace in Mantua; Leonardo da Vinci's map of Imola represents a unique fusion of Mercator projection and painterly perspective. Even earlier, Abraham Cresques, creator of the *Catalan Atlas,* combined the mapmaker's craft with the art of the miniature, and it is most likely his school that produced the famous Haggadah the Sephardi brought to the Balkans from Barcelona. On a tiny island near Krk in the Kvarner there is a monastery called Košljun where I saw an old edition of Ptolemy with separate copies of the fifth and sixth plates (which show the eastern and western shores of the Adriatic). Judging by the dark blue paint, they were made in the fifteenth century by the all-

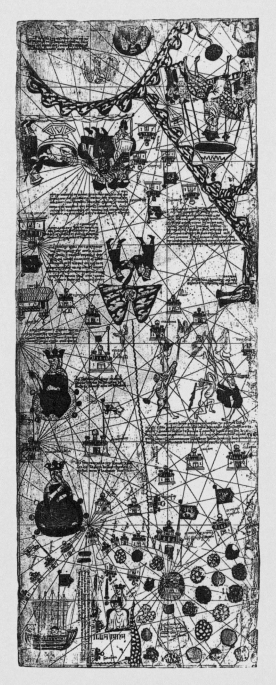

Narrative scenes.
Abraham Cresques,
Catalan Atlas.
Palma de Majorca,
1375.

but-forgotten Florentine Francesco Berlinghieri. Dalmatian sea captains, Venetian ship's chandlers, in short, the most prominent personages up and down the Mediterranean hung framed maps of the sea in the most prominent places in their houses—beside the crucifix, the ex votos, the family portraits—as a sign of respect.

As LITTLE IS KNOWN of mapmakers as of travelers. Conceptualizing sea and land is no run-of-the-mill occupation, and those who chose to do so were no run-of-the-mill people. Giacomo Gastaldi, an engineer by training, left Piedmont to make maps in Venice, while Pietro Coppo left Venice for Istria, where he became Petar Kopić and produced the most reliable map of the Istrian Peninsula; a Camaldolese from Saint Michael's Monastery in Murano, Fra Mauro by name, sent his map to King Alphonse V in Lisbon, the rival of the Serenissima; the Minorite Father Marco Vincenzo Coronelli founded the first geographic society in the world, the Argonauts, and, as official cartographer to the Republic of Saint Mark, constructed a huge globe for the Sun King, which is still on display in Versailles. Florence, Genoa, and several other Italian cities had their own mapmaking studios. But Italy's dominance in the field was abetted by foreigners, such as those who added the epithet Germanicus to their Latinized names or the modest founder of the Leghorn school of cartography, Vicko Demetrije Volčić, a native of Dubrovnik, who Latinized his surname to Volcius. Some masterpieces of the period—Behaim's globe, for instance, or Mercator's *Atlas*—originated far from the shores of the Mediterranean.

Among the mapmakers listed in the standard reference works, Piri Reis, cartographer to the Ottoman Empire and author of the famous *Kitab-i-Bahriye,* deserves special mention here. In the course of the naval battle at Valencia in 1501, Captain Kemal seized some maps from a Spanish galleon and turned them over to his nephew Piri, who used them to make a map of the world, of which only the western section is extant. Since the Spanish maps included Columbus's recent discoveries, Asia was able to see America from the shores of the Mediterranean in the time of Suleiman the Magnificent. And although it was a time of other great cartographers, we shall skip over them, their imaginations—and with them their maps—having strayed farther and farther from the Mediterranean to the oceans.

Fragment from a map of the world, with marginal notes. Piri Reis, cartographer to Suleiman the Magnificent. 1513.

Sketch of the island of Hispaniola. Christopher Columbus. 1492.

Mediterranean seafarers set sail with assumptions acquired on their own sea. Records of early oceanic voyages (logs and the like) indicate how amazed crews were to find coasts different from the ones they were accustomed to: at home they looked for other seas; abroad they seemed to be looking for the Mediterranean. Perhaps there is some basis for an anthropologist's recent hypothesis that the explorers set out more to confirm their ideas, legends, and beliefs—Atlantis, the Hesperides, the Golden Fleece, Eldorado, Arcadia, Eden—than to discover a new world. In any case, once the New World and its oceans were discovered, our relationship to the world and sea we inhabited necessarily changed: those of us who did not expose ourselves to the risk of the voyage became ipso facto loyal Mediterraneans.

THE MEDIEVAL *imago mundi,* a disk with three continents and two seas and the sea of oceans surrounding them, fell apart by itself. Its replacement had more to do than represent the new space that had been discovered; it had to find a new way to represent space. Mercator introduced the figure of Atlas into geography to distinguish science from myth: in the *Odyssey* the titan Atlas holds the pillars "dividing heaven from earth" on his shoulders; in Mercator's *Atlas* the world is both part of the universe and an entity in and of itself. An attempt by French cartographers to substitute Neptune's name for Atlas' to refer to a book of maps did not meet with acceptance. Titles of the great classics of cartography bespeak the search for a different image of the world: *De Summa Totius Orbis, Civitates Orbis Terrarum, Speculum Orbis Terrarum, Spiegel der Zeevaert, The Mariner's Mirror, Theatrum Orbis Terrarum, Teatro del cielo e della terra, Théâtre françois, Liber Chronicarum, Universalis Cosmographia, Cosmographicae Meditationes de Fabrica Mundi et Fabricati Figura.* The metaphors of the mirror (*speculum*), theater (*theatrum*), and circle (*orbis*) testify to the epic ambition of the Renaissance to represent the world as a scene, event, or narrative (the terms I use to open this book). Although the Mediterranean was no longer the center of the world but merely a part of it, it would be long in seeing and grasping its new status.

Newcomers to the art of mapmaking are impressed by giant mural maps reflecting the desire, need, or intention to enlarge the mirror of the world, the stage on which events play themselves out, the circle the earth makes. I have visited a number of their sites and found them

MAR DE AFFERICA

MAR DE ... ALM ...

Tapestry depicting the naval expedition of Charles V from Genoa to Tunisia. Historisches Museum, Vienna. Drawing by the Flemish painter Jan Cornelisz Vermeyen. 1535.

impressive as well: the Galleria delle carte geografiche in the Vatican, particularly the famous Terza Loggia, for which Pope Pius IV (a Medici) employed only the finest craftsmen; the part of the Palazzo del Laterano that Pope Zacharias IX (himself apparently a geographer) had adorned with geographic frescoes; the Palazzo di Caprarola, the country house of the Farnese family outside Rome, its walls covered with geographic motifs by Antonio Varese; the Palazzo Vecchio in Florence and the Palazzo Ducale in Venice; the altar of Hereford Cathedral, which was destroyed during World War II; the mosaic on the floor of what was once a Byzantine basilica in the ancient Moabite town of Madeba showing the contours of the Holy Land and parts of Egypt. In these figurations the sea itself may be less important than the desire to conquer or dominate it. The Nationalbibliothek in Vienna has a tapestry depicting a voyage from Genoa to Tunisia—Charles V's campaign against the Tunisians—based on a cartoon by the Flemish master Vermeyen. After taking Constantinople, the sultan Muhammad II commissioned the Greek geographer Georgios Amiruces to reproduce Ptolemy's maps with legends in Greek and Arabic as a basis for Anatolian kilims. (None is extant.) Many of the renowned French tapestries (the Beauvais tapestries, for instance) portray waterscapes, but the Atlantic is more common than the Mediterranean and landscapes more common than either.

It would be wrong to relate cartography to epic or dramatic genres alone: it offers many examples of modesty. The word *mappa* originally designated an ordinary piece of cloth waved at Roman circuses. It may come from Punic, though its precise etymology is unclear. For a long time biblical sea serpents were fixtures on maps, especially maps showing foreign waters. They resemble enormous fish baring their teeth and flapping their fins like the Leviathan or the Rahab. Mercator's work is revolutionary here as well: he exorcised the map. (His *Atlas* does contain monsters, but only on the pages done by others, such as Hondius.) In ancient times, as we have seen, geography served as a kind of criticism of the novel; Mercator turned it into a criticism of the imagination. (Voltaire later proclaimed it a criticism of vanity.) Rationalist cartographers in France (like Cassini, *père* and *fils,* who came from the south) combined rigor with moderation. Pope Paul V tried to refute the new ideas about the earth and defend biblical tradition in an early-seventeenth-century encyclical. The Enlightenment opposed both Christian and Islamic views on the subject. The meridian that

The map shows various place names including:

TABVLA EVROPÆ V

GERMANIÆ MAGNÆ PARS

IAZYGES

RHAETIA · VINDELICIA · NORICVM · PANNONIA · PANNONIA inferior

Venetia · Alpes · Padus · Ravenna · Ancona · ITALIA · Roma · Tiberis · Apulia

Genua · Liguria · Mare Thyrrenum · Napoli · Taretu · Brendisiu

Adriaticum · ILLYRIS · Salona · Corcyra nigra

CORSICA PARS · SARDINIÆ PARS

DACIÆ PARS · MACEDONIÆ PARS · EPIRI PARS

serves as the basis for standard time—and has done so since the middle of the eighteenth century—runs through Greenwich and not Jerusalem or the Kaaba. By then maps—like their views of the Mediterranean and other seas—had been thoroughly secularized.

LARGE MAPS NEED the support of power. We have only to read the *cartouche* testimonials thanking benefactors and praising patrons. Cartography was a state secret from the Phoenicians to the Byzantine Empire: as late as Chrysoloras' mission, Ptolemy's maps were under the official control of the Eastern Empire. If little is known of early Spanish and Portuguese maps (which we too have little to say about), it is because the great naval powers made a policy of silence until the Basque Juan de la Cosa, who accompanied Columbus, made a map of the New

The Tyrrhenian and Adriatic Seas in Ptolemy's fifth Tabula. Adapted and supplemented by Pietro Andrea Mattioli, Geografia. Venice, 1548.

World on donkey hide (though it too was long kept under wraps). Picture the large gathering of geographers convoked by the Portuguese Prince Henry the Navigator at Sagres near the Cape Saint Vincent at the far end of Europe and on the threshold of the great discoveries. Henry realized that a country on the edge of the continent with a less than propitious interior and the constant pressure of the sea was helpless without maps. The Lusitanians were saved by their sailors and their cartographers. The state-run Casa de India oversaw mapmaking as part of its official duties. The Castilian authorities set up an analogous institution, the Casa de Contratación, in Seville, its *patrón general* having the final say on which maps could be used. Thus the government "censored" navigation and in a way the sea itself. Venice imposed an analogous censorship on the entire Adriatic coast and a part of the Mediterranean (vis-à-vis Genoa, Byzantium, the Arab caliphs, and Turkish sultan), and even the tiny Republic of Dubrovnik censored a stretch of the eastern Adriatic, but Mediterranean politics was too particularist to censor the oceans. (Politics has to some extent retained its hold on maps in that it forces us to look at the sea as it does.) No country that failed to raise cartography to official status scored successes on the open seas. The desire to seize and conquer often stimulated mapmaking, but mapmaking stimulated the desire to seize and conquer. Nations taking or changing shape use maps now as mirrors, now as programs. Mediterranean history was instrumental in determining the nature of maps; maps were instrumental in determining Mediterranean history.

The golden age of Dutch and Venetian cartography is probably due to a common approach: both the Dutch and the Venetians reclaimed land piecemeal from the sea—the former using dikes to form polders, the latter using "underwater forestation" to reinforce lagoons—and reflected the resulting relationship to land and sea in their maps. Ptolemy set up chorography as an independent discipline consisting of drawings and descriptions of regions and settlements as seen from a boat or shore, from the mast or a nearby elevation, from the side or a bird's eye perspective; the Renaissance reawakened the interest in it. Chorographic maps were made by geographers and cartographers, engravers and typographers, studios and *botteghe* throughout Italy, but most of all in Venice. I have examined some at the Marciana and ferreted out others in specialized bookshops and private collections. I have also unearthed a number of their creators: Giovanni Vavassore, who published the first one of the Adriatic; the aforementioned Father

Coronelli; and men like Bordone, Rosaccio, Ballino, and in particular Camocio (or Camoccio, or Camutio—he used several spellings).
Camocio's studio, whose trademark was the pyramid (his publica-
tions often bore the motto "Al segno della Piramide" ["At the Sign of
the Pyramid"]), employed such craftsmen as the Dalmatians Natale
Bonifacio (Božo Bonifačić) and Martino Rota (Martin Kolunić of
Šibenik)—who were grateful no doubt for having escaped the fate of
the Slavonians (*schiavoni*), whose language they had no trouble understanding and whose laments they could hear coming from the galleys
in the neighboring port near the Basilica of Saint Mark—and the Greek
Zenon, known in Italy as Domenico Zenoi and known for a number
of fine maps, including one of the Spanish coasts. (I found the latter
as well as several others in the home of a hospitable collector in Valencia.) Zenon's name also graces the archives of the Venice police: he was
accused of making scurrilous sketches to illustrate the verse of a contemporary poet—they showed Aphrodite nude on an enormous shell
surrounded by a marine *veduta*—and both he and his publisher, Camocio, had to pay fines in gold. The censorship wanted cartographers to
be cartographers and nothing more. We hope the story of these cartographers will some day find its place in another work, preferably a
novel about their lives and their Mediterranean adventures.

I MADE SOME OF THESE NOTES on the *Dodekanesos,* island- and cave-
hopping. The *isolario,* or description of an island, makes for some of
the finest travelogues. Chorographic maps occasionally alter the forms
of islands, and rather arbitrarily at that. It is as if the chorographer were
interested more in the detail than in the whole, perhaps because many
islands are in fact details that have broken off from a whole. Besides,
islands themselves tend to change, and more than one have had to
change their names. Island-hopping on early Mediterranean maps is a
great pleasure.

The *isolario* is a genre all its own, a blend of art, literature, and geography. Its sources include Bartolomeo dalli Sonetti's *Isolario,* Cristo-
foro Buondelmonte's *Liber insularum archipelaghi,* Benedetto Bordone's
Isolario nel cui si ragiona de tutte le isole del mondo, Camocio's *Le isole famose,*
Tommaso Porcacchi's *Le isole più famose del mondo,* Coronelli's *Isolario*
and *Mari, golfi, isole* (Coronelli's name is bound to come up over and
over). Henricus Martellus Germanicus and Matthäus Merian visualized

The town of Hvar, on the island of Hvar, with the Pakleni otoci (Infernal Islands) in the foreground. G. F. Camocio, Isole famose. Venice, sixteenth century.

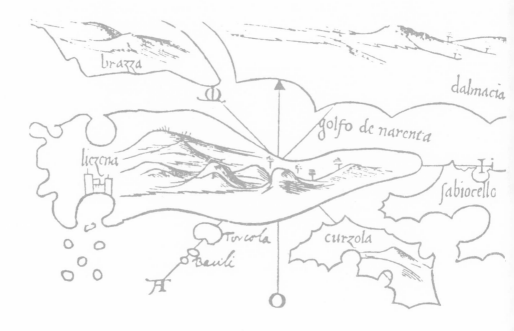

and drew the islands of the Mediterranean even though they were themselves from other shores. More than any other chorographer, Merian viewed Venice—from the bird's eye view of his mind, since there was no elevation from which he could look down—as a unified island. His example shows the importance of the view from outside, from the continent. Feelings inspired by islands are neither fleeting nor fortuitous. Modernity tends to valorize uniqueness: islands are unique. In the days when the center of the earth was shifting away from our sea, when it had ceased to be even its central body of water, chorographers pointed nostalgically in their *isolari* to the Mediterranean's unusually beauteous islands as proof of its primacy among seas.

Scholars claim that the *Odyssey* was composed with the aid of the *isolari* or *portolani* the poet had at hand, much as navigators compose their voyages with maps. We shall return to some of the major works in various genres with similar origins. Towards the end of the ancient period Salinus brought together a number of scenes, events, and narratives of the sea that baffled geographers for centuries. Giambattista

Ramusio, following his lead, published a huge, three-volume collection entitled *Delle navigazioni e viaggi* along with the maps to illustrate it. Imagination and scholarship having ever been rivals, it enjoyed more editions than Ptolemy's *Geography*. During the era of the great discoveries, Spain produced works combining scholarship and navigation like Hernández de Encis's *Suma de geografía* and Pedro de Medina's *Arte de navigar*. In Rome Bartolomeo Crescentio published a *Nautica mediterranea,* which included virtually everything that was known at the time about ships and shipbuilding, from a typology of wood, metal, cordage, and pitch to "the planisphere or maps for navigation," from winds and wind roses to "the temperaments of captains and crews." He especially praised the captains of Dubrovnik, men like the nobleman Nicolò Sagri (whom his fellow countrymen call Niko Sagroević today). Works like these specialize in taxonomies, a genre dear to the hearts of seditious medieval thinkers and one without which I feel it impossible to write on Mediterranean topics, as is amply evident in this Mediterranean breviary.

THOUGHTS ON THE WRITINGS of travelers and seafarers need to be supplemented by an examination of the form they take: the diary. People who invest so much energy in travel cannot manage to note every place they have been, every thing they have seen. Travel means more to them than travelogue. Not until he was thrown into prison did Marco Polo dictate his memoirs to Rustichello (Rusticciano), a Pisan *literatus* who made a conventional transcript of them in rather shaky French. Ibn Battuta, who never completed his *rihla,* also spoke through the pen of another, a certain Ibn Juzai al-Kaldi. Experts say he stylized several chapters in accordance with his own literary ambitions. Columbus wrote letters with scant descriptive passages: they were intended primarily for the personages on whom his voyage depended. His logbook was likewise scanty and remained unknown to contemporaries. The aforementioned Juan de la Cosa, who accompanied him on his second voyage, wrote more and better. Captains left logs to underlings: Magellan's records were kept, in French, by the Mediterranean Antonio Pigafetta (I particularly recall his description of a fish with pointed teeth and its desperate twitching); Vasco de Gama had a historian by the name of João de Barros on board, and without him his fame would doubtless have waned. Nor are these isolated cases. The great explorers devoted all their attention to navigation; no diary could compete with maps, maps and the Mediterranean often merging in their minds.

CERTAIN HIGH POINTS along the coast, which have served both learned chorographers and simple travelers as observation posts for studying the relationship between land and sea, have sonorous names like belvedere, mirador, panorama, miramare, faraglione, and the like, and even if the descriptions given of them typically leave much to be desired, they remain in our memory to resurface time and again. Some are famous and reputed dangerous: legend has it that both Sappho and Queen Artemisia of Halicarnassus flung themselves into the harsh waves of the Ionian from a cliff on the island of Leucadia (Levkas to the Greeks and Santa Maura to the Venetians); Icarus took flight from a similar promontory before plunging into the sea that ancient cartographers later called by his name; more than one geographer was tossed into the Tyrrhenian from the vertiginous terraces of the Villa Iovis on the island of Capri by order of Tiberius; the legendary King Arthur halted at Sainte Victoire, south of Aix-en-Provence near the convent of Sainte Marie de la Victoire, terrified of the waves dashing against the shore below; and many a geographer and poet have lingered on the bluffs overlooking Dubrovnik and Kotor to admire the view of the islands and gulfs. I have seen similar sites on the coasts of Spain and Turkey, the Kerkenna Islands, and Sardinia, sites where ecstasy and sacrifice derive from more than beauty or despair, where there is a verve at work, a vertigo, that the Mediterranean dares not name and that the maps too pass over in silence.

HISTORY CONGREGATES and accumulates more at certain points of the map than at others: events are more numerous and ominous, movements more frequent and determined. Such was long the case in ports, though they too have spaces, rather ample spaces, that history seems to have shunned, coves and inlets, for instance, that no one enters. Yet they show up on the map. "There are places," says a poet of the diaspora and friend of my Hydra helmsman, "that, when you examine them on a map, make you feel for a brief moment akin to Providence, places where history is inescapable, like a highway accident, places

where geography provokes history." I have sought out such places—
ports in particular—on the earliest maps of the Mediterranean.

CADASTRAL MAPS, the kind preserved in the local archives of port cities,
give additional insight into the relations between sea and land, the properties they show extending all the way to the coast and providing clear,
unobstructed views. Plots where the land/sea relationship has not been
resolved—plots exposed to the elements, for example—often change
owners or end up ownerless, the fear being that the sea will undermine or inundate the coast and reclaim it from land and landowner
both. On some maps (like the ones I came across in the small municipal museum in Trogir near the Ćipiko Palace) officials paint the coast-
line and the properties abutting on it in different colors to call attention to the relationship between it and the Mediterranean.

Picture postcards depicting seascapes, ships, and strands, and old
photographs—black-and-white or sepia—of the kind preserved in
family albums may be difficult to classify, but they deserve the effort:
they too play a role in familiarizing us with the sea and the coast. As
faded as early maps, they remind us how people made pilgrimages to
the sea, opened their bodies to it, sought rest or adventure in it; they
show us what the piers and wharves were like, and the boats docking
there (first steam-, then motor-driven), and the views they offered: a
beach scene, a port event, a narrative of bathers in a cove. Photographs
are not maps (as cartographers never fail to remind us), but they may
replace or supplement them: they too help us to know the face and
sweep of the sea. Indeed, for many of us the family album was the first
Mediterranean atlas: the sea on the eve of our first encounter with it.

The Viscount Ferdinand Marie de Lesseps had friends among the
early photographers, and although he invited them to record the digging of the Suez Canal, the modest capabilities of the cameras of the
time and the rigors of the Bitter Lakes, Ballah and Timsah, and the
construction sites at Port Said and Ismailia prevented them from ac-
complishing the task on their own. The Musée de la Marine in Paris
has an exhibit of paintings similar to photographs with titles like "The
Sixth Construction Site near Ismailia" and "Mediterranean Waters
Reach Lake Timsah." They give a good idea of the project, which follows parts of the canal dug by the slaves of the pharaoh Necho and

the subjects of Ptolemy II (Ptolemy Philadelphus) and later filled in by order of the Abbasid caliph Abu Jafar al-Mansur and by desert sands. De Lesseps's friend, Said Pasha, whom the Porte had placed on the throne of Egypt, could not proceed without removing an obstacle of faith: the Qur'an states that "Allah placed a barrier between the two seas." When the canal was at last opened, the internal sea became a strait, a passageway between two oceans. The human hand had altered the map of the Mediterranean and our conception of it.

SOME MAPS PLACE ancient theaters on a par with cities and ports, representing them in the form of a semicircle sunken into the ground with the stage and proscenium at the far end of the slope and seats carved into stone. Such theaters are to be found on all coasts of the Mediterranean and farther inland. They were first built by Greeks, but Romans and others followed suit. They are rarely situated in the center of a city, but their location is not of the essence: the theater of Dionysus was originally located on the outskirts of Athens in a swamp (*en limnais*). Moreover, there were times when the theater in far-off Syracuse was more important than its Athenian counterpart: Sicily hosted several premières of Aeschylus' plays. Like busy ports and rich markets, theaters often appear at points where sea and land routes come together. Mention should be made of the lesser known "semicircles" at Sagalassos, Termessos, Leptis Magna, and Caesaria. In addition to the numerous famous theaters scattered through Greece, Asia Minor, and Italy (like the Odeon at Corinth or the magnificent structures at Maillots or Pergamum), we would recall Mantenia and Eretria, Thugga in Tunisia and Timgad (the ancient Thumugadi or Thumugadis) in Algeria, the oasis of Palmyra in the Syrian desert, and Patara, half buried in sand, one of the chief cities of ancient Lycia. I have visited Stobi in Macedonia near the mouth of the Cherna River, which flows into the Vardar; Heraclea Lyncestis (near today's Bitola), past which the aforementioned via Ignatia runs; Scupi (today's Skoplje or Skopje), which was destroyed for the first time by an earthquake in A.D. 518; and a hill above Lake Lychnidus (today's Lake Ohrid), from which the famed blue of the water seems particularly intense and where ruins rise out of the ground like a shipwreck. The Adriatic island and town called Issa in ancient times (and now called Vis) were once the colony of a much larger island and town, namely, Sicily and Syracuse, and its nostalgic

Syracusan colonizers built a theater similar to their own on the tiny peninsula of Pirovo near the port and open to the winds of the south. It is older than the theaters in the Roman colonies of Salona, Narona, and Iadera (today's Zadar) or even Pietas Julia (today's Pula), older than the theaters in all the cities of the eastern Adriatic, though not of the Mediterranean as a whole.

The earliest Mediterranean theaters were of stone: the theater below the Acropolis, the Pompeo at Rome, the small theatron and large theatron at Pompei preserved by lava and ash, and the best preserved of all, the theater at Epidaurus on the east coast of Argolis. There were also theaters made of brick and, in times of want, even of wood. Excavations have brought to light such props as masks for actors playing maenads, sileni, and satyrs. The epitaph on the tombstone of an actor, a "magister mimariorium," by the name of Leburno who died at Sisak (Siscia in ancient times) during the third century A.D. reads: "Many a time did I die on stage, but never thus." Actors' tombs, like sailors' tombs, have no place on our maps, their pantheon being the Mediterranean itself.

COLLECTORS OF ANCIENT MAPS come together on occasion, and I recently attended a meeting they held in Amalfi. They gathered in that small city of great maritime renown on the Gulf of Salerno to commemorate the anniversary of the birth of Leo Barow, a Russian émigré— his real name was Leonid Barov—and perhaps the greatest cartographer of the twentieth century. He was born in 1881 and died abroad in 1957, having published—for decades and at his own expense—a cartographic journal called *Imago Mundi* with which he migrated from country to country. The meeting included an exhibition of wind roses in his honor, and the discussion among professional geographers and autodidacts like the ones we met earlier provides much of the material for this section. (The chart of early wind roses on page 134 was also part of the exhibition.) Although there is no way of proving Crescentio's claim in *Nautica mediterranea* that the Amalfians were the first to draw wind roses on their maps, they do seem to have been familiar with them—and with the compass, for that matter—before their rivals in Naples and the Gulf of Taranto. Nor is there any proof that they borrowed either the wind roses or the compass from the Arabs (al-Idrisi's maps have no wind roses) or the Normans, though there is no proof to the

1380 ? *(Combitis)* 1384 *(Pinelli)* 1422 Leon. (Goro) Dati 1426 Giroldis 1436 Andrea Bianco

1455 Bartol. Pareto 1470 Gr. Benincasa 1512 Maiolo 1556 Eufredutius 1562 Gastaldi

1375 Catalan Atlas 1462/68 Petrus Roselli 1456 Bertran and Ripol 1482 Jac. Bertran

1486 Arnaldus Domenech Anon. New York 1511 Pilestrina

1502 *(Cantino)* (1505) Pedro Reinel 1517? Indian Ocean Munich Portug. Anon. Dijon 1527/29 Spanish World Maps Weimar

contrary either. The famous *Carta pisana,* a parchment portolano dating from the late thirteenth century, contains two sets of directional lines, at Sardinia and at Rhodes, but they are not wind roses in the true sense of the word. In his *Periplus* Nordenskjöld claims that the oldest portolanos have no wind roses. The first we know of appeared in the 1375 *Catalan Atlas.* At that time, before the exodus from the Iberian Peninsula, Jews maintained close ties with the ports of Africa and Asia Minor, especially with Palestine. Early civilizations indicated the cardinal points by means of color. Reliable sources maintain that the Khazars used color to indicate winds. The colors of the wind roses may thus be connected with the designation of the cardinal points. At first black, red, and green predominated in the wind roses on Mediterranean maps; then came other transitional or arbitrary colors serving the eye rather than the mind.

Wind roses figure prominently in the poem "La Sfera," written and illustrated by the Florentine Gregorio (Gorio) Dati or his brother Leonardo. (The controversy in Amalfi over the author's identity is of no importance here.) The wind rose is often considered an emblem, but it is more than that; it is spoken of as a metaphor, but it is not only that. Its predecessors include the marble *Roman Fragment,* divided into twelve or sixteen winds and now exhibited in Prague, the *Tower of Winds* in Athens with Andronicus's clock atop a figure of Triton, the slab excavated by archeologists in Sippar on the Euphrates showing a rolling sea and four large stars, and the mosaic discovered in the Roman settlement of Thuburbo Majus in the vicinity of Carthage showing two circles with multicolored legs. There has been much discussion of sign and symbol in wind roses, their forms and meanings, the astrological and calendrical notes accompanying them, the division of the circle into four, eight, sixteen, and thirty-two sections or into twelve and twenty-four, which is temporal as well as geographic. "Compass roses," which were placed under the lids with indications of the car-

Wind roses,
as published in
Imago Mundi
vol. 7 (1950).
Fourteenth to
sixteenth century.

dinal points below the glass and the magnetic needle, are said to have originated in the northern seas. They were studied for many years by a sea captain named Albert Schück, who disseminated his findings in a multivolumed work entitled *Der Kompaß* and published far from the Mediterranean in the Hanseatic city of Hamburg at the beginning of the century.

In wind roses the letter *T* does not have the meaning it had on the T-O maps: it means the north (*tramontana*). The north is also indicated by a dot or arrow (as in Gastaldi) or by the north star (*stella polaris*). The heraldic sign of the lily of the valley (*fleur de lys*) appears quite often as well, because after the Crusades, thanks primarily to the Aquitanian seafarers, it came to represent respect for the French crown. There is a cross on the eastern side of the rose facing the Holy Land and Jerusalem, the center of the world according to Christian doctrine and the sanctuary of the Mediterranean.

THE COLORED PARTS of the wind rose are called rhombi on account of their form. In Italy, as the master cartographer Roberto Almagià points out, rhombi with the initials of the principal winds create a circle called a *rosone,* the word for rosette or rose window, the circular window with roselike tracery found in many cathedrals. (It is sometimes said that making a new and accurate map is more difficult than building a cathedral.) The petals of the rose outside the circle may be depicted as torches called *feu de joie* (fire of joy). Renaissance cartographers started reducing the number of wind roses or left them out altogether, apparently as a result of the occult interpretations that had accrued to them, but they were revived: navigators looked for them on their maps, believing that, like amulets or figureheads, they brought luck and could even save a crew. There is no reason to doubt that the wind rose originated on the Mediterranean.

THE AMALFI MARINE LIBRARY contains rich documentation of much of this. It was there I came across a work by Zacharios Lillius (who was probably of Greek origin) published in Florence in 1493 under the title *Orbis Breviarium.* I am thus not the first, unfortunately, to apply the word *breviary,* which usually designates a book containing hymns and prayers for daily use, to a geographic context. It is hard to overcome the temptation to turn an ordinary breviary into the Gospel and even harder here, given our biblical sea. Lillius was not alone in succumbing to it—which brings us back to the starting point of our periplus. The more we know of our sea, the less we view it alone. The Mediterranean is not a sea of solitude.

137

Maps

Clarifying the meaning of certain key concepts will be useful at this point, both for landlubbers less than familiar with the Mediterranean and for Mediterraneans familiar only with their own stretch of sea or coast: *campanilismo*—that is, the parish-pump (or, to be more precise, the parish-belfry) the parish perspective—is rampant from inlet to inlet and island to island, the Mediterranean being replete with parish belfries, *campanili*.

I will not go into the fine points of the climate, the ebb and flow of the tides, the natural harbors, the modest distances (the Mediterranean basin is only about two thousand nautical miles long and at most four hundred nautical miles wide), the advantages stemming from the many gulfs and rivers, the fact that the ancient world was plowing our sea while others were still peering timorously out at the ocean. Such points can be found in any marine encyclopedia. The history of the Mediterranean has been written many times over.

Various dialects have a Mediterranean koine of words and things, attitudes and ideas. It appears in various glossaries of various nautical disciplines. This section represents my own glossary of Mediterranean terms.

Glossaries offer more freedom than do dictionaries: the user can skip around on the basis of need or caprice; they are also more philological or literary by nature. They might best be compared to a Mediterranean satire, *satura* being originally a dish of mixed Mediterranean fruits, a *lanx satura* or medley, and only later, thanks to the writings of Horace and Juvenal, acquiring the meaning it currently enjoys.

139

OVERLEAF:
The Mediterranean and its cities: Marseille, Genoa, Naples, and Toulon. A chorographic map by François Olive. Marseille, 1662.

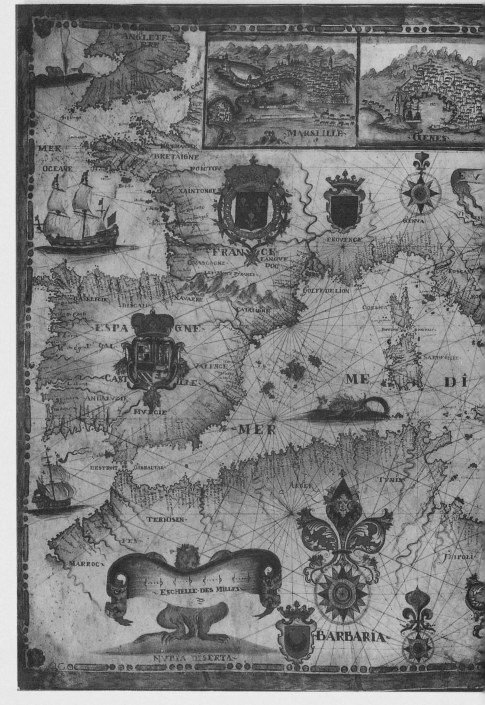

NAPOLI

CARTE PARTICVLIER DELA MER MEDI TERRANEE FAICTE PAR MOY FRANÇOIS OLIVE A MARSEILLE

TARTARIE

HONGRIE

PODOLIE

CHERSON

MOLDAVIA

MER MAGIOR

BOSSINE

DALMATIE

MER NOIRE

GRECE

ROMANIE

DESTROIT DE COSTANT

NOPLI

ARMENIE

ASIA

ANATOLIE

CARMANIE

TER

ALEP

LARCHIPELAGO

NEE

CHIPRE

SVRIA

RA

DAMAS

MARMARIQVE

LEGITE

IERVS
ALEM

AFRICA

LIBIA DISERTA

LA MER
ROVGE

In the foreword to his *Glossaire nautique,* dedicated to "sailors who do not disdain the science of history and scholars who deal with the sea" and published in Paris in 1848 in two enormous volumes at the expense of the Ministry of the Navy, Augustin Jal, seafarer and enthusiast, notes that "a glossary enables us to include a number of details impossible to include even in the most extensive treatises with the most copious notes" (p. 9). Footnotes are generally unassimilated additions to the text; the glossary is a genre intended to do away with them. I offer the glosses that follow as a dish of mixed fruits—some philological, others literary—hoping to expand upon a number of issues merely touched upon in the previous sections and to introduce the reader to the sources I have unearthed and the helpful people I have met in my travels. Like Ibn Khaldun and Mercator, I have followed Ptolemy's lead and used the testimonies of travelers who have been where we have not been and seen what we have not seen. The result is less a glossary of the Mediterranean than a glossary to my breviary.

"The Mediterranean takes on a number of names in accordance with the lands it touches," Mercator points out in his *Atlas* (Amsterdam 1609, p. 30). The name of a sea depends on its location and its links to the lands along its shores and to their peoples. Ancient peoples like the Egyptians and Sumerians called the Mediterranean the Upper Sea because of its position with respect to them. It had many names in the Bible: the great sea (*yam ha-gadol,* Joshua 1:4), the uttermost or utmost sea (*yam ha-aharon,* Deuteronomy 11:24, 34:2), the sea of the Philistines (*yam pelishtim,* Exodus 23:31). At times it was called simply The Sea, everyone assuming the sea in question was the Mediterranean.

The Semitic word *yam* refers to all great waters: seas, lakes, and rivers alike. In ancient Egypt all bodies of water were indicated by MW (we do not know whether the vowel following the M was pronounced *o* or *u*), the waves of the sea and of the Nile showing up hieroglyphically as long, broken lines. The word *yam,* which was preserved by the Copts, also features the M indicating our sea, but the sea of reeds (Red Sea) comes from a different root and is probably of later origin. In the First Book of the Kings we read that "King Solomon made a navy of ships in Ezion-geber, which is beside Eloth, on the shore of the Red Sea. And Hiram sent in the navy his servants, shipmen that had knowledge of the sea, with the servants of Solomon" (1 Kings 9:26–27), from which we deduce that in Old Testament times the sea of reeds was more important to the king of Israel than the Mediterranean of the Philistines lapping the shores of Palestine.

Both Hecataeus and Herodotus call the Mediterranean the Great Sea, as do the Phoenicians, who appear to have been the first to navigate it. In *The Peloponnesian War* Thucydides calls it the Hellenic Sea (1.4) because it belongs to Greece. The Greeks called it, accordingly, "our sea," which nomenclature the Romans borrowed (*mare nostrum*) as did many after them. Plato is a bit more circumspect when he says, "the sea beside us" (*par' hêmin thalassa,* from *Phaedo* 113a). In a text known under the title "De mundo" and perhaps wrongly attributed to Aristotle we find the fateful designation of "inner sea" (*hê esô thalassa,* 3.8) as opposed to the outer sea or ocean: it is this designation that will later give rise, in Latin translation, to the term Mediterranean.

Philology will help us to trace our sea's history. The adjective *mediterraneus* was not a particularly refined word. Festus, a grammarian of the golden age, recommended that it be replaced by *mediterreus,* but recommendations of the sort are rarely heeded once a word has come into common use, and this was a time when Rome was on its way to becoming a major sea power. (By then the epithet *meditullius*—from *tellus* [earth] and possibly related to the Greek *mesogaios* [inland, in the heart of a country]—was archaic.) The word *mediterraneus* designated a landlocked space on the continent as opposed to *maritimus.* Cicero calls inland inhabitants "the most mediterranean of people" (*homines maxime mediterranei,* from *In Verrem* 2.5). Similarly, the noun *mediterraneum* designated the heart of the country (for example, and in the plural, *mediterranea Galliae* [the continental parts of Gaul]). The epithet *mediterraneus* came to be linked with the "inner sea" because the "inner sea" was itself landlocked. Such is the meaning used by Solinus in his geographic compilations and tales (*Collectanea Rerum Memorabilium* 18.1), which was read with great curiosity by the ancient world in decline and the Middle Ages as a whole. But it was Isidorus Hispalensis, or Isidore of Seville, who turned the adjective into a proper noun: "The Great Sea [Mare Magnum] flows from the ocean in the west; it faces south and reaches north. It is called 'great' because other seas pale in comparison; it is called the Mediterranean because it washes against the surrounding lands [*mediam terram*] all the way to the east, dividing Europe, Africa, and Asia" ("De Mediterraneo Mari," *Origines* 12.16). And so—it being difficult to judge just how influential Solinus's "fantastic tales" were—our sea became the Mediterranean thanks to the authority of a Christian polygraph and saint. The ocean took its name from the mythical figure of Titan's son. The Mediterranean is more concrete than myth.

The Greeks had a number of words for the sea: *hals* is salt, the sea as matter; *pelagos* is the open sea, the sea as scape; *pontos* is the high sea, the sea as space, scene, and road; *thalassa* is the general concept (and of unclear origin, Cretan perhaps), the sea as experience and event; *kolpos* is bosom or lap and in the strict sense of the word refers to the part of the sea embraced by the coast; *laitma* is the deep, dear to poets and suicides. Much as the forms of the sea complement one another and blend, the words for the sea expand their meanings when juxtaposed in the works of the great poets and storytellers—matter/space, deep/ high or open, scene/event—thus reflecting the rich experience of the ancient Greeks living and sailing on the Mediterranean.

The Romans were more laconic. The Latin word *mare* (which they share with such branches of Indo-European as the Slavic and Italic and which they passed on to the Romance languages), like the Semitic word *yam,* originally designated all bodies of water: seas, lakes, and rivers. Later, imitating Hellenic models, Roman writers borrowed words like *pontos* and *pelagos* or lent Latin words (*sal, salum, aequor*) Greek meanings. Their metaphors and figures of speech conceal continental biases, an attachment to the land: *campi aequorei* was one expression for the open sea; Virgil conflates navigation and plowing (*vastum maris aequor arandum* [the vast plain of the seas to be plowed], *Aeneid* 2.780). The Mediterranean peoples differ not only in how they use the sea but also in how they name it.

The Arabs—and the Turks after them—called the Mediterranean the Rumelian (that is, Romano-Byzantine) Sea: *al-bahr al-rum.* Ibn Khaldun also calls it the Syrian Sea at various points in his *Al-Muqaddima,* as does al-Idrisi in the *Book of Roger.* The word *al-bahr* also designated all great bodies of water and still designates the most important of them: the Nile. The Semitic term, *al-yam,* has survived, but is considered bookish and archaic. The Muslim peoples have translated the name for the Mediterranean from the name given it by Isidore of Seville: *al-bahr al-mutawassit.*

Our sea changes gender from coast to coast: it is neuter in Latin and the Slav languages, masculine in Italian, feminine in French, and either masculine or feminine in Spanish; Arabic has two masculine words

for it, and Greek numerous words of all genders. It is difficult to draw
the borders between seas: one tends to favor one's own. According to
an old Greek saying, a Greek has not left his homeland until he passes
Cape Malea (at the extremity of the eastern peninsula of Peloponnesus).
"Our sea is vastly superior to others in all respects," writes Strabo, "and
hence is our point of departure" (*Geographia* 2.57). The *Iliad* mentions
only two seas: the Thracian and the Icarian; the *Odyssey* uses no specific
names: everything is sea. "Is the sea of other lands fair?" asks the poet
(Fernando Pessoa, in "The Sailor"). Many would answer in the negative or fail to ask. "Only the sea of other lands is fair" (ibid.). Such is
the answer of those who have left the Mediterranean for other seas,
for the New World.

Many signifieds connected with wonder or fear of the sea have no
signifiers to express them. Here is Xenophon describing how the Greek

*Rome, Sovereign
of Peoples. Père
Philippe Briet.
Paris, 1687.*

warriors reacted to the sight of the sea after a long overland expedition: "'The sea! The sea!' The words traveled from mouth to mouth. All the men bolted towards it . . . and began kissing one another, weeping" (*Anabasis* 4.7). They all gazed at the same sea, yet each one saw his own. A similar scene has been recurring since man's first encounter with the sea: signifieds get lost in whoops and shouts, expressions for which no signifier suffices. And while there are differences between people experiencing the sea for the first time and people merely returning to it, there are times when everyone seems to view it for the first time. It depends on the sea—Mediterranean or not—and ourselves.

THE SEA IS ABSOLUTE, its designations relative, as the glossarist Augustin Jal would say. The Mediterranean has been called both the North and the South Sea. On his travels through Egypt Herodotus saw it to the north and therefore called it *boreia thalassa* (4.42). Renaissance maps sometimes use the term South Sea, as did Giuliano Dati in his geographic poem "La sfera," and early in *Orlando furioso* Ariosto calls the Mediterranean *d'Africa il mare*.

Scholars familiar with dead languages have pointed out that civilizations using colors to indicate the cardinal points tend to call our sea green or white. The Arabs have preserved the name White Sea (*al-bahr al-abyad*), white being used for designating its western part. The Turks and the Bulgarians use White Sea as well. The early songs of the South Slavs refer to the sea as white in addition to blue—and not only when the waves are up. Nor is the reference completely alien to modern Greek, despite its strong ancient tradition. The Red Sea (Erythros Pontos) once referred to the Indian Ocean, red being used to designate the East. What we call the Red Sea the Egyptians call the Sea of Reeds (as noted in Amadeus Peyron's 1835 *Lexicon Copticum*, p. 304). The Black Sea, or Pontus Euxinus, has an unusual etymology, the Greek adjective *euxeinos* (hospitable) having replaced *axeinos* (inhospitable), which is how the sea appeared to sailors seeking the golden fleece, though perhaps it comes from the Old Persian stem for black or dark, *axšaina-*, by way of folk etymology. In any case black was the color associated with the north. (Much color symbolism is confirmed by the Cabala.) Certain Balkan toponyms and especially hydronyms on or near the Mediterranean coast hint at the cardinal points: the Black and White Drim Rivers, whose waters are identical, and the White and Black

Timok in Serbia or the Black and White Iskar in Bulgaria. The same may be said for Montenegro (Crna Gora, that is, Black Mountain), Albania (from Latin *albus* [white]), and Red Croatia (Croatia Rubea, Dalmatia Superior) and White Croatia (Croatia Alba, Dalmatia Inferior), which are the forms used in the notes on Croatia by the famous Duclean priest we call Dukljanin. Hungary too, let us recall, was divided in the Middle Ages between black in the north and white in the west. The connection between color and cardinal points would explain why there is a White Nile and a Blue Nile when the Nile is everywhere green; it would explain the azure in the Côte d'Azur, which goes back to the Arabic *azraq* (blue) as a result of its geographic location rather than of any particular blueness. Some linguists make so bold as to posit the Pelasgi—the pre-Hellenic inhabitants of Greece who allegedly brought us the grape and the olive—as a "white" people (*pelasgus*) who gave their sea (*pelagos*) the name White. But let us put an end to these all-too-Mediterranean conjectures.

Seen from the coast the sea has many hues—all shades of blue and green, silver and gold in the moon and sun, oil and salt in the day and night, sky bright in Virgil's metaphors (*caeruleum mare*), wine dark in Homer's epithets (*oinops*)—though where we thought there were only hues or images, we sometimes find practical signs like directions or cardinal points. This is not to deny the influence of our thoughts or fantasies, serving as they do to help certain names take over. We have only to recall the multicolored wind roses designating the cardinal points on early maps to recognize modestly, with Borges's lyric "La navigación," in the 1925 collection *Luna de enfrente* (The Moon across the Way): "The sea is a primordial language we cannot decipher." I have kept his words in mind while looking into the various names for the sea, leafing through lexicons of seagoing peoples, putting together this cultural landscape of the Mediterranean and especially this glossary.

The Mediterranean is made up of many smaller seas which, as Isidore of Seville pointed out, tend to take the names of "regions" and "peoples" ("a gentibus: Tuscum, Ligusticum, Dalmaticum," and so on), "islands," "human destinies," "kings remembered," "local customs," and even "cattle paths" ("a bovis transitu: Bosphores," *Origines* 13.16). Everyone seems to want his own sea by his own shore. Thus in ancient times we had the Phoenician, Cilician, Lydian, and Icarian Seas, later the Seas of Alborán and Biban, the Balearic Sea, the Seas of Genoa, of Taranto, of Marseille, the Upper Sea and Lower Sea, the Sea of Candia (or Crete), and the Sea of Morea (or Peloponnesus). The names change. For Apollonius Rhodius, the Adriatic was no more than an "Ionian gulf," while for Strabo, the entire Ionian Sea was a part "of what today we call the Adriatic Gulf" (*Geographia* 2.5). According to the Acts of the Apostles, Saint Paul sailed the "Adria" (27:27), which at the time extended as far as Crete and Malta and—in several versions of Ptolemy's maps—all the way to Sicily. In a document dating from 1069 the Croatian king Petar Krešimir calls it "mare nostrum Dalmaticum," which is precisely what the Byzantine emperor and chronicler Constantine VII Porphyrogenitus (V.31) had called it a century before. The Turkish traveler Evli Kelebi gives it two names in his *Seyahatnamesi* (Travelogue): the Venedik Korfezi (Gulf of Venice), as it was called in his day and his part of the Mediterranean, and the Korfez Deryasi, as it was called on the basis of the older Persian model.

THE ISSUE of the Mediterranean's borders, which I have mentioned several times, comes up in Plato's *Phaedo* as well when Socrates refers to "those of us who dwell in the region between the Phasis and the Pillars of Hercules along the borders of the sea like ants or frogs along a marsh" (2.56). The coasts are the borders of the sea and sometimes include the word for sea: *ta epithalattia, ta parathalattia,* and *ta paralia* all designate the seacoast in their own ways. The word for dry land, firm ground, terra firma is *êpeiros* (which gives the toponym Epirus), while *khersos* means land as territory (and is the origin of the toponym Kherson). The word for either the coast of a sea or the bank of a river is *êiôn,* while *aigialos* is the seashore or beach. (We find it in the name of the medicinal sands of Igalo in our Gulf of Kotor.) The word for a rugged seacoast or river bank is *aktê* (hence the name of the unfortunate Acteon in Greek mythology); a *rakhia* is even steeper. The reason the Greeks have so many names for coast is that their coast is so varied and uneven; besides, their language offers paradigmatic ways—valid for many Mediterranean languages—of conveying what it means to look inland from the coast: *epithalattidios* is a coastal dweller; *khersaios* is an inhabitant of the hinterland, and the difference between the two is evident in Plato's *Laws* (704b). Herodotus notes the opposition between islander (*nêsiôtês*) and inlander (*êpeirôtês*). In Aristophanes' *Frogs* we find the characteristic notion of *athalattôtos,* a person who has never set foot in the sea. The Attic spirit looked upon the inland Boeotians with disdain: Gregory of Cyprus mocks their mind (*Boiôtion nous*); Macarius calls them swine (*Boiôtia hys*). We can find similar instances of derision fanned by the endless pejorative epithets and images introduced into classical culture by the Greek philosophers and spanning all periods, languages, and coasts of the Mediterranean.

Italy probably has the greatest number: the most widespread of them, *cafone* (boor), was born in Naples, but quickly spread over the entire country, north and south; the word *terrone* originally meant tied to the land and is now a general pejorative term for Southern Italians, much as *polentone* (polenta eater) is a general pejorative term for Northern Italians (regional and more specific insults like *gabibbo* in Genoa or *tamarro* in the Abruzzi abound); Strabo tells us that the Pompeians spoke derisively of their neighbors a stone's throw from the coast (in today's Nocera, Nola, Acerra). The Apocryphal Book of Sirach mentions the incompatibility between the Jews from inland and the coastal Philistines, though the Holy Scripture does not see fit to record the names one group gave the other. Arabs call their mountain dwellers *jibali;* the Bulgarians call them Balkans plus a pejorative suffix ("Balkaneers," as I rendered the epithet in the Breviary section). The Croatian word *žabar* (frog catcher) can have different deprecatory meanings at different points along the coast: for some it designates a landlubber, for others a neighbor—an Italian, for instance. The scabrous *cul-terreux* (peasant) has wheedled its way into an otherwise refined French terminology, and the Provençals have their pejorative names for the French, the Catalans for the Aragonians, the Dalmatians for the Vlachs, Kotor Gulf residents for the rest of the Montenegrins, and so on. The roles, comic and tragic, are known to all on the open stages of the Mediterranean.

PEOPLES GOING DOWN to the sea call it by different names. Arriving at the shores of the Adriatic, the Southern Slavs heard Greek and Roman words for what they saw. Philologists tell us that they kept some words of their own and adopted—or adapted—others. They kept their own Slav word for sea, *more,* but turned the Greek word, *thalassa,* into several words having to do with waves. Thus the sentence *More se talasa* means "The sea is agitated, covered with waves." The word *pelagos* survives in the dialect of the south Adriatic island of Šipan, where the verb *pelagat* means to go fishing far from shore, on the open sea; moreover, the Palagruža, or Pelagosa, Islands in the central Adriatic and the Pelagian Islands just south of Sicily take their names from it. And the word *kolpos* has not only left a trace in the dialect of the Elafit and Jelenji Islands (where to go on a *kulaf* means to go fishing on the open sea) but also gave the word *gulf* first to Italian (*il* golfo *di Venezia*) and thence to all Mediterranean and European languages.

Besides *more,* the word for sea (which landlubbers—but not old salts—often call simply "the water"), our ancestors brought from their ancestral homeland various words for boat (*brod,* the generic term; *ladja,* a river boat; *korab[lja],* a seagoing vessel) and the words for oar (*veslo*) and sail (*jedro*). Having no word for mast, they borrowed *jarbol* from the Latin word for tree (*arbor*). They did, however, have their own words for fishhook (*udica*), harpoon (*osti*), fishing trap (*vrša*), and net (*mreža*). The latter, which refers specifically to the net used in freshwater fishing, has—as we have had occasion to point out in another context—entered Romanian as *mreajă.* The word *vlak,* which the ancient Slavs used for "dragnet," has permeated northern Greek dialects, replacing the older Greek term *griphos.* (For an exhaustive study on the subject, see Petar Skok, *Naša pomorska i ribarska terminologija na Jadranu* [Our Nautical and Fishing Terminology on the Adriatic], Split 1933.) The Slavs also inherited words from the Illyrian and Dalmatian-Roman populace of the earlier Roman and Byzantine provinces, words for fish they had not yet eaten, for tools they had not yet used. And everyone learned from the Italians—particularly the Venetians—though it is sometimes difficult to establish which Mediterranean people did the inventing and which the inheriting.

The Czech historian and philologist Konstantin Jireček has shown that the Slavs share more names for rivers than for coasts and seas (see *Geschichte der Serben* I, Gotha 1911, p. 63), while the Croatian scholar Petar Šimunović writes, "Neither Croatian toponymy nor Croatian geographical terminology offers proof that the Croats ruled the waves or found linguistic equivalents for the essential concepts in navigation, fishing, shipping, and ship-building—for living on and from the sea— that is, that they created a complete and completely autonomous 'thalassonymic' vocabulary" (*Istočnojadranska toponimija* [East-Adriatic Toponymy], April 1986, p. 252). By way of consolation, let me append the opinion of the Italian scholar Matteo Cortelazza concerning the Western coast of the Adriatic and thus our teachers: "Italian nautical vocabulary is predominantly continental in origin" (*Bollettino dell'Atlante linguistico mediterraneo,* 8–9, 1966–67, pp. 67–77). Even Mediterraneans were born on dry land.

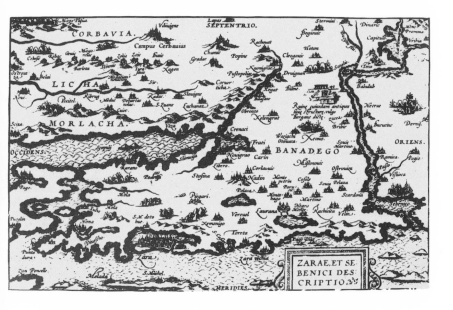

NAMES FOR SHIPS ARE NOT easily categorized in terms of origin. Not even the word *barca*—which so many peoples have naturalized (it was used by Phoenicians and Punics, Greeks and Romans)—has a clear etymology. It is presumed to stem from the ancient Egyptian, but the Egyptians presumably borrowed it as well. The oldest *barca* bore the name of "wood" in many languages (*al-'ud* in Arabic, which gives *leut* [boat]). Our Croatian word for boat, *ladja*, is of Balto-Slav origin (*lodia* from *oldia*) and originally meant "tree trunk." Traces of the Latin word for boat, *navis,* occur in Sanskrit, Greek, Celtic, and even Armenian dialects, but no one can say what its true Indo-European prototype is. The origin of *galley* (*galea, galeone, galera,* etc.), though it plowed many a sea and occurs in all European languages, remains unidentified in Meyer-Lübke's *Romanisches etymologisches Wörterbuch.* The Italian etymologists Carlo Battisti and Giovanni Alessio presume it to be "a relict from the Illyrian substratum reaching from the Dalmatian coast to Venice" (*Dizionario etimologico italiano,* Florence 1951, vol. 3, p. 1749). The *galea,* as they would have it, was a tortoise (*testuggine*), which, when it moved, resembled a boat with one or two ranks of oars. The Greek word *korabion,* which entered Slavic before the great migration of peoples, derives from the name of a beetle or crab (*kara-*

Description of Zadar and Šibenik by Božo Bonifačić (Natale Bonifacio) of Šibenik. Abraham Ortelius, Theatrum Orbis Terrarum. Venice, 1595.

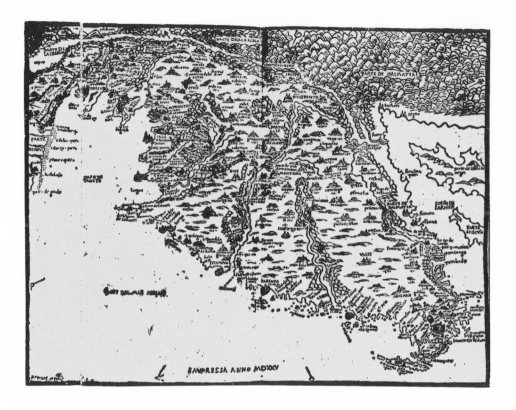

Istria. Pietro Coppo (Petar Kopić). Venice, 1540.

bos, cf. Aristotle, *Historia Animalium* 531b.25). These examples, along with many others I shall refrain from enumerating here, share certain structures and metaphors. Having failed to trace them back to their etyma, we may as well conclude that they originated in the Mediterranean itself.

The Croatian word for boat, *brod,* is related to Slav *bred-,* the stem of the verb *bresti,* "to wade across, ford (a body of water)," and hence clearly of continental origin. Radovan Vidović's *Pomorski rječnik* (Nautical Dictionary, Split 1984), much like Augustin Jal's *Glossaire nautique,* gives a long list of words at the entry for boat, most of which are of Greek, Latin, and Romance origin: "*banzo, barca (barka), bastasia, bastassiza (bastašica), batel, bergantinus (brigantin), biremis (= fusta), barcon, barcosa, barcusius (bragoč?), carabus (korablja), caraca, carachia, casselata, chelandia, cocha, codura, drievo, dromo, frigada, fusta (fušta), galea (galija), galera, galion (galiun), grippus (grip), gumbara, kravela* (cf. R. *korabl'*, Gr. *karabos*), *katrga (katurga), ladja, lembus, lignum (drievo, legno), linter, londra, marziliana, navicula, navigium, navis, ormanica, plav, saeta, sagittea, saita* (from which *šajta* is perhaps derived), *saena, šebeka (šambek), tartana, treciones (galeae), triremis, zolla, zopula*" (p. 70). Vidović also puts to rest any illusions one may have harbored concerning the food crews were fed. He cites sailors' diaries, an unusual practice in normative reference works of this nature:

> The salt beef was purchased by the barrel in Trieste, Italy, England, or Marseille and was as black and stringy as dog meat; the ship's biscuits were as tasteless and hard as boards and refused to dissolve even in water or coffee, but most captains preferred them because they cost less than the ones made in Odessa or Genoa that came apart with the flick of a finger. The menu on board did not change very much: in the morning we had hard tack, and rare was the ship that gave us coffee or tea with it; for the noon meal we had soup with salt beef, for the evening meal stew and sometimes salt beef on potato salad. In port they would buy fresh beef rather than salt-beef, but it was really only the head minus the brain and tongue to save even more. Small ships with a crew of five or six would buy half a head each, and the cook was supposed to save enough to make two steaks for the captain and the clerk. They used almost no fat because the onions that went into the stew were fried in the grease from the salt-beef soup. . . . The crew ate below deck out of a single bowl. Only the *nostromo* had a plate of his own. As for water, everyone from the captain to the *mozzo* drank from a cup attached to the barrel. In port the ship's boy would fill a bottle for the captain and the clerk and the boatswain and the crew would drink out of jugs." (Vidović, pp. 301–2)

This passage comes from *Uspomene iz pomorskog života* (Memoirs of a Life on the Sea, Split 1933), by a sailor named Vlado Ivelić. Mediterraneans read glossaries as if they were memoirs, which they sometimes are. Take, for example, the huge *Atlante linguistico mediterraneo* (Linguistic Atlas of the Mediterranean) that has been coming out in installments for years now in Venice (and was once edited by Mirko Deanović [1890–1984] of Dubrovnik). Mediterraneans greet each new fascicle with excitement, protest, and increasing nostalgia.

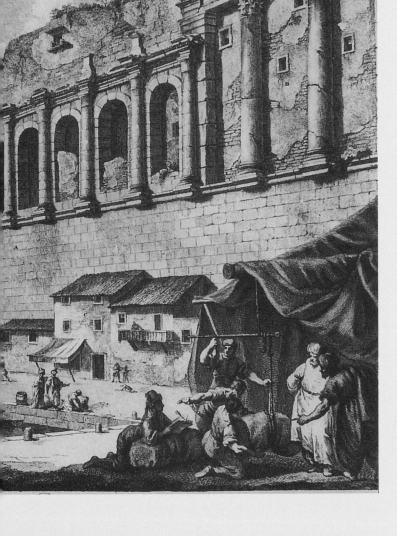

*The old harbor
of Split with the
Palace of Diocletian,
by Ch. L. Robert
Adam,* Ruins
of the Palace
of Diocletian.
London, *1764.*

Glossary

IN THE WAKE of the First World War Božo Cvjetković of Dubrovnik, a true Mediterranean, accepted the challenge of the critic Jovan Sker-lić to put together a kind of nautical breviary of his own—shorter than this one—under the title *Estetska oceanografija* (Aesthetic Oceanography, Dubrovnik 1920). He concentrated on the Dubrovnik shipbuilding trade. The small Dubrovnik Republic—small in area—had numerous shipyards in Dubrovnik proper and in the outlying towns of Gruž, Cavtat, Župa, and Rijeka Dubrovačka, in Zaton, on the islands of Lopud and Šipan, and in Slano and Ston on the peninsula of Pelješac. These shipyards "launched large numbers of galleons, polacres, carracks, and other large sailing vessels that spread the glory of Saint Blasius [the patron saint of Dubrovnik] from the fabled Levant to the Pillars of Hercules and thence to dark and perfidious Albion, the land of Columbus, and—following the routes of Vasco da Gama—all the way to Calidas' homeland and Bhagavat's heavenly throne." He describes the most famous of the shipyards, founded in Gruž in 1526, in similar terms: "It furnished all the necessary equipment: winches, nets, vats, axes, measuring rods. . . . Large warehouses for lumber, tar, rope, anchors, etc. stood close at hand." The yard included a house where the owner could live while overseeing the construction of his ship. Precious lumber came from the bountifully wooded slopes of the Srdj, from the island of Mljet, from Albania, from the Neretva region, from Senj, but primarily from Mount Sant'Angeleo and Mount Gargano in Apulia. In the correspondence of the scholar and patriot Cvjetković, which his family put at my disposal, I learned that the Alexandrian ship on which Saint Paul sailed to the Apennines from Malta had a figurehead "whose sign was the Dioscuri," that is, Castor and Pollux (as is corroborated by Saint Luke in the Acts of the Apostles 28:11). We may assume that other ships plowing the Mediterranean at the time boasted similar figureheads on bow or stern.

Further valuable facts about ships and shipbuilding crop up in the works of inspired dilettantes. While taking a vaporetto tour of the islands in the Lagoon of Venice, I stopped at Torcello, Burano, Murano (where my fellow travelers and I were much impressed with the glassblowers), Mazzorbo, the one-time government seat of Malamocco, the Realtine Islands, and finally Chioggia. There I came upon a two-volume glossary of sorts entitled *Calafati, squeri e barche di Chioggia* (Chioggia's Shipbuilders, Shipyards, and Ships). Compiled by Dino Memmo and published in 1985 with the assistance of the local authorities, it has

Within the image: CIVITAS VENECIARV · Ecclia · S. Maca · Palaci ducis

The City of Venice.
Breydenbach, Pere-
grinationes in
Terram Sanctam.
Mainz, 1486.

much to offer. It tells how a tiny town contributed to the great sea power that was Venice, how shipbuilding (*galafa'*) came to develop there and at what cost, when the corporative statutes for shipbuilding or *mariegole* originated (the first reference to a *mariegola* dates from the spring of 1211), what kinds of anchor predated the Renaissance model (*l'ancora rinascimentale*), and what kinds of rudder predated the Navarra rudder. It also gives the provenance of various tools and their names: *curiaga, canagola, chissa, gala* or *gala verta, catarafa* and *cartabon, polacchina, cortelo, verna, becanela a due* or *becanela a tre, alzana, berlasso* or *imberlasso*, none of which made their way into Giuseppe Boeri's wonderful old glossary (*Dialetto veneto* [Venetian Dialect], Venice 1829). There is no need to define them here: they are incomprehensible to Venetians, to say nothing of other Italians, just as the Dalmatianisms I have cited are incomprehensible to Pannonian Croats, to say nothing of Serbs, Bosnians, or Montenegrins. The same incomprehensibility characterizes linguistic relations between coast and hinterland from the Maghreb all the way to Libya, Palestine, Syria, and southern Anatolia and back to Provence, Catalonia, Aragon, and Gibraltar; indeed, it is one of the most salient features of the Mediterranean region.

TIMOSTHENES, THE ADMIRAL of Ptolemy II, was the author of a ten-volume study entitled *On Ports*. How much more we would know about the Mediterranean had it come down to us.

Harbors and ports should be viewed not merely in practical terms of freight loaded and unloaded, of import and export: they existed before boats. They served the first sailors setting forth for the other shore in hollowed logs. The Greeks paid special attention to *limên autophyês*, a "self-occurring harbor," one that comes about by the will of the sea. Thucydides is among the first to speak of them (1.93). *Pelagolimên*, according to the description by the strategist Polyaenus (3.9), lay on a stone embankment with a long wharf. The Phoenicians built ports with two piers to accommodate opposing winds. They chose the best sites along the Mediterranean and marked them with the consonants MHVZ (we do not know what vowels they pronounced between them).

There has been much investigation of early ports in the twentieth century, much diving among their sunken algae- and shell-covered piers and digging in the silt, sand, and earth that buried them. When I read the account of the French archeologists who excavated Byblos (Maurice Dunand, *Les Fouilles de Byblos* [The Byblos Excavation], Paris 1937), I could not get over the number and variety of objects lost and found in the port that probably provided the name for the most widely read book in the Mediterranean world and beyond.

The writings of an engineer by the name of Gaston Jondet, who conducted underwater explorations of the remains of the port on the ancient island of Pharos near Alexandria, testify to the skill of the men who built it. It consisted of two breakwaters—two and a half kilometers long and over sixty meters wide on a foundation made of stone from a quarry in Mex and assembled without mortar or cement after a Minoan model—between the island itself (now a peninsula jutting into the Mediterranean) and the mountain Abu Bakar.

I have also seen the sunken shores of Pozzuoli not far from Naples (Portus Iulius, Baia, Campi Flegrei in Campania), a historic feat of port engineering accomplished with the aid of vulcanized sand (*puteolanus pulvis*), which turns into the firmest of cement upon contact with fresh or salt water. Seneca includes it in his *Naturales Quaestiones* as one of the wonders of his world. It also occurs in Vitruvius's *De Architectura*. Not far from the Temple to Serapis, now about ten meters underwater, there was an important sculptor's studio. Saint Paul departed for Rome from Pozzuoli. The via Domiziana ran through it. It is also where Petronius set the crowning glory of his *Satyricon,* Trimalchio's Feast. On my way out of town I happened upon Martial's epigram about the matrons at the nearby summer resort of Baia (it too now under water): they arrived like Penelopes and left like Helens (*Epigrammaton Libri* 1.63). It was the most famous pier on the Mediterranean.

Some time later I came across a little-known work by Ruggero Bošković, *Del porto di Rimini* (On the Port of Rimini, Pesaro 1765). Bošković—a cosmologist who had come close to the theory of the atom, an astronomer who had measured the length of the meridian between Rome and Rimini, a native of Dubrovnik who had thrown in his lot with the Jesuits yet vied in mathematics with d'Alembert—was invited by the city fathers to solve the problems of their seaport, which goes to show the importance of ports in the Mediterranean scheme of things.

Many glossaries deal with the relationship between port and gate (see the chapter "Ports et portes" [Ports and Gates] in Georges Dumézil's *Fêtes romaines d'été et d'automne* [Roman Summer and Autumn

Festivals], Paris 1975), perhaps because in Latin and the Romance languages they have the same root. The feast of Portunas, the god of ports and protector of gates (*deus portuum portarumque praeses*), takes place at the end of the canicular, or dog-day, season on 17 August. His sanctuary was traditionally located near a river, bridge, and port, *in portu Tiberino* in the words of Varro (*De Lingua Latina* 6.9). Early calendars show that port celebrations or *portunalia* (we can only guess what they entailed) were alternatively called *Tibernalia*. The connection between ports and gates in Mediterranean culture is reinforced by the fact that the Etruscan word *culś,* which figures in the most extensive text we have in the language—that is, the inscription on the famous linen mummy cloth in the Zagreb Anthropological Museum, the *liber linteus zagrabiensis*—also appears to mean not only port and gate but also a divinity (*culśanś*) uniting them. Thus the Etruscans, a seagoing people if there ever was one, determined the status of many ports along the Apennine side of the Mediterranean.

But let me return to the issue of sunken ports, which was in fact a primary factor in motivating me to write the current book. A sunken port is a kind of necropolis. It shares the fate of sunken cities and islands, holds out the same secrets, questions, lessons. Some have been studied to death, others barely broached. The port of Tiro, among the oldest known, once tied island to land (as many of the best ports do). Its breakwater could tame the fiercest of waves; its remains rose out of the water like mountain tops until recent times. (I once saw them on an engraving dated 1836.) Even now they can be spotted in the depths on days when the sea is calm. A statue of Poseidon brought up by divers is defiantly clutching a seahorse in his hand. The port of Helice on the Gulf of Corinth and its sudden and tragic destruction by a tidal wave have been the subject of centuries of fearful and cautious conversations, of chronicles and histories. The famous seaport of Apollonia on the Libyan coast with its two large ports built in the Phoenician manner (that is, connected and with breakwaters) once provided great wealth to neighboring Cyrene by exporting its grain to Ostia, yet despite the patron from whom it takes its name, it too ended under water. (Its remains, like Tiro's, can be seen in the depths when the sea is calm.) The African coast offers a number of such scenes: Utica, for example, near Carthage, where it is hard to tell what was destroyed by human evil and what by the wrath of the sea. (Utica, I should point out, was another island port.) The military port of Misenum, not far from Pozzuoli, suffered a similar fate, invincible as it seemed: it rested on giant blocks of stone and massive caissons dug into the sea floor with all the skill the Romans had learned from the Etruscans and Carthaginians. Near today's Marseille, divers have uncovered pine and oak logs that supported the old port of Massilia. Massilia—established by Greeks from Phocaea eight centuries before the birth of Christ (Pytheas set forth from Massilia on his periplus to the far north, the Ultima Thule)—Massilia sank as well. Just west of it, near what is today the Gulf of Saint-Gervais off Fos-sur-Mer, I saw a stone pier, some columns, and what may have been statues of divinities at a depth of four to five meters in the mire deposited by the Rhône. (Rivers often play a role in such plots.) Just next to Posilipo, not far from Naples, lie the remains of the Greek Parthenope and the marketplace Paleopolisa, and the remains of the ports of Gaiola and Marchiaro in the sea east of the point called Casa degli Spiriti are occasionally visible. Motya, well known during Sicily's golden age, has disappeared without a trace. The Adriatic island of Pag had and lost the port of the Illyrian Liburnians— Cissa or Kissa by name; scholars are still searching for its remains. I have met people from nearby Rovinj who believe it to be their place of origin. The Brijuni Islands off the Dalmatian coast also have a sunken port. Sunken ports are common; I have not visited them all. They represent something we do not wish to identify with, perhaps because we Mediterraneans all have something of the sunken port in us.

ISLANDS LIKE SEAS CHANGE NAMES. Whether such has always been the case is not clear. Both the rulers and the inhabitants who name them change as well. Diodorus Siculus devotes an entire volume of his *Bibliotheke,* a world history from the earliest times, to islands, telling how and why his native Sicily, "which was originally called Trinacria for its shape (it has three large promontories like three points), later took the name Sicania from the Sicani who inhabited the island" (5.2). The Prophets called Cyprus Chittim (Ezekiel 27:7); the ancient Greeks called it Alasiotas. In the Old Testament Crete is Caphtorim (Genesis 10:14), but the Arabs later called it Candia. The Lipari Islands were once better known as the Aeolyan Islands. The Peloponnese was called Morea by the Venetians because it abounded in *moro,* mulberry. Ibiza in the Balearic group was called Pitiusa for its pines. Hvar had a similar name, but the Italians changed it to Lesina. The Kerkenna Archipelago was once known as Kyrannos, but when Hannibal was defeated on land and sought salvation on the sea by setting sail from that point on the Punic coast for the Phoenician coast, historians called it Cercina. In ancient times the largest island in the Adriatic, Krk, was called Curicta or Curicum (Kurikon or Kuriatika in Greek) after its town; the Italians called it Veglia, and the local population uses Veja, or simply "the island" (that is, Bodulija). The steep reef between Krk and the shore now known as Saint Mark was once Almis; all rock with no vegetation whatsoever, it supports a long bridge over a canal that at one point bore the name Calm and at another Wild. Pag was once Cissa or Kissa, like its port; Vis (Lissa in Italian) was Issa. Some Mediterranean islands, however, have always been what they are: Rhodes was Rhodes from the outset; Lesbos was always Lesbos.

Peninsulas change their names as well. In ancient times the Mediterranean coasts of the Iberian Peninsula took the name of the Hesperides (from the Greek word for evening or west). The Romans called them Baetica, and the mountain chain separating the southern coast from the hinterland is called even today the Sistema Penibética (from the ancient name of the Guadalquivir, Baetis). The name for (V)andalusia would appear to come from the Vandals. Names like the Caliphate of Córdoba, the Empire of the Almoravidians, or the Kingdom of Granada reflect administrative concerns, while Costa Blanca and Costa del Sol are purely geographic in nature. In any case, names came more from land than sea, and changes in name from changes in situation or, to put it the other way round, changes in Mediterranean borders and political relations led to changes in form and content.

Even the Pillars of Hercules acquired a new name in the post-mythological era. The name, Gibraltar, testifies to the power of the southern coast: it derives from a combination of the Arabic word *jabal* (mountain) and the name of the conqueror Tarik, distorted in the mouths of the peoples along the northern coast of the Mediterranean.

ISLANDS ARE USUALLY DISCUSSED separately, that is, apart from the mainland. They are a perennially popular subject. Etymologists associate the Greek word for island, *nêsos,* with the Indo-European root meaning "floating." The origin of the Latin and Romance words—*insula, isola, île,* and so on—remains obscure. The Italian verb *isolare* (to isolate), which has entered many European languages, comes from the word *isola:* islands have traditionally been symbolic of detachment and solitude. The Croatian word for island, *otok,* comes from *tek-,* the stem of *teći* (to flow) plus the prefix *o-* (around); most other Slav languages use *ostrov,* or variants thereof, which derives from the word for current, *struja,* with the same prefix. Petar Skok, whom I have cited before in matters etymological, claims that "they are not nautical terms; they were transposed from land to sea: they exist as toponyms on land" (*Etimološki rječnik hrvatskog ili srpskog jezika* [Etymological Dictionary of Croatian or Serbian], Zagreb 1970, vol. 3, p. 350). Our Mediterranean islanders were transposed from inland as well.

Pliny the Elder, who sailed through the Adriatic islands, characterizes them as follows: "The Illyrian coast has more than a thousand islands. The sea is shallow, the currents insignificant, running through narrow inlets" (*Naturalis Historia* 3.151). Pomponius Mela, though not particularly gifted, followed his lead: he fell in love with the Adriatic and composed fulsome praise to it (*De Chorographia* 2.55). Every part of the Mediterranean would appear to have its Pomponius: we owe him our gratitude.

The oldest known description of "the islands of the blessed" occurs in Hesiod's *Works and Days:* "The blissful heroes inhabit the islands of the blessed near the ocean's deep swirl, their hearts free of care: the fruitful land yields three sweet harvests a year" (169–73). But islands are fruitful and their inhabitants generous in the Psalms of Solomon as well: "The kings of Tarshish and of the isles shall bring presents" (Psalms 72:10). The notion of an island as something apart, undisturbed by the outside world and hence capable of establishing absolute order, has given rise to the most zealous utopias. Plato portrays a luxuriant Atlantis in the *Critias* and the *Timaeus,* "a blessed island illuminated by the sun and productive of fragrances . . . , with temples, royal palaces, ports, and harbors" (*Critias* 115). It was bound to sink and thus teach us the transitory nature of happiness. But what has become of other such islands, the subject of much conjecture? Where are Antilia, Satanazes, the Island of the Seven Cities? Did they suffer the fate of Atlantis? Did they ever exist in the Mediterranean or elsewhere for that matter?

ISLANDS ARE NOT ALWAYS places of happiness and bliss: great dangers and temptations lurk between Scylla and Charybdis. Islands are also

places of incarceration and exile. Such was the case not only in myths and epics but also in the practice of tyrants Greek and Roman, Arab and Turk, German and Slav. Daedalus built the most abominable of prisons, the labyrinth, on the island of Crete; his son Icarus tried in vain to fly from a cliff on the island and plunged into the sea that bears his name. Many are the islands to which despots have banned their adversaries. Leafing through the writings of a little-known historian of the fourth century, Ammianus Mercellinus, I came upon the concept of *poena insularis* (island punishment [15.7]), which seems to have entered Roman legal terminology before the decadent period. The tiny island of San Nicolo was a *colonia penale* as early as the Kingdom of Naples. Seneca spent eight years in exile on Corsica. The Dubrovnik poet Ivan Gundulić withdrew late in life to Daksa, one of the smallest of the Elafitic Islands, to repent the sins of his youth. Many lost their lives there. Roman rulers, *consules atque proconsules,* sent their worst enemies to the island of Mljet (whose name is etymologically related to honey: *melite nesos* [island of honey]) in the southern Adriatic between Lastovo and Šipan. The sweet little island (with its picturesque saltwater lake) was so crawling with poisonous snakes that it required no guards. The Dubrovnik Republic adapted this Latin tradition to its own more modest needs and possibilities by turning the same island into a minor Mediterranean Siberia.

It was a frequent phenomenon. Buonaparte the Corsican was imprisoned twice on the Mediterranean island of Elba before being exiled to Saint Helena. Lev Trotsky spent the first stage of his exile on the island of Prinkipo (Büyükada in Turkish) in the Sea of Marmara. ("In Prinkipo in 1932, nothing less dark or violent was to be seen on the horizon than Trotsky's pale blue eyes," writes Max Eastman in "Problems of Friendship with Trotsky," *Great Companions,* New York 1954, p. 152.) The Lipari Islands served as a concentration camp, the old Austrian fortress on the tiny island of Mamula off the Gulf of Ko-

The Island of Utopia. Anonymous engraving from the first edition of Thomas More's Utopia. *Louvain, 1516.*

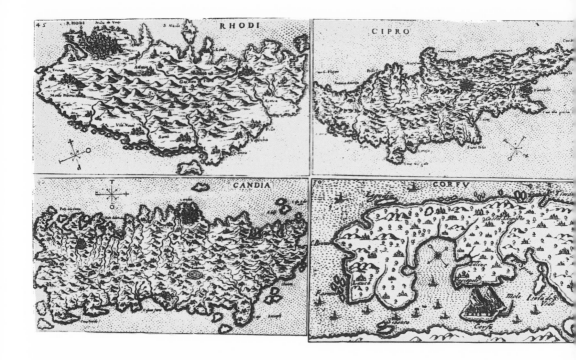

tar as a prison for leftists and anti–Fascists. Between 1941 and 1943 there
was an Italian camp for Jews on the island of Rab (perhaps on the spot
where the insane asylum is now). On the small island of Iaros, as well
as the larger island of Makronisos (to return to the Greeks), the Colonels
built camps for intellectuals and other advocates of democracy after
the Second World War (along the lines of the Soviet camps on the
Solovetskie Islands in the White Sea during the "personality cult,"
though with milder climatic conditions). Naked Island (*Goli otok*) in
the northern Adriatic near the Kvarner Archipelago served as a prison
for Yugoslavs who refused to accept Tito's break with Stalin in 1948.
It was an exercise in futility worthy of a Sisyphus: the prisoners did
nothing but break stones and throw them into the water, as if trying
to stop up the Mediterranean.

  The Spaniards transferred certain customs to their colonies: the max-
imum security penitentiary nicknamed "The Rock" and located on
the island of Alcatraz in San Francisco Bay (that is, in the bay of a city

honoring a Mediterranean saint) reputed until recently to be "the safest prison in the world." In French Guiana a series of prisons with religious names (the Îles du Salut [Salvation Islands], Île du Diable [Devil's Island]) far outdid their ancient models in cruelty. Nor should we forget that three of the great navigator-explorers—Magellan, La Pérouse, and Captain Cook—perished on three godforsaken islands. The island Kafka used as the basis for his "Penal Colony" is not clear. What is clear is that the possibilities—Mediterranean and otherwise—are legion.

While Goethe was making ready for the journey to Italy that would inspire the *Römische Elegien* (Roman Elegies, 1788–90), he had a dream of an island utopia: "I landed in quite a large boat on a fertile, richly luxuriant island which I knew had the most beautiful pheasants. . . . They were in fact pheasants, but as dreams tend to transform everything, they had long tails with multicolored eyes like peacocks or rare birds of paradise" (*Italienische Reise* [Italian Journey], 19 October 1786). Sicily reminds the poet of "Asia and Africa, and it is no mean experience to stand at this wondrous juncture of so many radii of world history" (26 March 1787). Mediterranean history often ends up on islands.

As it is virtually impossible to visit all the Mediterranean islands, I have had recourse to testimonies of those who have explored some I have not. In his little-known book on Sardinia, for example, D. H. Lawrence writes, "They say neither Romans nor Phoenicians, Greeks nor Arabs ever subdued Sardinia. It lies outside; outside the circuit of civilisation" (*Sea and Sardinia,* New York 1921, p. 15). Sardinia reminds him of Malta, lost between Europe and Africa, belonging nowhere, beyond history and time. History and time are less than evenly distributed over the Mediterranean.

Lawrence Durrell spent much time on the islands of Sicily, Rhodes, Corfu, Cyprus, and Patmos and wrote extensively about each. Moreover, he saved the word *islomania* from oblivion: "Somewhere among the note-books of Gideon I once found a list of diseases as yet unclassified by medical science, and among these there occurred the word *Islomania,* which was described as a rare but by no means unknown affliction of spirit. There are people, Gideon used to say, by way of explanation, who find islands somehow irresistible. The mere knowledge that they are on an island, a little world surrounded by the sea, fills them with an indescribable intoxication. These born 'islomanes,' he used to add, are the direct descendants of the Atlanteans, and it is to-

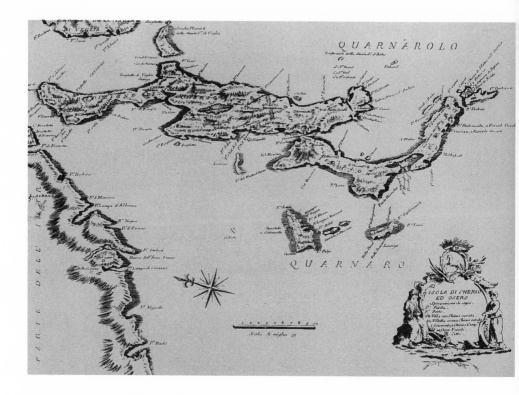

The Kvarner islands. Alberto Fortis, Saggio di osservazione sopra l'isola di Cherso e Osero. *Venice, 1771.*

wards the lost Atlantis that their subconscious yearns throughout their island life. I forget the other details. But like all Gideon's theories it was an ingenious one. . . . This book is by intention a sort of anatomy of islomania" (*Reflections on a Marine Venus*, London 1953, pp. 15–16). And this book is by intention a means of freeing the spirit of various Mediterranean maladies, including islomania, which once plagued me and even now returns from time to time.

SINCE MUCH OF THE MEDITATION on islands leads to the subject of exile, I should like to devote a short midrash to it. The ancient Hebrews were more inclined to establish institutions and hierarchies in questions of faith and ritual than were the ancient Greeks. They elected "leaders of exile," considering them descendants of David and vesting great power, both spiritual and secular, in them. The officials were called *resh golutha* in Aramaic and exilarchs in Greek and Latin; French-Jewish Talmudic scholars called them *princes de l'exil* (see *Écoute, Israël* [Hear, O Israel], Paris 1953, by the unusual poet Edmond Fleg). The *Midrash Rabba,* a work about exiles and their persecutors by the exilarch Rabbi Huna, proved highly inspirational. The diaspora long preserved and honored the title *resh golutha,* and generations profited from the office, but when the exilarchiate died out with Rabbi Ezekiel, all attempts to revive it were in vain. The meager data I have been able compile show exilarchs to have been exceptionally patient and tolerant, lighthouses on capes of good hope, commandants on islands of exile. The Mediterranean can be proud of having given birth to such an institution.

I LEARNED HOW TO CONTEMPLATE the sea and pray from a monk by the name of Irineus. I met him at the Coptic Monastery of As-Surian, between Alexandria and Cairo, not far from the coast and on the edge of the desert. Irineus was born in Odessa of Uniate parents who had fallen prey to religious persecution. He was taken in by one of the many Greek families in the cosmopolitan seaport that Odessa has always been. During the war the family managed to flee to Salonika. Irineus took his monastic vows at the Iviron Monastery on Mount Athos, then served the Lord on Mount Sinai and on the Lebanese plateau, in monasteries on Cyprus and in cells of Greek "meteors." He often contemplated the sea while praying. He told me about the Coptic hermits Saint Anthony and Saint Pachomius, who had done penance in the desert near the sea, and about Saint Macarius's Monastery and the monastic precepts of Saint Basil: withdrawal from the world and renunciation of country and family, property and goods, friends and secular concerns (I cite from memory). Saint Jerome, no stranger to the desert or the Mediterranean himself, translated Saint Basil's harsh precepts into Latin, and Saint Athanasius wrote a biography of Saint Anthony the Anchorite.

Irineus the Anchorite was dignified when he spoke, handsome when he gazed into the distance, and confident when he argued that Christians die in Christ. His Russian was pure, archaic at times, and without metaphors. He knew several languages, including Coptic. He had lived in Alexandria, where he deepened his knowledge of early

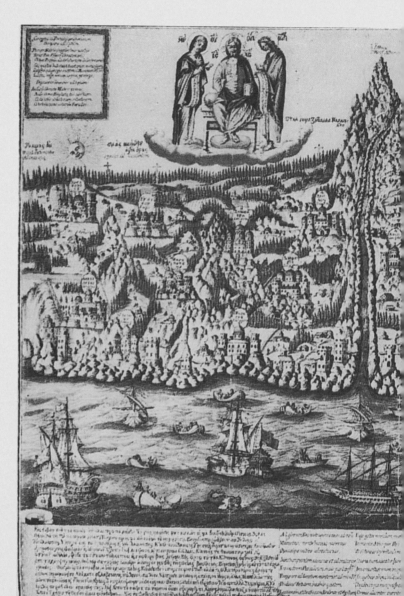

Mount Athos. Alessandro dalla Via. Venice, late seventeenth to early eighteenth century.

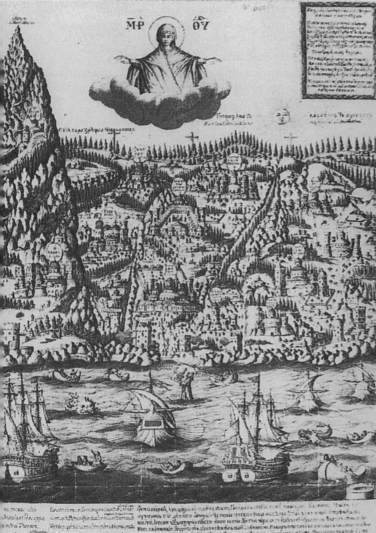

Christianity and the theologians and exegetes who had made this "first Christian university" famous. He was particularly interested in Cyril of Alexandria, who had perused Christ's teachings for a synthesis of earlier mystical aspirations rather than a break with them. He told me about the lighthouse of Sostratos of Knidos and the rectangular foundation for the long *tholos* topped by an enormous light. It appears to have been a model for ancient mausoleums, the steeples of the first Romanesque churches, and the towers of Byzantine basilicas. Each time I see a new lighthouse, I think of what he said and cannot help comparing it with Mediterranean churches.

The spirituality brought to the shores of the Mediterranean by the prophets and apostles was, he claimed, inherited by the great anchorites. Philo's *De Vita Contemplativa* was one of the purest manifestations of the new Hellenism: *theôria* means both "sight" and "insight," and contemplation is experience and theory, *praxis kai theôria*. He explained to me the original meanings of *anakhôresis* and *koinônia*, of *xeniteia* and *laura*, of *apatheia* as self-control and *diakrisis* as inner determination, and he spoke of it all as part of the spiritual tradition of the eastern Mediterranean that later spread west and north and must not be ignored, its ways leading to Cappadocia, to the Kiev Monastery of the Caves (*Kievo-Pecherskaia lavra*), to Sveti Naum and Sopoćani, to the Sanctuary of the Forty Martyrs in Bulgaria and the Armenian monasteries on the saltwater lake of Van and the freshwater lake of Sevan. He spoke of many works both religious and secular. Hölderlin's Hyperion dreamt of becoming a "hermit in Greece." In ancient cultures the "attitude of the viewer" had prevailed; philosophy had sought "intelligent points of view." (Irineus laid special emphasis on the words I have put in quotation marks.) Given that every force calls forth opposing forces, the Hellenic tradition developed a tendency to move beyond the realm of the visible, and wisdom—that is, the attempt to penetrate mystery—came to be identified with blindness: Tiresias is blind (like Homer), but intuits what he cannot see. Oedipus puts out his own eyes when they deceive him; the first Christian preachers tell the Greek pagans, "If thy right eye offend thee, pluck it out, and cast it from thee" (Matthew 5:29); when Dante reaches the infinite light of Paradise, he loses his sight. The Mediterranean sun is blinding.

The end of antiquity was characterized by great advocates of silence. "The *logos* must be preceded by silence," the Neoplatonists warned, and Plotinus sought "understanding in silence." The ideal of the ascetic was a "wordless dithyramb" to God. The emphasis on equanimity in speech and prayer was not exclusively Byzantine, Irineus insisted; it was to be found in the West as well—in Palermo (in the thirteenth-century Chiostro di San Giovanni degli Eremiti), throughout Spain and France (in the Cistercian, Paulist, and Trappist orders), on several Adriatic islands (Košljun near Krk and the Island of the Madonna of Škrpjelo in the Gulf of Kotor)—and even on the southern coast of the Mediterranean in Sufic *tariqats,* and it should be factored into any consideration of Mediterranean borders.

I do not know whether Irineus ever completed his study of Saint Simeon Stylites and the motivations behind his thirty-year abode on a pillar. Like many Slavs, he does not answer letters, though who can tell whether mine ever reached his desert monastery by the Mediterranean.

ACCESS TO THE SEA is closely connected to the sacrament of baptism in both the Old and New Testaments. "All our fathers were under the cloud, and all passed through the sea. And were all baptized unto Moses in the cloud and in the sea" Saint Paul wrote (I Corinthians 10:1–2) during a voyage through the Mediterranean.

Faiths changed people's names along the Mediterranean. Christians of all tongues and nations adopted Hebrew names from the Holy Scripture; Muslims adapted them, Abraham becoming Ibrahim, David Davud, Solomon Suleiman, Joseph Jusuf, Miriam Meryema, and so on. But some names differ from one faith to the next. Many have to do with light, with the sun or the earth, virtually none with the sea. The Son of God said to Simon Peter, "Thou shalt be called Cephas, which is by interpretation, a stone" (John 1:42), the Greek *petros* being a translation of the Aramaic *kepha.* Saint Jerome tried to interpret the name of Mary as a compound made up of the Hebrew words *meir* (light) and *yam* (sea)—the *Stella maris* known to sailors from time immemorial—but despite Jerome's authority as saint and translator, the etymology has long been confuted. The sinful Mary Magdalene takes her name from the town of Magdala on the Sea of Galilee. Lydia comes from the eponymous ancient country in Asia Minor. As legend has it, the modest *Lydia purpuraria* (scarlet Lydia), having come to Philippi, the capital of Aegean Macedonia, and heard Saint Paul (it was the place where he first preached the gospel in Europe), became the first Macedonian Christian (see *Martyrologium Romanum* 3.8). While there are no important holy names connected with the sea, an entire new human nomenclature grew up on the Mediterranean.

LIKE NAMES, COASTS ARE either Christian or not; like people and boats, they may be baptized, and they are often named after saints or the Virgin Mary. Along the coast of Sardinia, for example, we find names like Santa Maria Navarese, Isola di Santa Maria, Santa Caterina di Pittunari, Santa Lucia, Monte Santu, Sant'Antonio de Santadi, Capo San Marco, Stagno di San Giovanni, Santa Teresa di Gallura, La Maddalena, and Costa Paradiso. The name Marsala in southern Sicily dates from the period of Arab rule and comes from the words *mars* (port) and Allah. The Greek islands show much ancient pagan influence, but Crete, for instance, has many Christian toponyms, names like Hagia Triada, Hagios Nikolaos, Hagios Ionannis, Hierapetra, Apanosiphis. The municipal marketplace and fish market in Barcelona bear the name of Saint Joseph. Nor is the southern coast of the Mediterranean devoid of examples.

Along the Adriatic the word for saint, *sveti,* occurs in the abbreviated forms *su-* or *sut-,* making the names sound, if anything, more intimate than elsewhere: Supetar (Saint Peter), Supavo (Saint Paul), Sutivan (Saint John), Sustipan (Saint Stephen), Sućuraj (Saint George), Sumartin or, with metathesis, Sumratin (Saint Martin), Sutorina (Saint Irene), Sutmiho (Saint Michael), Sutvara (Saint Barbara), Sutomišćica (Saint Euphemia), and so on. Besides these, we have punta Križa (Point Cross), punta Madona (Point Madonna), vala od Marije (Maria Bay), zaljev Svetog Pavla (Gulf of Saint Paul), and finally otok Svetog Grgura (Saint Gregory Island, which does not enjoy the best of reputations). Sailing into Pula, we are greeted by three islands: Sveti Petar (Saint Peter), Sveti Andrija (Saint Andrew), and Sveta Katarina (Saint Catherine). Saint Elijah gave his name to Sutlija, the hill and quarry that put Trogir on the map ("Tragurium marmore notum," wrote Pliny the Elder [*Naturalis Historia* 3.141]: "Trogir is noted for its marble."). Thus the land along the Mediterranean is sanctified, while the Mediterranean itself is either holy in and of itself or cursed.

Seaports have often taken saints as protectors, and many in the central Mediterranean region have taken patrons from the East (which confirms the existence of spiritual as well as commercial ties). Genoa,

Barcelona, Tarragona, and our tiny Senj have all singled out Saint George of Syria. The exarchate of Ravenna preferred Byzantine patrons. But it is the eastern Adriatic that has seen the greatest merging of East and West: Saint Domnius of Antioch and Saint Blasius of Sebastia are the patron saints of Split and Dubrovnik; Saint Theodore, patron of the Byzantine army, defends Korčula; Saint James, Šibenik; and Saint Tryfonius, Kotor. The inhabitants of Renaissance Trogir enjoyed the confraternity of Saints Damian and Cosmas. Zadar built churches to Saint Anastasia and Saint Chrysophorus. Dalmatia dedicated a shrine of precious metal to Saint Simeon. The beautiful, prosperous cities of the Mediterranean would never have been able to withstand the onslaughts of the barbarians were it not for the providential aid of their saints.

LAWMAKERS IN ANCIENT GREECE looked out for salt. Salt mining was an honored profession; salt mines were protected. Homer sings the praises "of divine salt" (*halos theioio*) in the *Iliad* (9.214), and Aristotle mentions it in the same breath as morality and friendship in the *Nicomachean Ethics* (1156b.27). Pliny the Elder sees its influence "on the pleasures of the spirit [*ad voluptates animi*], so that of many different delights— life's greatest joys, rest after hard work—we say they are of salt, which no other word expresses quite so well" (31.88). Cicero owned several salt mines and speaks of them with pride: "salinarum mearum possessio" (*Ad Familiares* [To Friends] 7.32), which goes to show the connection between rhetoric and salt. One of the main Roman roads was called the via Salaria because the Sabines used it to transport sacks of salt into the Eternal City. (The cartographer of the Tabula Peutingeriara draws it with great clarity.) Salt opened the roads from the sea inland and vice versa. It is impossible to count all the salt mines along the Mediterranean or overestimate what we owe them.

HARD AS IT IS TO BELIEVE, the olive was brought to the Mediterranean by outsiders: it was transplanted before the grape but after the fig (though all three plants appear in the Talmud, the Bible, and the Qur'an). Olive culture is responsible for terminology on a par with philosophical and religious terminology: the man who cultivated olives was called an *elaiologos,* the man who sold them an *elaioparokhos,* the man who stood watch over them an *elaiokhristês* (the watch itself being the *elaiokhristia*), and the production of olive oil was *elailourgia*. Gethsemane comes from the Hebrew words for garden (*gath*) and olive press or mill (*shemanim*). The olive and olive tree enjoy a special place in the Holy Scripture: olive oil is said "to honor God and man" (Judges 9:9). The Hebrew word *Mashiah* (Messiah, that is, the anointed one), becomes *Khristos* in Greek. The Qur'an swears by the olive (*al-zeitun*) and the fig: Sura 95 begins "By the fig and the olive, by Mount Sinai and the city of peace" and is called "Al-Tin" after the fig tree. These institutions and rituals are as essential to Mediterranean civilization as routes and voyages.

"The Mediterranean lies on the fringes of [a] desert belt and the olive is its tree," Aldous Huxley writes, "the tree of a region of sun-lit clarity separating the damps of the equators from the damps of the North. It is the symbol of a classicism enclosed between two romanticisms" (*The Olive Tree,* London 1947, p. 295). Huxley sees the olive tree as a emblem of Latinity. "As well as for peace and for joy, it stands for all that makes us specifically English rather than Teutonic; for those Mediterranean influences without which Chaucer and Shakespeare could never have become what they learned from France and Italy, from Rome and Greece, to be—the most essentially native of our poets" (p. 293).

Lawrence Durrell, who spent his youth on the Greek islands and his old age in Provence, sees the olive as the synthesis of what it means to be Mediterranean: "The whole Mediterranean—the sculptures, the palms, the gold beads, the bearded heroes, the wine, the ideas, the ships, the moonlight, the winged gorgons, the bronze men, the philosophers— all of it seems to rise in the sour, pungent taste of these black olives between the teeth. A taste older than meat, older than wine. A taste as old as cold water" ("Landscape with Olive Trees," *Prospero's Cell,* London 1975, p. 105).

The bibliography of any Mediterranean glossary would not be complete without Apicius's *De Re Coquinaria,* which deals at several points with the olive and its role in Mediterranean cuisine. ("How," he asks, "can we preserve green olives in such a way as to make oil from them at any time?" [1.28].) But he is only one of the many writers and poets, to say nothing of painters, who have depicted olives in their work. Olives have also made their way into city statutes and national consti-

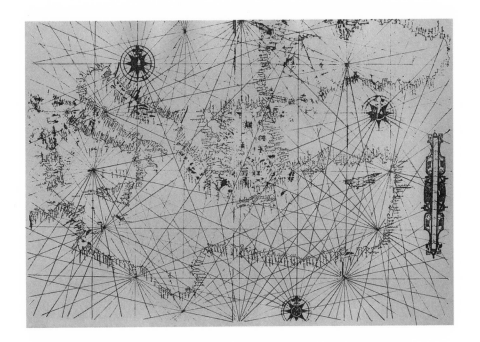

Portolano of the Mediterranean. Vicko Demetrije Volčić (Vicentius Demetrius Volcius).

tutions. *Works and Days* only began with Hesiod; Mediterraneans are constantly rewriting it.

A concluding example: the description of the olive harvest and pressing process in the picturesque, folksy language of a lively Franciscan from Poljica near the Adriatic coast, Don Frano Ivanišević. "You harvest your olives on All Saints Day or thereabouts, in early November. . . . You need ladders and sticks because there's lots of climbing and batting to do. You don't want to wait till they're overripe and start to rot, but then you don't want to take them when they're green either. Anyway, once you've picked them, you gather up the sacks and take them home and pour them into basins or vats or, if you haven't got any, you spread them out on the floor. Then you let them rest a day or two and ripen up, come into their own. If the piles are big, you'll want to stir them and air them out because otherwise they'll burn and their oil will burn your mouth. Next you crush them in a press. The women throw them in and the men work the press. But you don't pour out the liquid then and there. No, you let it stand for a bit so the best oil—what we call *lanbik* or *lotnjak*—rises to the surface. You pour that into wooden barrels and put what's left in sacks you've rinsed out a few times with boiling water. Then the men roll up their trouser legs and trample on it to squeeze the rest of the oil out. You scoop that oil up with a soup plate and pour it into a barrel and throw out the dregs— what we call *murga* (*Poljica—narodni život i običaji* [Poljica—Folk Life and Folkways], Zagreb 1903, p. 304).

THERE ARE MANY ANCIENT TEXTS, both theoretical and practical in nature, devoted to vinegar. The fermentation and acidification processes have been known since Greek and Roman times. Even earlier, engravers used a mixture of vinegar and acid to etch the outlines of land and sea on copper plates. Such was the process most likely used in the maps of the Mediterranean region (*pinax*) that Herodotus saw in the Levant (5.49).

Our ancestors believed that vinegar cured all kinds of maladies. It was used to treat fever and headaches; it was used to alleviate Christ's sufferings on the cross. "Now there was set a vessel full of vinegar: and they filled a sponge with vinegar, and put it on hyssop, and put it to his mouth" (John 19:29). According to the Old Testament, bread dipped in vinegar made a modest Mediterranean meal: Boaz offers it to Ruth in the field beside the reapers (Ruth 2:14).

Southern countries have long discussed the hot and tangy, the sour and acerbic qualities of vinegar. The pungency of the Italian product (*italicum acetum*) was applauded in theaters (Plautus) and lauded in epigrams (Juvenal). While the manuals emphasize the auxiliary role of vinegar in the preparation and conservation of food, I should like to keep alive the memory of several dishes which are closely tied to Mediterranean topography and in which vinegar comprises the prime condiment: mixed grill *alla torinese,* Turkish maize, Maghreb desert consommé, and "four rogues from Marseille" (with marjoram, rosemary, and root of *nulla-campana,* which grows along the coast). Or *garum,* a fish extract; *verjus,* made of juice squeezed from unripe Mediterranean fruits; and the lesser known *crista-marina.*

As broad in scope and refined in taste as the culinary treatises and encyclopedias dealing with the Mediterranean tend to be (and my modest glossary makes no attempt to synthesize their findings), most have overlooked stone soup. I will therefore give the recipe here. Take two or three stones from a spot where the low tide does not reach. (They should be neither too large nor too small, and dark from having lain on the bottom of the sea.) Cook them in rainwater until everything in the pores has had a chance to seep out. Add a few bay leaves and some thyme, a teaspoon of olive oil and a teaspoon of wine vinegar. You will not need to salt if you have chosen the proper stones. Stone soup is known on virtually all islands of the Ionian Sea, from the Adriatic to the Tyrrhenian. It was made by the Illyrians, the Greeks, the Liburnians, and probably the Phoenicians, the Etruscans, and the Pelasgi. It is as ancient as Mediterranean poverty.

THE LITTLE I KNOW ABOUT SPONGES and sponging I owe to the German scholar H. Schmid, who devoted his life to the subject and published the results under the title *Die Spongien des Adriatischen Meeres* (Sponges of the Adriatic Sea, Leipzig 1852). Romantic that he was, he proclaimed the Adriatic a sponge garden (*Spongiengarten*), though it is doubtful that he could have been familiar with all its beds and deposits: besides Krapanj near Zlarin, which is the best-known site, I would cite Žirje and Murter, several locations in Istria (near Rovinj and Poreč), and major promontories like Kamenjak and Pelegrin (in the vicinity of Proiz); then Prigradica and Vela Luka, the Infernal Islands, Premuda, Silba, and Olib (not far from Žut), Sit, Milna, Smrikova, Lavdara and Balabra, Kurba Major and Kurba Minor, Glavoč Major and Glavoč Minor. (I have intentionally chosen sites redolent of the Mediterranean past of both original settlers and colonists.)

From time immemorial sponge hunters have dived after a purple shell called *murex* by the Latins: "The sea along the coast of Laconia near Corinth is rich in shells containing the ingredients to dye raiments purple. They are surpassed in value only by those in the Phoenician Sea" (Pausanias, 3.21). Sponge hunting was prevalent on the islands of the Aegean and Ionian near Rhodes and Crete, off Tabarca in Tunisia, between the Kerkenna Islands and Jerba in the Gulf of Gabès, from Tarvah to Misurata in Tripolitania, off Malta, opposite the Torre del Greco near Naples, along the coast of Turkey, especially in the Syrian Sea, which once competed with the Red Sea and Eritrea, home of the finest sponges in the ancient and medieval world. In the mid-nineteenth century a device called *gangava* or *gannegava* came into use. It consisted of a net in an iron frame that was attached by a chain to the boat's capstan and scraped along the bottom of the sea. Diving equipment was not used in the Adriatic until 1893, nor did it appear much earlier anywhere on the Mediterranean: until then sponges, like coral and *murex,* were gathered in the classical manner.

NO ONE KNOWS WHAT WAS IN the eight books devoted to fish and fishing mentioned by Athenaeus: all we have is Oppian's *Halieutica.* Ovid wrote on fish, though it is hard to identify many of the varieties he heard of as an exile on the Euxine shores: there were more then than there are now. Apicius, in the ninth book of the aforementioned culinary manual, proposes a feast of the kind that still feeds Mediterranean dreams.

Since many have described the myriad types of fish and ways in which they can be prepared, I shall not do so here. I cannot understand why some fish were embossed on coins found through the towns of Graecia Magna—the crab found in Motya, the octopus in Syracuse, the shell in Oxentum, the dolphin in Taranto—while others, equally attractive and no less valuable, failed to catch the minter's eye.

In a study entitled *De situ Illyriae et civitate Sibenici* (On the Location of Illyria and the City of Šibenik), a fifteenth-century canon from Šibenik and occasional poet by the name of Juraj Šižgorić (Georgius Sisgoreus Sibenicensis) recounts the meeting of various types of fish at the mouth of the Krk (Tyrus fluvius), where freshwater and salt water come together. "Here we find unusually large tunny (*thynni*), dolphins (*delphines*) at play, and, frequently, seals (*vituli marini*) as well. When the sun is in the signs of Cancer, Leo, and Virgo (*in Cancro, in Leone et in Virgine*), the fisherman bring in much dentex (*dentrices cristatae*), which is considered a great delicacy: the only other waters in which it is found are supposedly the Dardanelles (*in Hellesponto*). They also bring in oysters (*ostreae*), flavorful because they taste of the Dalmatian Sea, mullet (*capitones*), salpa (*salpae*), scorpions (*scorpenae*), mule-fish (*muli*), wolf-fish (*lupi*), gudgeon (*gobiones*), gilthead (*auratae*), crab (*pagri*), cuttlefish (*loligines*), and mackerel (*scombri*). When the sun is in the sign of Taurus (*ingrediente Taurum*), they catch great quantities of picarel and bream (*copia menarum et sparulorum*) from the bottom of the sea using rods. Sometimes sea monsters (*piscium monstra*) never before seen emerge" (13.45). Note that Šižgorić mentions oysters but not other types of shellfish, from ordinary mussels to delectable lobsters (which colonists

from the north saw for the first time on the trays of indigenous gour-
mands). Judging by statistics of the major fish markets (I have investi-
gated Barcelona, Naples, Marseille, Athens, and Istanbul as well as Trogir, Trapani, Tripoli, and Trieste), few types of fish that trace their origins
to other seas—with the exception of cod and perhaps salmon—are
bought for and consumed at the otherwise tolerant Mediterranean
table.

Vojmir Vinja's *Jadranska fauna: Etimologija i struktura naziva* (Adriatic Fauna: The Etymology and Structure of Its Nomenclature, Split/
Zagreb 1986), which is itself a kind of glossary, gives a systematic treatment of fish names. In his introduction the author pays fitting tribute to our mutual teacher Petar Skok (who unfortunately did not live
to put together his notes—lost after his death—on the etymology of
Mediterranean fauna nomenclature) and to Henrik Barić (1883–1957),
Romance linguist and Albanianist and one of the leading experts on
language issues in the Mediterranean region. He notes an interesting
phenomenon, one that goes beyond the confines of ichthyolexicog-
raphy: "One may almost establish a rule to the effect that the less valuable a fish or other marine animal, the more names it has. The words
salpa and *tuna* are recognizable through the Mediterranean region,
while the *Paracentropristis hepatus,* which is inedible and hence devoid
of interest to fishermen, has as many names as sites" (vol. 1, p. 24).

It would be interesting to look into the ichthyomorphic figures we
meet in early, especially medieval, paintings. What Mediterranean fishes
did Jonah find in the whale's belly? What Mediterranean fishes did the
apostles catch in such great quantity? And what Mediterranean fishes
did Christ use to feed the multitudes?

NETS OFTEN ACQUIRE NAMES from the names of the fish they are meant
to catch (sardine nets, conger nets, etc.) or the way they catch them
(dragnet, pound net, etc.). Alberto Fortis, an abbot who published his
Viaggio in Dalmazia (Journey to Dalmatia) in Venice in 1774, saw a
net in Zlosela near Šibenik "which in their dialect is called *fružata*
(frights.) By shouting, beating oars and poles, and throwing stones into
the water, they frighten the mullet, which, when attempting to flee,
land in the net" (p. 161). The learned abbot notes that such a means
of catching fish shows how lazy and ill acquainted with the ways of

the sea the local populace is and that "the only way to assure the felicity of this coastal people is to use the club, ill advised as it is for the inhabitants of a Mediterranean country."

Paintings on the walls of the palace of the Emperor Titus in Rome show figures casting nets into the sea and hauling them out—and looking rather dour and heavy-handed about it. (Roman rhetoric uses the same kind of dour, heavy-handed devices—it is a style reminiscent of the style of Roman wrestlers—and has been passed down through the generations.) The Spartans built a temple to Dictina, the goddess of nets and fishermen, *diktyon* being the Greek word for net (Pausanias, *Description of Greece* 2.12); on Crete she was called Briotmartis. The most respected fishermen were those who went after tuna. Like warriors, they enjoyed the assistance of scouts, theirs being called ichthyoscopes. Their glory has not dimmed on the Mediterranean even in modern times, especially in Sicily and Corsica, along the Tunisian coast, on the Balearic Islands, on the Sea of Marmara, and on the Bay of Saint-Paul, not far from La Valette (near which the apostle was shipwrecked and which he blessed after surviving the ordeal).

THE COASTS ARE FRAGRANT with grasses, with pines, with all kinds of vegetation. The mixture differs from coast to coast. There are regions where the plants are more fragrant than the sea itself. Some plants capture the spirit, others leave it cold. The fruit of the vine appears in both the Old Testament (Genesis 9:20) and the Qur'an (16:12) and comes together with figs in the New Testament: "Every tree is known by his own fruit. For of thorns men do not gather figs, nor of a bramble bush gather they grapes" (Luke 6:44). Grapevines and grape clusters adorn sarcophagi and gravestones, frescoes, icons, and missals. The capitals of the pillars Solomon used for his palace were decorated with pomegranates, "two hundred in rows round about" (I Kings 7:20). The people of Jerusalem greeted Jesus with palm branches in their hands (John 12:12–13). The palm occurs as frequently as the olive in the role of Mediterranean image. Its presence is also a determining factor in drawing Mediterranean borders. In the north it is confined to a narrow belt; in the south it makes deep inroads into the heat. "The palm likes salty soil," Theophrastus notes in his *History of Plants* (2.6.2). The almond tree, wild or cultivated, is a common motif in Gothic paintings and sculptures, where it gathers the rays of the sun or evokes the

Tuscany. Royal Library, Windsor Castle. Detail from a chalk drawing by Leonardo da Vinci. 1502–3.

sun. It also serves as an artistic device in the biblical scenes so favored by Mediterranean painters: the large almond-tree halo surrounding the figure of Christ in the Last Supper, the Virgin Mary at the time of the Annunciation, or the seven doves bearing the seven gifts of the Holy Spirit.

MY KNOWLEDGE OF MEDITERRANEAN flora would have been even more modest than it is had it not been for the work of Theophrastus and the *Materia Medica* of Dioscorides of Anazarbus. And it would have been limited to book knowledge had I not come to know an Arab herbalist. He was born on one of the Kerkenna Islands, but worked on the island of Jerba on the road to Humt Suk, not far from the old Spanish fortress (and presumably works there still). Many sought him out for advice, calling him simply *tabib* (doctor or pharmacist). He lived by himself in a small house with two modest rooms and reed matting on the floor. He began his study of medicine in the south of France, in Montpellier, and although he did not complete it, he did make a French translation of Ibn al-Baytar's *Treatise on Medicinal Plants,* which experts say serves to supplement Dioscorides. He told me about the medicinal plants he grew up with and why there are so many names for one and the same herb, bush, or tree. On the Algerian coast the fig has three names—*kerma, tagerut,* and *telukat*—besides the name it has in the Qur'an, *al-tin;* broom is called *shedida* in some regions and *tellegit* in others. As in the Balkans and on the Iberian Peninsula, there are many words for sage: *kusa, takruft,* and—in Egypt—*safsaf.* (I was unable to ascertain whether the word is Coptic in origin.) Rosemary is called *iazir, klik,* and *hasalhan;* mint *mersit, hana,* and *nana* (the latter was brought to Bosnia by the Turks). He showed me a pine that he called *snuber* (or *senuber*—my transcription is not clear) but that people from Kayblia call *azumbei.* I saw a type of vine discussed by Theophrastus: if it comes in contact with smoke, it yields dark grapes at some times and light grapes at others (*History of Plants* 2.3). He explained the differences between palms: some tend to grow by the sea (they actually need "salty soil"), while others grow farther away, on the mainland; some yield fruit—dates—while others do not. The date palm is called *nekla.* The dwarf variety, called *dum,* has fingerlike leaves, yellow when masculine, green when feminine, yellow-green when both. There were three myrtles near the *tabib*'s house. They are called *tehan* or *mersin* in Sahel near the Mediterranean and *tafeltest* in the Sahara and the Hoggar Mountains. The semantics involved is radical in the literal sense of the word. We have seen it at work in the plant nomenclature along the eastern Adriatic coast and in the Apennines, and it makes itself felt in Aristotle's botanical classifications as well. The plethora of names stems not merely from their multifarious origins but also from a desire to preserve a certain individuality in the face of common, uniform, linguistic constructs. This too is a phenomenon known throughout the Mediterranean region.

I was skeptical about the *tabib*'s claim—on the basis of how and where certain types of grasses grow—that the Mediterranean leans more to the south than to the north, in the direction of Africa rather than Europe, but I later found it confirmed in the work of a specialist on African flora: "The discovery of a genuinely Mediterranean flora in the mountains of the Sahara proved one of the greatest surprises of the botanical exploration of the region. . . . The vegetation in the Hoggar Mountain wadi beds is indisputably Mediterranean" (Pierre

Quézel, *Contribution à l'étude de la flore et de la végétation du Hoggar* [Contribution to the Study of the Flora and Vegetation of the Hoggar Mountains], Algiers 1954, p. 155).

WHEN INVESTIGATING RAINFALL and other sources of water in the desert, I had a look at the Talmud in its Palestinian and Babylonian versions. I learned that because rain never falls during the month of Adara, the faithful fast, and that while the temple was under construction, rain fell only at night and work could therefore proceed. The Gemara says that he who knows not the joy of ablution knows no joy in life, and Leviticus devotes an entire chapter to ritual cleansing. As we have seen, the Semitic word *iam* is a generic term for water, and in the Qur'an it designates freshwater and salt water (35:13), the desert sources and the billows of the Mediterranean.

THE LITERATURE DEALING with Mediterranean markets is generally of a practical nature: it focuses more on trade than on the market as such. Much has thus remained obscure. In ancient Greece the market authorities, *agoranomoi,* were prominent personages; their counterparts in Rome were chosen from among the magistrates known as *aediles.* In the Arab world they were given the title *mukhtasibi* and *mukhtakir;* in Spain, the resonant *señores del zoco,* "gentlemen of the market." Scholarly works treating the marketplace—its origins and history, layout and typology—are rare (I would cite Pedro Chalmeta Gendrón, *El "señor del zoco" en España: Edades media y moderna* [The "Gentleman of the Market" in Spain: The Medieval and Modern Periods], Madrid 1973, published by the Instituto Hispano-Árabe de Cultura, with a preface—in French—by the marketologist Maxime Rodinson), but the works of ancient historians contain valuable remarks on the subject. Herodotus visited many Egyptian marketplaces and notes the traits of their denizens in several passages (1.93–94, 2.141, 4.183). Pausanias speaks of small shops strung one next to the other in his *Description of Greece* (6, passim). Aristophanes warns of the temptations lurking in such places in *The Clouds.* And Aeschylus in *Seven Against Thebes* made special mention of *theoi episkopoi agoras,* the gods who watch over the market: they were among the most important Mediterranean deities.

In Athens and Thebes the agora was both marketplace and public square. Aristotle wanted to separate the two: he felt that the space for trade (*agora ôniôn*) should not be confounded with the space for political rallies or celebrations (*eleuthera agora*) (*Politics* 1 3 3a.3 1). Golden-age Athens distinguished marketplaces for retail trade (*kapêleia*) from marketplaces for wholesale trade (*emporia*). For a time they were open mainly to men; then, for practical reasons, *agora gynaikeia* (women's markets) came into being. The market was a major Mediterranean institution.

Markets sold more than food. History has preserved records of Egyptian and Phoenician urns of aromatic salves, Greek and Roman phials of rich perfumes, rouges and powders from the coasts of Libya and Asia Minor, oils from Syria and Assyria to make patrician houses smell sweet: *Syrio fragrans olivo,* "fragrant with the Syrian olive," and *fragrans Assyrio odore domus,* "a house fragrant with Assyrian scents" (Catullus c.6.8 and 68a.146). Venetian galleons, having made the rounds of the Mediterranean markets and followed the paths of the great faiths from East to West, sailed home to Renaissance Italy from the Orient bearing not only spices but also scents theretofore unknown.

Aromatic plants were an especially valued commodity in the marketplace: markets would take on their fragrances and be differentiated thereby. (The information about myrrh, cinnamon, incense, cassia, and labdanum in my "Breviary" section comes from Herodotus 3.1 13.) Many sources testify to the popularity of herbs, both culinary and medicinal. The Bible speaks of hyssop as a remedy for leprosy and rue as an antidote for various poisons; calendula, lemon balm, and all varieties of mint fortify the system; basil is the king of herbs; and thyme is said to derive from the ancient Egyptian word *tham* and to have been used to embalm the pharaohs. Many herbs have been found in the pyramids, where they were preserved for the occupants' life after death. Although they still grow on the coasts and islands, they seem to be losing their medicinal properties, and their fragrance wafts less and less over Mediterranean marketplaces.

To DISTINGUISH THE ARCHAIC from the Ionic style of marketplace, we have only to examine its structure. Both are rectangular in form; what makes them different is their position vis-à-vis the street and the city as a whole. The topography of the Athenian agora partakes of features going back to both the geometric and classical periods. The marketplaces of Pireus and Corinth were also well known, as were those of certain islands and of important colonies in Asia Minor such as Miletus, Phocaea, and Pergamum, which even then exhibited colonial attributes not to be found in the metropolitan Mediterranean region.

Like the Athenian agora, the Roman forum was simultaneously marketplace and public square. The word *mercatus* originally had a semi-vulgar ring to it: it meant trade as an activity and the arena where that activity took place. The word *horrea* designated a large warehouse, mostly for grain and salt, the most famous of which was in Ostia. Historians say that small fish markets along the Tiber preceded the construction of the great *macellum* (food market) of the classical period. The floor plan for the Roman *castra* (fort) seems to have included space for trade, and Romans encouraged the construction of marketplaces in their colonies, bringing in water, for example, and building fountains similar to their Roman models. If I adduce such details, it is because I want the glossary to include as many institutions as possible: they make Mediterranean civilization; they *are* the Mediterranean.

THE CENTER OF POMPEII provides a revealing picture of the inner connections among institutions. The forum had temples to Jupiter, Apollo, and the Genius of Augustus, a basilica (the palace of justice), a municipal *curia* for political affairs and regulating the goods coming in from the nearby Porta Maritima, a *comitium* for elections, a *mercatus* and *horrea,* offices for the bureau of weights and measures (*mensa ponderaria*) and for bankers (*argentarii*), workshops for the famous Pompeii wool (*aedificium eumachiae*), and stalls for displaying merchandise. Slightly removed from the center—though within easy reach—was the *lupanar* (house of ill repute), another major Mediterranean institution.

Municipal statutes defined duties and privileges with greater or lesser success, medieval towns following ancient models. The statutes of such Adriatic towns as Korčula, Split, Vinodol, and Trogir are instructive in this regard. I focused in my research on the sections dealing with fish markets, weights and measures, and punishments for cursing and other minor infractions. "Fishmongers must remain on their feet; they must wear nothing on their heads" (*stare debeant in pedibus, nihil tenere debeant in capite*), I found in the appendix to Trogir's statutes (*Reformationum liber* 1.11). Clearly the city fathers were concerned with the theatrical aspect of the marketplace: an actor who is seated—with his head

covered to boot—is neither visible nor credible. (In Genoa they were concerned with its philological aspect as well: the fish market there still boasts the mandated *Mercato Ittico* sign.) Thus did Mediterranean fish markets outgrow pier and port and enter world theater.

ORIENTAL MARKETPLACES and the roads leading to them are legendary, literally so, because the legends involved have in fact come down to us. The word *bazaar* is of Persian origin, *wazar* meaning "square" in the Pahlavi dialect. The Crusaders marveled at the opulence and variety of the bazaars. Both the Turks and the Arabs helped to introduce the Eastern art of trade to the West. Muhammad II built his famous bazaar in Istanbul as a symbol of sultanic wealth and power. The Kapali Market (*kapali* means "covered") in the same city was a major institution. The celebrated Bezziastan (*bezistan* means "silk market") vied in splendor with the ancient cities of the East. The Turks brought our word for shop, *dućan* (from the Arabic *dukkan*), to the Balkans; the Arabs took it to the shores of the Atlantic. The French word for shop, *magazin,* comes from the Arabic *makhazin* (plural of *makhzan* [storehouse]) and has traveled the world over. Not surprisingly, then, banks are an invention of the Near East and its financial acumen. I sometimes feel that all good and all evil comes from that part of the Mediterranean.

The word *suk* (a marketplace in Muslim countries, also spelled *souk, sukh,* and *suq*) has had an unusual fate. In the early Semitic dialect of Arcadia it meant narrow or tight; in Aramaic it came to designate a row of small stands closely packed together. On the maps drawn by al-Idrisi the Strait of Gibraltar is called a *sukak* (narrow passageway); in Bosnia a narrow street or passageway is called a *sokak*. The Arabs took it to the lands they conquered, and the word itself became a conquistador when it crossed the ocean with the Spanish and Portuguese, its derivatives having entered by then the languages of both the former—

The Gulf of Trieste. Biblioteca Marciana, Venice. Anonymous drawing. Seventeenth century.

zoco (marketplace), *azoche* or *azogue* (public square)—and the latter—*açougue* (butcher shop). Seville and Toledo, Navarra and Teruel, Majorca and Sicily had a number of famous suks. Market days were holidays. For festivals of the vine (which were celebrated on the Greek islands as well), when shop windows brimmed with grapes of every hue from pale yellow to deep purple, the entire city—the entire region at times—would turn suk. Much more fruit, many more seeds and spices were sold than were produced in the area, and where they came from remains a secret to even the most dedicated Mediterranean watchers.

Islam perhaps showed more insight into the marketplace than did Christianity: while the New Testament reports the money changers being driven out of the temple (John 2:15, Luke 19:45), the Qur'an speaks of the Messenger "eating food and walking through the markets" (25:7). The role of the suk (and it is currently expanding in the basest possible forms throughout the world) must not be ignored, and more's the pity that we more often than not turn to chance guides rather than classic texts like Maupassant's description of a Tunis suk overflowing "with rugs, fabrics of every color, and leathers; with gilt-embroidered bridles, saddles, and reins; with garlands of red and yellow Turkish slippers" ("Tunis," *La Vie errante,* Paris 1890, p. 149). Many people are suspicious of the peddlers in Mediterranean suks, but few stop to think of the time they and theirs spend with the goods they sell, how much patience their trade requires, and how little it pays. Avoiding exoticism, a bugbear not limited to commentators on topics Mediterranean, the moral philosopher seeks meaning: "There are no names, no signs; there is no glass. Everything for sale is laid out. One never knows what the objects will cost: the prices are neither fixed nor affixed. . . . One can find everything, but one finds it many times over" (Elias Canetti, *Die Stimmen von Marrakesch* [The Voices of Marrakesh], Munich 1967, p. 16). These lines might stimulate another approach to the matter (the scholarly literature is wanting in methodology): the Eastern word, *bazaar,* represents a spatial concept, while the Western word, *mercatus* (from *merx* [merchandise]) implies utility. The opposition between the imagination and the matter-of-fact that this difference brings to the fore is as old as the opposition between East and West. Yet perhaps the opposition itself is misleading: the Mediterranean is a place for overcoming oppositions.

SOME READERS REFUSE to open a book of this ilk if it fails to mention carnivals; some writers purposely avoid the topic. Carnivals are not an exclusively Mediterranean phenomenon; they take place elsewhere, though in different forms. Wherever they take place, however, they ruffle the authorities and undermine faith and the law. Their connection with the theater—they all use costumes and masks—is also universally acknowledged. But the stages that are the cities of the south provide a particularly congenial place, time, and reason for carnivals: the fresh air invigorates the spirit, the sun invites the body to change, even shed, its clothing, and the mind, unable to resist the promptings of body and spirit, yields to play, antics, folly. Any blanket interpretation would be risky: a mask is not only a mask, a role not only a role, desire not only desire in Mediterranean festivals.

THE ANCIENT HEBREWS HAD a finely developed sense of measurement and coordinated it with their laws. Significantly, there is a table of measures among the scrolls discovered in the late forties in a Qumran cave near the Dead Sea ("for the whole deposit it is now felt . . . that the most satisfactory designation is 'The Dead Sea Scrolls'" [Millar Burrows, ed., *The Dead Sea Scrolls of St. Mark's Monastery,* vol. 1, New Haven 1950, p. xi]). It figures in the scroll bearing the title "The War of the Sons of Light with the Sons of Darkness." The names for the measurements of length listed there illustrate an often neglected link between the human body and units of measurement. The section of the scrolls containing measurements of weight has not come down to us. Documents referring to weights and measures have a tendency to disappear from Mediterranean archives.

The passage in the "Breviary" section devoted to weights and measures is therefore particularly important. It needs to be amplified by the statement that measurements are constantly undergoing adjustment and change. The following list of units of measurement used at various times in Dubrovnik was compiled for "The Golden Age of Dubrovnik," an exhibition held in the Rector's Palace there in 1987:

Weight: *litra* (or *libra*), which depending on the circumstances can be heavy (381.6 gr in the seventeenth century) or light (327.9 gr during the same period, though probably even scantier outside the city proper); *oka* = 1.3 kg (for trade with

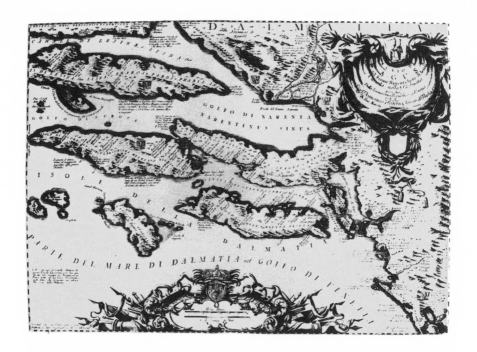

Turkey); *kantar* (of Greek origin) = 55.96 kg (for trade with the rest of our lands);

Volume: *star* (for grain) = 98.4 kg in the sixteenth century; *spud* (here it was used more for salt, while the Russian *pud* was used mostly for grain) = 42.27 kg in the seventeenth century (that is, during the Republic's heyday);

Liquids: *vjedro veliko* (large bucket, used exclusively for wine) = 21.97 l (in the sixteenth century, and it probably increased with time); *vjedro malo* (small bucket, during the same period) = 19.22 l; *bario* = 64.38 l (in the eighteenth century, that is, before the Napoleonic occupation that deprived the Republic of its independence but gave its citizens the *code civil*); *star* (for oil) = 9.61 l or, sometimes, less;

Length: *lakat* = .512 m (*lakat* literally means "elbow," and the standard was perhaps the oversized arm of a Herzegovinian peasant); *ped* (or *pedalj*, "span of the hand") = .256 m; *noga* (or *stopa*) = .341 m (*noga* and *stopa* mean "foot" and "footstep" respectively, and the standard may have been a mountain dweller); *sežan* (or *paš*) = 2.025 m;

Surfaces: the *sežan* squared = 4.194 m² in the eighteenth century; *solad* (or *zlatica*) = 1600 m²; *ral* = 840 m² (also in the eighteenth century, before the French Revolution).

The public scales in Dubrovnik hung from a stone arch amidst the columns in the atrium of the Sponza Palace. The Latin inscription on them is still legible and takes the form of an elegiac couplet:

> FALLERE NOSTRA VETANT ET FALLI PONDERA MEQUE
> PONDERO CUMMERCES PONDERAT IPSE DEUS

> Our scales do not allow us to deceive or deceived be,
> and as I measure goods so God Himself doth measure me.

God would appear to have had his work cut out for him: there is an enormous literature on the subject (see in particular the Marciana in Venice, the municipal archives in Genoa and Marseille, and miscellaneous sources in Valencia and Barcelona, Naples, Cairo, and Istanbul). Many coastal dwellers (in the broad sense of the word) believe that all visitors from the mainland (on a seaside holiday, for instance) are gullible or naive, that they have no understanding of "our ways," and that they are therefore easy to get the better of. Their attitude is one of the reasons why Mediterraneans strike mainlanders as unrestrained. Wise men have long advised moderation in all things: *mêden agan, ne quid nimis* (nothing in excess). Mediterraneans often mock them.

THE LANGUAGE USED FOR CURSING—language per se and body language—deserves closer attention than scholars have been wont to give it. It occupies an important place in the Mediterranean's "secret dictionary," to use the term Camilo José Cela gives his glossary (*Diccionario secreto,* vol. 1, *Series* coleo *y afines,* and vol. 2, *Series* piš *y afines,* Madrid 1979), which has been of great practical assistance to me.

Curses are as old as language. Our verb *psovati* (to curse, swear) comes from *pas* (dog); the corresponding verbs in other Mediterranean languages have more religious connotations (cf. Italian *bestemmiare* [to

Within the image:

TE ALLEGHIERI POETA FIORENTINO CONALTO INGEGNO ELCIELO ELPVRGHATORO ET ILREGNO INFE
EZO DEL CAMINO DINOSTRA VITA POSE INREL LAVORO OVAL NELIMOSTRA ILPOEMA

NEL
MEZO
DEL
CA
MINO

DIMO
STRA
AT
A
DNO
STRA

*Dante in Florence.
Albertina, Vienna.
Anonymous en-
graving. Fifteenth
century.*

curse, blaspheme], French *jurer* [to swear, give one's word]). The Old Testament condemns to death "whosoever curseth his God" (Leviticus 24:15–16). Apart from Aristophanes and Plautus, Greek and Roman authors left little evidence of their curses, though they are common enough in Pompeii graffiti and on jugs and vases to justify the conclusion that the content of Mediterranean curses—the frequency of the verb for copulation, for example—has changed little between then and now.

Like the Old Testament, the rigorous Justinian Code condemns blasphemers to death; the Qur'an is no milder (see sura 7). In the *Inferno* (3.103–105) Dante depicts a group of blasphemers crossing the fatal Styx in Charon's boat:

Bestemmiavano Dio e lor parenti,
l'umana specie e 'l loco e 'l tempo e 'l seme
di lor semenza e di lor nascimenti.

They cursed God and their parents,
the human race, and the place and the time and the seed
of their begetting and their births.

The Croat Marko Marulić devotes an entire chapter in his *Evangelistarium* to blasphemy ("De Maledicendi Nequitia" [On the Evils of Blasphemy], Cologne 1529), placing it in the company of the most heinous vices (7.29) and citing the support of such authorities as Solomon, the prophets Jeremiah and Hosea, and above all Saint Paul, who lumps "revilers" together with fornicators and idolaters as unworthy of inheriting the kingdom of God (I Corinthians 6:9–10). The Statute Book for the City of Split, which dates back to 1312, is much more lenient than the Christian Marulić (himself Split born): it contains a special clause ("De Blasphemantibus Deum et Sanctos") fining "those who curse God and the saints" ten pounds, half of which was earmarked for the individual reporting the guilty party. The archives are silent as to how much accrued thus to the municipal coffers. On the island of Korčula the rate was only a perper a curse. Those unable to afford even a perper would have to "remain bound to a pole for an entire day" (Statute Book for the City and Island of Korčula, 55). Chroniclers have failed to mention how many poles were occupied on dog days, when blasphemy on the Mediterranean tends to reach a pinnacle.

According to the Austrian Criminal Code of 1853, paragraphs 122 and 124, the Empire deemed blasphemy punishable by "from six months to a year in prison." My research in the legal archives reveals that the number of perpetrators of the delict was incomparably greater in Istria and Dalmatia (and in the parts of Italy under Austrian rule) than in Pannonia or Austria proper. Fortunately the law was applied less than rigorously, or the damage would have been greater than the ravages inflicted on the Mediterranean by the phylloxera.

Some theoreticians claim that outright obscenities—those featuring the verb of copulation, for instance—were brought from the mainland by the Turks or Magyars (cursers extraordinary), but their hypothesis is hard to verify. My personal fieldwork has been supplemented by two studies: *Bestemmia e turpiloquio* (Blasphemy and Obscenity) by Giuseppe Carpetza, published in Bologna in 1923 but still fresh and timely, and *Bludna psovka* (The Lewd Curse), a doctoral dissertation by Father Ignacije Gavran published in Sarajevo in 1962 by the author himself. In the latter I found a touching description—in Latin—of a Mediterranean curse, more theatrical or gestural than linguistic and perhaps more female than male, namely, the *denudatio partis posterioris,* which, Father Ignacije points out, is known in a milder form as well, a diminutive or hypocoristic form, so to speak: *eiusdem levis percussio* (p. 13). I sought out the reverend father and found him in a monastery in the coastal town of Zaostrog near Makarska, that is, not far from the island of Hvar, where he was relaxing by translating excerpts from the work of Hippocrates, the *Corpus Hippocraticum* being part of the monastery's collection. He carried on at great length about the motives for the spite, indignation, rage, and other such excesses that gave rise to the curses—the heat and aridity, for instance—absolving his fellow Mediterraneans, "for they know not what they do."

Restraint is surely the only reason his fine book does not include the expression of disdain or protest contained in a gesture that in Italy is called *la pernacchia* and in Spain *el pito catalán,* that is, the raspberry, an artificial fart made with the mouth and fingers. Some attribute its origin to the Sicilians, others to the Neapolitans (the word itself apparently comes from the Neapolitan dialect). In fact, it has been current from ancient times on virtually all shores of the Mediterranean.

CRICKETS OFTEN CROP UP in accounts of Mediterranean moods, not only in the works of numerous Greek poets, ancient and modern, from Homer to Elytis ("a tiny cricket in a night of fools" in the poem "Laconic"), but also in most of the national literatures as well—the verse of Vladimir Nazor in early-twentieth-century Croatian literature, for example. Aristotle speaks of the way the tiny insect "produces a sound by rubbing against the air" (*Historia Animalium* 4.9). Whether it is a song or a noise is not clear. Many writers have noted that crickets can withstand the hottest weather and outshout the stormiest sea. They chirp in the knots of the spruce, in the branches of the pine (which must intoxicate them with its fragrance), beneath the fig tree's decorous leaves or on the vine, on the common thistle, by the road, in the brush or a heap of stones; they chirp without letup or by fits and starts, one by one or in chorus. But they can be silent too, at high noon, in summer, in the heat, and then an eerie still descends, and nothing happens, and people sit and wait for someone or something to start up again. A teacher I once met on the island of Samos had studied crickets closely, listened closely to their trochees and iambs, and he contended that cricket metrics had influenced the prosody of Greek verse. He also claimed that islander crickets differ from mainland varieties in that their orgies merge with space and time. I owe the quotations from the ancients above to this modest schoolmaster from the Sporades. My conversations with him also led me to note here the splash and splatter of the sea against the shore, the remains of waves—exhausted, moribund—as they lap the hull of a ship or the piles of a pier. The sound or possibly song of the cricket does not disturb insomnia—I know from experience—on summer nights when staying awake is easier than going to sleep, and the spirits keep watch over the Mediterranean.

CONFLICTS BETWEEN the Latin and Byzantine worlds and the Western and Eastern churches stymied the development of the Balkan Peninsula even before the period of Turkish rule. History prevented the southern Slavs from synthesizing the Byzantine and Roman, the Greek and Latin elements that had come together on their territory. Had they not been prevented from doing so, they might have served as a model to the rest of Europe, which a divided Christianity was in the process of dividing. Instead, the Mediterranean coast broke up as well: "There are divisions at every point from East to West," Leonardo remarked in one of his notebooks ("Codice Atlantico," *Scritti scelti,* Turin 1966, p. 326).

The Adriatic coast and its hinterland were crossed by multifarious peoples and tribes before and after the Slavs settled there. In *De situ Illyriae,* cited above, Šižgorić—himself citing Pliny, Strabo, Appian, Callimachus, Boccaccio, and other authorities—lists "the people known under the common name of Illyrians": "Some are called Pannones according to the Romans or Peones according to the Greeks; then there

are the Himani, the Encheleae, the Bulini or Dudini, and the Peuce-
ciae according to Callimachus; then the Soretes, the Serapilli, the Iasi,
the Sandrizetes, the Colaphiani, and the Breuci according to Pliny; the
Norici, the Antintimi, the Ardiei, the Retii, the Pallarii, and the Iapodes,
who live in the Alps, according to Appian; the Salasii, the Segestani,
the Daysii, the Daci, and the Gethae or Gothi; the Boii, the Istri, the
Liburni, the Curetes [that is, Croats], and the Dalmatae; and finally the
Mysii, the Tribali, and the Prusi, who live as far from the Mediterranean as the Black Sea" (3.19).

The multiplicity of peoples in Illyria will make for major problems
when the time for nation-building comes to the Balkans. They so be-
wildered even our fifteenth-century canon Šižgorić (who made a point
of his heritage by collecting Slav proverbs) that he opted for the Venetian scepter: "What can be more pleasant in our time that to live out
one's days under the reign of Venice? Venice has always been free, never
subject to tribute, and Christian, never sullied by idolatrous cults. Venice
is the queen of the sea, the creator of all wealth, the delight of the
world, the permanent custodian of faith and justice" (16.53). Nation-
ality has often been tenuous along the Mediterranean.

BALKAN PEOPLES, LIKE MANY OTHER Mediterranean peoples, have opposed one another at certain times and come together at others; differences between them may disappear or increase. Some treat the phenomenon with alarm, others with irony; writers treat it in odes or
parodies. The Qur'an says, "For all peoples there is a term, and when
it arrives, they cannot slow it by even an hour, nor can they hasten it"
(7:34). What concerns us here is the Mediterranean peoples' relationship with their sea.

The anthropologist-geographer Jovan Cvijić makes the following
general remarks on the subject in his *Balkansko poluostrvo* (Balkan Peninsula, first published in French as *La Péninsule balcanique,* Paris 1918):
"The South Slav population underwent certain changes under the influence of the sea and the Mediterranean climate. Some groups in the
region [the east Adriatic coast from Istria to the Gulf of Kotor] adapted
to the Mediterranean way of life and became renowned sailors; they
were the only ones to come in contact with overseas peoples and civilizations. The coastal dwellers lived in an environment permeated by
Roman civilization, though they also show traces of Byzantine civi-

lization, principally from the seventh to the tenth centuries, and a few barely visible remains of Eastern civilization. . . . It is a composite of what they themselves experienced and what they borrowed, borrowed it would seem, twice over: from the East and from the Venetians" (Belgrade 1931, vol. 2, pp. 86–99). The Slav layer, which covered the autochthonous layer, was deeper in some places than others. If it nonetheless imposed its language on the former inhabitants, it did not thereby obliterate their differences, and in that the Mediterranean played its part.

Most of the east Adriatic coast belongs to the Croats. It is inhabited by the Dalmatian Croats, whom their neighbors are wont to call simply Dalmatians. Here the Kingdom of Croatia—in all likelihood the first Slav state—arose during the early middle ages. The kings and princes crowned here usually had names ending in the Slav suffixes -*slav* and -*mir,* which tends to belie the allegations that the Croats have other than Slav roots. They built a navy that in the tenth century attracted the attention of the Byzantine emperor Constantine VII Porphyrogenitus. (Croatian historians cite with pride the passage in Chapter 31 of his *De Administrando Imperio* referring to eighty large *sagenae* and forty smaller *condurae.*) History records various types of relations between Dalmatian Croats and their inland Pannonian brethren. It recounts attempts, internal and external (Mediterranean passions being what they are), to separate one from the other or separate one and the other from the South Slavs. We Croats have failed to make the most of the possibilities for distinguishing ourselves—independently or with others— on the sea (not that the possibilities have been overly attractive). Yet we still love it and consider it the most beautiful part of the Mediterranean.

The Slovenes occupy only a small part of the Adriatic. It is in the north, in Istria, along the Bay of Trieste. Their past, like ours, is more connected with the coast than with the sea. Popular legend tells what befell "the fair Vida" when she set sail to see the world, and poets sing their attachment to the limestone plateau in the Dinaric Alps known as Kras and to the Mediterranean climate. Of course there are differences between coastal and Alpine Slovenes, as there are between those from, say, Carniola and Styria, but their common language, *slovenščina* (Slovenian) binds them together. It has proved stronger than the contrast between mainland and sea, Central Europe and the Mediterranean.

The Serbs seem to make their way to the warm sea when they are at their most powerful or most beleaguered. In the fourteenth century, for example, their Stefan Dušan, "lord of the Romaioi" and heir to the East Roman Empire, expanded his dominion to include two seas beyond the Adriatic—the Ionic and the Aegean. Yet his state preferred land to sea: he sold Pelješac, the largest peninsula of the southern Adriatic, to the city of Dubrovnik. Centuries later, during the throes of the Great War, the Serbian army retreated across Albania, hoping to reach the island of Corfu. The parched horses rushed to drink of the waves and neighed piteously when they tasted salt; the exhausted men too saw the sea as salvation, and for many it proved—as the poet put it—a "blue grave." Such scenes are symbolic: in the Balkans Europe has continually defended itself against the East. Serbia is a fortress destroyed and rebuilt many times over, always relying on the continent, hoping the Danube will replace the sea. Serbian artists have painted "Belgrade on the Sea," and Serbian writers have described it as part of the Mediterranean.

The state of the Bosnian king Tvrtko I touched the sea as well: indeed, it embraced the stretch of the coast between Split and Dubrovnik. Herceg Stjepan (Duke Stephen) gave his name to the town of Hercegnovi on the north shore of the Gulf of Kotor. That gulf (which, like so many others, aspires at times to sea status) has produced a number of important Slav mariners, including several admirals of the Russian navy. Montenegrins gaze longingly down at the sea from their mountains. (*Gorski vjenac* [The Mountain Wreath, 1847] is the greatest poem of their greatest poet, Prince and Bishop Petar Petrović Njegoš.) Surrounded by enemies, they have led an islandlike existence and developed something of a Mediterranean-island mentality.

The Bosnian Muslim Slavs have likewise formed an island within the Balkans—at least since the fall of the Ottoman Empire. I am not the first to use the metaphor: I found it in Meša (Mehmed) Selimović's novel *Derviš i smrt* (Death and the Dervish, 1966). My knowledge of words of Arabic and Turkish origin in the languages of the South Slavs designating phenomena found up and down the Mediterranean comes from the Muslim Slavs, and it is because of them that I cite so many here.

Finally, a few words about the Macedonians. Though near the sea—they feel it to the south—they are not part of it: their neighbors, who have tended to overpower them, have denied them access. Part of their people lives on the Aegean, and sea winds waft over the Vardar, but the only "sea" Macedonia proper can lay claim to is a large lake by the name of Ohrid. Saint Naum's Monastery has fig trees, almond trees, and rosemary growing nearby, and the frescoes of Saint Sophia's in old Ohrid feature an extraordinary blue. When the wind rustles the wheat on the plain called Pelagonia, it looks like the sea (whence its name), and, bluish at dusk (like other Macedonian plains), it turns dark like Homer's night sea. Quite far inland there are threshing floors made of petrified salt, where the sea was once but has long since disappeared. Macedonian poetry exhibits a "longing for the South," but Macedonian folk tales (I recently had another look at the tales recorded by Marko Tsepenkov) hardly mention the Mediterranean.

MUCH HAS CHANGED SINCE the times of Šižgorić; much has not. The peoples he speaks of have been united, but the divisions still hold. It is difficult to explain to outsiders (a thankless task I am often called upon to perform and am performing to some extent here and now) the differences that existed and continue to exist among Dalmatians, Morlacians, Vlachs and Karavlachs (Black Vlachs), Ducleans, Red and White Croats, Green and White Montenegrins, onetime inhabitants of Ragusa and current inhabitants of Dubrovnik, yesterday's denizens of Fiume and today's of Rijeka, Konavljians and Kotorians; it is hard to talk about the Škutorians, the Bodulians, the Makaranians, and the Pulians, the people of Šibenik and Split, of Bekija, Cista Prova, and Imotski, Vrgorac and Zagvozd, of Klis, Livno, and Duvno (the ancient Delminium, which some say gave its name to the whole of Dalmatia), of Sinj horsemen, Senj pirates, Dubrovnik lords, Poljica republicans, Pelješac and Kotor captains, Montenegrin sirdars, anti-Turkish high-waymen and their cohorts, patresfamilias on the Kvarner Gulf and the Kornati, islanders from Hvar and Brač, Korčula and Pag, Rab and Cres and Vis and more, the Croatian Istrians, the Slovenian Istrians, the Italian Istrians, the Dalmatian autonomists and the anti-autonomists, the newcomers and the oldtimers, the people who look like their ancestors and the people who look different, the Catholics (Croats, Slovenes), who are in the overwhelming majority, the Orthodox (Serbs, Montenegrins, and some Kotorians), and the Muslims (the Bosnians and Herzegovinians, some Albanians, and an occasional Rom), and, last but not least, the Jews, who used to flourish here as they did elsewhere on the Mediterranean, but who are here no more.

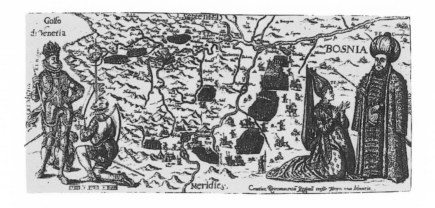

THE ETHONYM VLACH or Wallachian deserves a special gloss. The Croatian historian Ivan Lučić (Lucius) was among the first to point out the term's polysemantic quality (see "De Vlahis," *De Regno Dalmatiae et Croatiae* 6.5, published in Amsterdam in 1666 by the cartographer Joan Blaeu). The Teutons used the word to designate Romans and Celts; the Croats, Slovenes, and Hungarians to designate Italians; the Serbs to designate Romanians; the Turks to designate all Christians; the Catholics to designate the Orthodox; coastal dwellers to designate peasants and shepherds in the hinterland; dwellers of the plains to designate mountain dwellers; natives to designate recent arrivals; and recent arrivals to designate more recent arrivals. It also occurs in the word *Morlak* (an obsolete designation for the inhabitants of mainland Dalmatia), which is composed of the root *maur-*, "black" (as in Moor), plus *(V)lach.* Such was the word used by Father Alberto Fortis and by Napoleon's traitorous Marshal Marmont, Duke of Ragusa and of the Illyrian Provinces, in the latter's *Mémoires,* which are more read in Dalmatia than in France. The multifarious uses to which the word is put speaks volumes about the way Mediterranean neighbors treat one another. The Mediterranean is, as I have had occasion to state with enthusiasm, a sea of close neighbors.

THE INTERPRETATION OF WINDS inevitably goes back to Greek mythology and Homer's taxonomy in the *Odyssey* (Euros, Nôtos, Zephuros, and Boreês, 5.295–96). What I wish to pursue here is something I touched upon in the "Breviary" section in another context, namely, the foreign origins of the names we have given our winds. The *bura,* which blows from the north, comes from the Greek via Latin (cf. aurora borealis); the *levanat* blows from the east and comes from the Italian (*levante* [east]); the *pulenat* blows from the west and comes, it too, from the Italian (*ponente* [west]); only the *jugo,* which blows from the south (and means "south"), is Slav in origin, the desire for a warmer clime having lured the Slavs in that direction. Like most European languages, we take our *silok* or *siroko,* from the Italian *scirocco,* which designates the same hot wind as the *jugo* throughout Southern Europe and Northern Africa. (The Italian word comes from the Arabic *sharq* [east], which is not without significance for certain rains and their color.) We also have *burin* (a weak *bura*), *buraca* (a quiet breeze, from the Italian *burazza*), *buraska* (a squall, from the French *bourrasque* via the Italian), and *nevera* and its diminutive *neverin* (a sudden snowstorm, from the Italian *neve* [snow]— which does occasionally flutter over Mediterranean coasts—though also linked by folk etymology to *nevjera* [infidelity, treachery]). The *garbin* and *garbinada* blow from the southwest (*gharbi* meaning "west" in Arabic) and can be quite unpleasant; the *lebić* and *lebićada* are southwest as well, though not in every region (the name coming to us via the Italian *libecco* from Libya and a rather skewed notion of geography not unheard of in these parts). Finally, the *tramuntana* (from the Italian *tramontana* [north wind], but meaning literally "wind between [*tra*] the mountains") blows across the mountains from the mainland, the mainland's revenge, so to speak, for the insults the Mediterraneans heap upon it.

Students of literature even more than of linguistics should be attuned to gradations like *levantić* or *levantin* (a minor *levanat*), *levantun* (a major one), *levantarun* (a particularly strong one), and *levantar* or *levanćar,* which are pronounced only in rage. I have also seen *leventora* and *livanterina,* but have not been able to determine their connotations. Nearly every wind has analogous variations. The myriad diminutives and hypocoristics are particularly interesting in that they imply a desire to mitigate natural (and supernatural) forces. According to Aristotle's *Meteorology,* storms occur "when winds blow in the midst of other winds" (2.6). Gaston Bachelard draws an analogy between storms and epics: "Violent waters provide one of the first schemes of universal wrath. Hence no epic is without its storm" (*L'Eau et les Rêves* [Water and Dreams], Paris 1942, p. 239). Wind and water have often wreaked their consorted violence on the Mediterranean.

HOMER EVOKES THE SOURCE of the rivers I speak of in the "Breviary" section such as "the lovely Titaresius whose clear waters do not mix with the silvery waves of the Peneus but run along its surface like oil, for the Peneus is a branch of the Styx of the dreadful oath" (*Iliad* 2.752–55). Plato speaks in the *Phaedo* of "inexhaustible rivers of immense proportions with waters warm and cold" (2.60). Aristotle reacts to Plato's romantic hydrography with characteristic realism in his *Meteorology* (2.2). Homer poses many questions I have felt bound to respond to. How, for instance, does the seagull make contact with the water's surface: with its breast or legs, its beak or wings? In the *Odyssey* the seagull "dips its thick wings into the sea's salt" (5.53). The *Odyssey* also details the construction of Odysseus's ship (5.234–61) and the custom of implanting oars on sailors' graves—"the oar I rowed with while alive with my companions" (11.77–78)—as the young Elpenor's companions did for him and as we place crosses on our graves. Homer has much to say about swimming as well: about the match between Dionysus and Ampelos, the bet between Karpos and Kalamos, the Satyr's mischievous water games. Classical literature as a whole abounds in references to swimming: the woman from Herculaneum who used the sidestroke, the Etruscan diver, the Achaean vase from the Louvre depicting a gigantic bath for young women, Hero and Leander on the frescoes and coins of Pompeii, and Leander's "multiple bathings" (*copia nandi*) immortalized by Ovid in his *Heroides* (16.147), which recur repeatedly in literature up to Marlowe and Grillparzer (see Erwin Mehle, *Antike Schwimmkunst* [The Art of Swimming in Antiquity], Munich 1927). Let us pay homage to the unjustly forgotten French abbot Ameilhon, who made one of the first contributions to the study of the art of swimming in the journal of the Académie des Inscriptions in 1777. The notebooks of Paul Valéry, to whose Mediterranean inspirations I alluded in the "Breviary" section, contain a passage about swimming that he did not dare convert into poetry (Paul Valéry, *Cahiers,* vol. 2, Paris 1974, p. 1273).

VALÉRY HAS THIS TO SAY about Mediterranean discourse: "Nowhere was the power of the consciously disciplined and directed word more fully and advantageously developed—the word ordered according to logic and used to discover abstract truths, to build the universe of geometry or of the relations necessary for justice, the word as mistress of the forum, as a basic political device, a natural instrument for acquiring or maintaining power" (Paul Valéry, *Cahiers,* vol. 1, Paris 1973, p. 1097). No one can dispute Valéry's statement about the "disciplined word." The problem is that the word all too often dissipates in wordiness and thus loses all sense of discipline, and the problem—recall Daudet's Tartarin de Tarascon—is very definitely a Mediterranean one.

I HAVE ALSO PONDERED the following statement by Camus about the superiority of Mediterranean cultures: "Whenever a doctrine comes in contact with the Mediterranean basin, the Mediterranean has emerged intact from the resulting clash of ideas; the country has dominated the doctrine" (Albert Camus, "La culture indigène," *Essais,* Paris 1965, p. 1323). I would contest the point: the Inquisition and Fascism were both "doctrines," that is, ideologies, and the basin did not remain totally "intact" upon contact with them, nor did it "dominate" them. I find other reflections of his more interesting: for example, the idea that Christianity repressed the body and introduced history as a kind of punishment. And when writing about Mediterranean darkness, I recalled the Algerian twilights he experienced as "promises of happiness" ("L'été à Alger," *Essais,* Paris 1965, p. 76) and thought that Mediterranean twilights needed to find a new poet.

MARCO POLO'S ACCOUNTS—to Kublai Khan—of the cities he passed through form the basis for Italo Calvino's unusual book *Le città invisibili* (Invisible Cities, Milan 1984). I have kept his imaginary guide close at hand while writing. "Despina can be reached in two ways: by ship or by camel. The city looks different when approached by land and when approached by sea" ("La città e il desiderio" [The City and Desire], p. 25). "One must never confuse the city with the discourse describing it, yet there is a connection between the two" ("La città e i segni" [The City and Signs], p. 6). "In Maurilia the traveler is invited to tour the city and at the same time to look through old picture postcards showing it as it used to be" ("La città e la memoria" [The City and Memory], p. 37). All along the Mediterranean there are cities that have sunken into the mainland and become sealess ports, cities Italo Calvino knew well.

PRISONS BUILT ON and even overlooking the sea are no rarity. They are to be found in Dubrovnik, Rijeka, Split, Naples, Marseille, Barcelona, Algiers, Istanbul, Casanova's famous dei Piombi in Venice, and elsewhere. The title of Ivo Andrić's famed novella *Prokleta avlija* (The Damned Yard) refers to the old Istanbul prison by the Bosporus. Andrić treats it as the meeting place of all human journeys. Physical imprisonment is perhaps harder to bear by the sea. Mediterranean languages, living and dead, contain many words describing the hardships it entails; some of the languages may have died from them. The Dalmatian coast probably has more mental than penal institutions, the most famous being the Šibenik asylum and the asylums on Rab and Ugljan. Nor was there an excessive number of them: the Mediterranean sun may enlighten the mind or derange it.

THE APOLLONIAN/DIONYSIAN dichotomy does not need much discussion, and not only because enough has been said or because I am not sure whether what Nietzsche says on the subject needs supplementing. If we understand the Apollonian principle to represent form and rules, restraint and reason in the individual or society, that is, discipline and order, and the Dionysian principle to represent individuality and originality rather than the commonly invoked inclination to impulsiveness and ecstasy, then Mediterranean cultures partake of both, and whenever the balance tips too far in one or another direction, the coast is the worse for it and suffers accordingly (though this applies more to civilizations than individuals).

Nietzsche also sets forth the possibility of acquiring or inheriting Mediterraneity no matter where one is from, citing Goethe and Winckelmann and defining the transparency of Mozart's music as "a belief in the South." Zarathustra's admirer wants us to seek the meanings behind the mysterious cry "Great Pan is dead!" heard as the ship with the Egyptian Thamous at the rudder sailed past the island of Paxos (see Plutarch, *De Defectu Oraculorum* [On the Disappearance of the Oracles], 419b). The Mediterranean is made up of such riddles.

LITERATURE HAS ATTEMPTED to classify dreams of the sea according to the age and sex of the dreamer, dividing them, for example, into masculine and feminine, early and late, fateful and routine, memorable and forgettable, night dreams and daydreams, dreams of sailing and sinking, coast dreams, island dreams, high sea dreams. But literature does not have an easy time of it: dreams vary from sea to sea, and the Mediterranean itself surpasses all Mediterranean literature.

Elation in the face of the sea generally deserves the parodying it provokes. Rare are the passages in which physical or spiritual delight at contact with the Mediterranean element sounds anything but inflated and comic. Let me cite an exception by a writer born far from the shores of our sea. He is reporting his midsummer encounter with Crete: "The earth grows wan and weird, defertilized, dehumanized, neither brown nor gray nor beige nor taupe nor ecru, the no color of death reflecting light, sponging up light with its hard, parched shag and shooting it back at us in blinding, rock-flaked splinters that bore into the tenderest tissues of the brain and set it whimpering like a maniac. This is where I begin to exult. This is something to put beside the devastation of man, something to overmatch his bloodiest depredations. This is nature in a state of dementia, nature having lost its grip, having become the hopeless prey of its own elements. This is the earth beaten, brutalized and humiliated by its own violent treachery. This is one of the spots wherein God abdicated, where He surrendered to the cosmic law of inertia" (Henry Miller, *The Colossus of Maroussi,* New York 1941, pp. 156–57). As I say, you will not find many such truly Dionysian passages in the Mediterranean literature.

THE MEDITERRANEAN is often the site of symposia on the Mediterranean. The custom clearly goes back to Plato. In 1973 Zagreb was the site of a symposium called "Mediterranean Cultural Traditions." The papers were published in *Most* (The Bridge), the multilingual review of the Association of Croatian Writers. (The issue in which they appeared [39–40, 1974] contains an extensive bibliography of works on the Mediterranean, which is why I do not include one here.)

The Polish panelists had much to say about the work of Jan Parandowski on Mediterranean myth and history. I found much food for thought in the essays "Rzym czardziejski" (Magic Rome), "Eros na Olimpie" (Eros on Olympus), and "Dysk olimpijski" (The Olympic Discus). A Hungarian panelist quoted extensively from Mihály Babits, poet, essayist, and editor of the influential interwar journal *Nyugat* (The West). In the essay "Olaszország és Pannónia" (Italy and Pannonia)

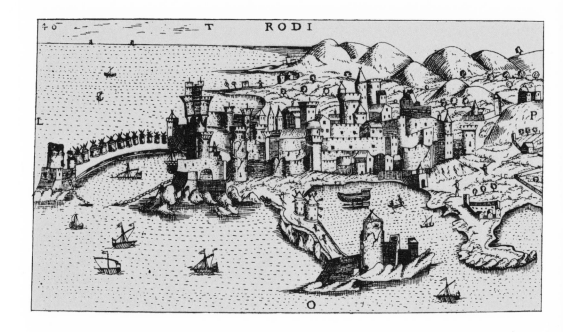

The island of Rhodes. Giuseppe Rosaccio, Viaggio da Venetia a Costantinopoli. *Venice, 1606.*

Babits speaks of the "deep, mysterious Latinity of the Pannonian region," "the similarities between the Italian and Hungarian landscape," and "Janus Pannonius' love of Italy." The South has never ceased to influence Hungarian culture, woo it, prepare it for surprises. Pannonia is an antechamber to the Mediterranean. When the grain ripens and the wind is up—especially at noon and dusk—it ripples like the sea. An ancient sea once spread all the way to the foothills of the Carpathians. There are traces of it still. Some (the novelist Danilo Kiš in Peščanik [The Hourglass], the poet Vladimir Vidrić in "Ex Pannonia") claim to remember it. Lake Balaton has something of the sea about it, though its water has no salt. The same holds for several other Central European lakes, though they have to be approached at the right time, in summer, and without Mediterranean prejudice.

The symposium (which I moderated, if poorly: I was incapable of stemming the tide of voluble southern extrapolations) provided many of the impulses for the thoughts I explore here. It also gave me a chance to experience firsthand the characteristic clash of views and discourse between Mediterraneans and mainlanders on the one hand and established Mediterraneans and newcomers on the other. Dalmatians spoke as natives and as settlers, as representatives of sea and of land. Islanders were the most sensitive. A participant from Agrigento in Sicily left the hall after hearing the following read aloud: "Sicilians have been Greek, Carthaginian, Roman, Byzantine, Arab, Neapolitan, or Italian; they have never been Sicilian or ceased to be long ago. Their tragedy is that belonging to so many periods and races they do not know who they are" (Dominique Fernandez, *Mère Méditerranée* [Mother Mediterranean], Paris 1965, p. 198). The author of these lines is very much at home in both Italy and Sicily and a great lover of the south and the Mediterranean.

In response to a suggestion that we address the issue of why the adjective Mediterranean seemed increasingly to have negative connotations, one of the participants quoted from "Rapporto sulle coste siciliane" (Report on the Sicilian Coasts, 1968) by the Sicilian novelist and essayist Leonardo Sciascia. Sciascia has little patience with "mainland islanders," those who argue that "Sicily is not an island" and would "withdraw from the sea." His article includes a compendium of anti-sea sayings in dialect, such as *Lu mari è amaru* (The sea is bitter), *Cui po jiri pri terra, non vada pri mare* (If you can go by land, do not go by sea), and *Mari, focu e fimmini, Diu noi scanza* (God protect us from sea, fire, and women) (Leonardo Sciascia, *Opere 1956–1971*, vol. 1, Milan 1987, pp. 1167–68). Variations on such sayings turn up all along the Mediterranean.

(Even Greek, which abounds in expressions evincing a rare love, a veritable passion for the sea, has epithets that convey—or reveal—fear and mistrust: *pikrokymatoussa* [having bitter waves], *leventopikhtra* [drowning the bold], *farmakeri* [poisoned], *ghoissa* [enchanting], *maghissa* [bewitching]. I thank Vassilis Vassilikos for reminding me of such epithets. They too turn up all along the Mediterranean.)

My account of the symposium would not be complete were I not to invoke at least some of poets and novelists whose works came up in the discussion. Poets included Constantine Cavafy with his Hellenistic and Byzantine Alexandria; Dino Campana (*Canti orfici* [Orphic Hymns]) and Salvatore Quasimodo (*Odore di eucalyptus* [The Scent of Eucalyptus], *Acque e terre* [Waters and Lands]); George Seferis (*Imerologio katastromatos* [The Log Book]); Rafael Alberti, firmly anchored in both the Atlantic and the Mediterranean (his *Marinero en tierra* [Sailor on Land] epitomizes the sea's gender-identity crisis in the famous line "¡El mar, sólo la mar!"); René Char with his own south (*Le Soleil des eaux* [The Sun of the Waters]) and Saint-John Perse, who lives on other seas but belongs to them all (*Anabase,* which was translated by T. S. Eliot, *Amers* [Seamarks], and *Vents* [Winds]); Salvador Espriu from Catalonia (*Centiri di sirene* [Sirens' Paths]); Frédéric Mistral and the Félibrige from Provence; and of course Eugenio Montale and his *Mediterraneo.*

Among the novelists, I should mention Nikos Kazantzakis (*Odysseia* [The Odyssey]), Jean Giono (*Naissance de l'Odyssée* [Birth of the Odyssey]), and Julien Gracq (whose novel *Le Rivage des Syrtes* [The Sidra Shore] I expounded and defended, having translated several chapters from it). As usual there was little talk of Arab and Turkish writers, though works with a Mediterranean bent by Taha Hussein, Mohammed Dib, Kateb Yacine, Ahmet Hasim, and Abdülhak Hâmit did come up.

The few South Slav authors discussed at the symposium were largely unknown to the non-Slav participants. Even the closest Mediterranean neighbors are woefully ignorant of one another; nor do they show much desire to learn.

Marko Marulić, humanist (he was the first to compose verse in Croatian) and author of *De Institutione Bene Vivendi* (On How To Live Well, Venice 1524), was more inclined to Christian asceticism than to pagan, Dionysian excess, and a similar bias in Croatian literature may be traced in part to his works. The only works Saint Francis Xavier took with him on his mystical journey to India were his own breviary and Marulić's *De Institutione* (in the Cologne edition of 1531). The monument to him in Diocletian's Palace in Split, the work of Ivan Meštrović, favors Marulić the Croat over Marulić the Christian. Marin Držić, master of the Renaissance comedy, was of course much more secular a writer, but his humor unfortunately spawned no heirs. History books never fail to point out that the Croatian nobleman Nikola Zrinski in the incarnation of Zrinyi Miklós was one of the founders of the Hungarian literary language, the language in which he composed his poem *Adriai tengernek Syrénája* (The Siren of the Adriatic Sea, 1651). His brother Petar translated it only a few years before he was executed in the Wiener Neustadt by the Austrians. The idea of the Adriatic siren's lure reaching all the way from the Mediterranean to the *puszta* gave the work a certain popularity among the South Slavs.

There was also a comparison of three twentieth-century South Slav writers—a Croat, a Serb, and a Slovene. Miroslav Krleža (of whom more below) was judged more Central European than Mediterranean, Miloš Crnjanski more Pannonian than Mediterranean (even in his *Lirika Itake* [Ithaca Lyrics]), and Srečko Kosovel (in "Pesem z Krasa" [Song from Kras]) equally divided between his love of the Alps and of the Adriatic.

THE THEME OF the south Slavs as the "third component" between East and West (a theme I touch upon in the "Breviary" section) runs through much of the work—prose and poetry—of Miroslav Krleža, but his ideas about our presence on the Adriatic take their purest form in the essays "Illyricum sacrum" (Holy Illyria, 1963) and "Zlato i srebra Zadra" (Zadar's Gold and Silver, 1950). They are less romantic than his theory about the connection between the Bogumil sect and the Albigensian heresy: himself inclined to heretical ideas and thus often isolated, he sought support in the past when he failed to find it in the present. He was never partial to the sea or an admirer of the Mediterranean. Much as he denied it, he was a Central European writer: Zadar meant more to him than Dubrovnik. He resented the Mediterranean.

CENTRAL EUROPE SOMETIMES makes its way to the Mediterranean—at Trieste, at Rijeka and Opatija, at various points in Venice and Dubrovnik—and I have more in mind than some comfortable old Habsburg hotels and resorts. The meeting of Mitteleuropa (Central Europe) and the Mittelmeer (the Mediterranean) was taken for granted by the nostalgic cavaliers of the *kaiserlich-königlich* (imperial and royal) Dual Monarchy of Austria-Hungary at its twilight. Here is the Austrian writer Hermann Bahr at the head of Dubrovnik's main thoroughfare, the Stradun, in 1909: "I am standing at the second gate looking down the Stradun, and suddenly something within me says, 'It could be Vienna's Getreidegasse with its bells ringing and the colorful little street of goldsmiths' houses in Prague's Hradčany district and the Cloth Hall in Cracow with Mickiewicz standing by and the square in Trent where Dante lifts his hand to the North and the Platz des Vogelweiders in Bolzano. Here in the reflection of the Comneni you feel at home'" (*Dalmatinische Reise* [Dalmatian Journey], Berlin 1909, p. 56). Bahr goes on to say how glad he was that the Croatian playwright and poet of the Mediterranean Count Ivo Vojnović was working on a history of his native city. He would have been less glad had he known that rather than embracing Central Europe, Vojnović looked to the unification of the South Slavs (which is sometimes held against him today). The Mediterranean does not submit easily to the mainland.

AND NOW A FEW WORDS about books dealing with our sea. Many have been written; more come out every day. But as Fernand Braudel warns, "The history of the Mediterranean constitutes a mass of knowledge that defies all reasonable synthesis" (*La Méditerranée: l'espace et l'historie* [The Mediterranean: Space and History], Paris 1985, p. 157).

Mussolini liked to stress Italy's Mediterranean mission. During his rise to power the authorities supported the publication of two large tomes with more than a thousand pages and the title *Il Mediterraneo* (Turin 1924–26). The authors, Attilio Brunialti and Stefano Grande, suggest that the name of Tripolitana be changed to Triolitalia; they call Libya "Libia italiana" and Albania "Albania veneta" (vol. 2, p. 1076); they state that "Dalmatia derives its climate, vegetation, and the basic factors of its economic development from Italy" and call the 1920 Treaty of Rapallo "miserly" and "a sorry renunciation" (vol. 2, p. 1056) because it did not annex the entire Adriatic coast to Italy. But this was not the first time ideology excluded the rational interpretation of facts on the Mediterranean.

Das Mittelmeer—Schicksal eines Ozeans (The Mediterranean: Fate of an Ocean) is of a completely different nature. It was written in the thirties by a German emigrant named Emil Ludwig and first appeared in New York in 1943 in French translation. Ludwig, a noted biographer, used "a biographical approach highlighting the human factor" (p. 12). His two ample volumes tell the stories of historical figures like Agrippa and Augustus, Pericles and Justinian, Lorenzo de' Medici (Lorenzo il Magnifico) and Suleiman I (Suleiman the Magnificent), Ferdinand de Lesseps and Said Pasha, and shows how they shaped the Mediterranean. What he fails to show is how the Mediterranean shaped them; that is, he does not show the Mediterranean itself.

Fernand Braudel does not confine himself to the period of Philip II in *La Méditerranée et le monde méditerranéen à l'époque de Philippe II* (The Mediterranean and the Mediterranean World in the Age of Philip II, Paris 1949, 1966), which also consists of two hefty volumes. He takes an "anthro-geographical" approach: he is concerned with *la géographie*

The oldest preserved globe. Martin Behaim. 1492.

humaine. Rather than use the Mediterranean as a test case for his theory of *longue durée,* he deduces the theory from the data. Although the work is somewhat academic in nature and does not reach the highest level of French historiography in terms of style or synthesis, it is the best study we have, the pinnacle of historical discourse on the Mediterranean for the foreseeable future. "Poetic discourse" on the Mediterranean (sun, sea, sand, etc.) tends to dissolve into kitsch, and as there is little room to navigate between the discourses, the danger of veering into a pastiche is very real.

Yet there always seem to be reasons to return to the topic. Some are all but irresistible. Not even Braudel resists them all, and Leonardo Sciascia actually put his name to a coffee-table book with the title *Il Mediterraneo* (Milan 1984). Published by the Touring Club, it is basically a lavishly illustrated anthology of texts he provided with an introduction. As he admits, it is hard to find the proper discourse, "the point of comparison [*ragguaglio*] between literature and history, reality and imagination, human existence and myth" (p. 10). It is perhaps harder than even he imagined. Michelet, who in *La Mer* (The Sea, 1861) observes the water from two coasts, the Atlantic and the Mediterranean, goes so far as to replace historical discourse with a literary diction all his own. His descriptions of lighthouses prove more successful than his descriptions of the sea itself. "One likes to sit near lighthouses, beneath their friendly fires, the true hearth of the seafaring life. . . . When no star is visible, the sailor still sees the lighthouse and takes heart, finding his own star in it, the star of Fraternity. . . . The lighthouse was an altar, a temple, a column, a tower. The Roman Empire lit up the entire Mediterranean from headland to headland."

AUGUSTIN JAL GIVES NO ACCOUNT of his methodology in the *Glossaire nautique;* he simply combines his own research with quotations from the research of others in a perfectly straightforward manner (though I might point out that on page 952 in volume 76 of the *Catalogue général de la Bibliothèque Nationale* I found that the author and seafarer Augustin Jal occasionally used the pseudonym Fictor, which gives him a special place in our narrative). I have been prevented by the more modest size of this exclusively Mediterranean undertaking from identifying my every source, though I wish to set forth certain of them here.

The Portuguese poet Fernando Pessoa beautifully conveys my preference for earlier ships (and, in the event, earlier maps of the Mediterranean) in his "Ode marítima" (1915):

> I would see nothing but schooners and timbered ships,
> Hear of no seafaring life but that of the seas of old . . .

I found much helpful material in *Imago Mundi,* the cartography journal edited by Leo Barow at great personal expense. I also made extensive use of Nordenskjöld's *Periplus,* whose first English edition came out in Stockholm in 1889. (The remarks on wind roses and early maps appear in his second chapter.) Dante's lines on Ulysses' exodus from our sea come from Canto 26 of the *Inferno,* Saint Augustine's condemnation of the "absurdity of the antipodes" from the *Civitas Dei* (The City of God, 16.9). In Isaiah (17:12) the "multitude of many people" who have turned against God are likened to "the noise of the seas," in Psalms (89:9) God rules "the raging of the sea," and in Revelation (21:1) there is "a new heaven and a new earth" and "no more sea." I put together the voyage across the Valley of Eshcol from passages in the Old Testament (Numbers, books 11 to 32). I also plagiarized the New Testament and several other holy books (the Talmud, the Qur'an). I hope believers will forgive me if they recognize them (though nowadays religious instruction is much neglected—even on the Mediterranean).

Wise men and poets of ancient times have, as I have observed, sought the reasons why we so relish picking up pebbles from the beach and playing with them or drawing figures in the sand and molding figures out of it. I have incorporated their jottings and added more recent ones. A child romping by the sea in the *Iliad* "makes a toy of sand, then scatters it again in jest with his hands and feet" (15.363–64). Pindar singles out a special pebble (*psêphos*) in the *Olympian Odes* (10.9), and Heraclitus sees time as "a child playing with pebbles" (*pessos* [stone in a board game], fragment 52). The pebbles Osip Mandelshtam gathered on the Mediterranean-like beach of Koktebel in the Crimea—as he himself puts it and as his wife Nadezhda confirms in her memoirs—"are nothing less than weather itself removed from the atmospherical and concealed in functional space" and were "a great help" to him as he worked on the *Razgovor o Dante* (Conversation About Dante, Moscow 1967, p. 53).

Irineus the Anchorite was well acquainted with contemporary Hellenists and Byzantologists, especially Sergei Sergeevich Averitsev, who long languished in internal emigration in the shadow of the Kremlin. Rumor has it that his *Poetika rannevizantiiskoi literatury* (The Poetics of Early Byzantine Literature) was copied and translated by monks on Mount Athos for use among the Orthodox before it was published in Moscow in 1977. In 1990 I met the pale and pious Sergei Sergeevich at the Monastery of Saint John of the Hermits in Palermo while putting the finishing touches on this book. I never met the poet Vyacheslav Ivanov, another Mediterranean Russian, who in "Son Melampa" ([Melampus's Dream], 1907) describes an unusual maritime phenomenon I touch upon here:

Seas move within the deep sea, some to sunrises, others to sunsets;
Waves on the surface aspire to noon, waves below to midnight:
Many are the streams flowing in the darkling deep
And underwater rivers rolling in the purple ocean.

And the "poet of the diaspora" whom I cite in the "Maps" section and who speaks of "places where geography provokes history" is yet another Mediterranean Russian, Joseph Brodsky (see his "Flight from Byzantium," *Less Than One,* New York 1986, pp. 406–7).

The quotation about maps indicating the coasts of the Rumelian Sea but not of the ocean comes from Ibn Khaldun's *Al-Muqaddima* (Beirut 1967, p. 92). The wall in Alexandria on which I found the fragment from Ibn Battuta about the four gates of the port has since been destroyed. The most accurate version—and the one I used to correct mine—occurs in his *Rihlat* (Travels, Beirut 1985, 1.37). Nor did I invent the portrait of Manuel Chrysoloras: I found it in the Cabinet des Dessins of the Louvre under the inventory number 9849 *bis.* The *hadith* the Prophet used to exhort the faithful to conquer the seas by telling them that "a battle on the sea equals ten on land" and "the *shehid* who falls in battle on the sea equals two who fall on land" comes from one of the most rigorous compilations (A. J. Wensinck, ed., *Concordance et indices de la tradition musulmane* [in Arabic], Leiden 1933–38, vol. 2, p. 160). I owe my first acquaintance with Arabic maps to Konrad Müller's *Mappae Arabicae* (vols. 1–4, Stuttgart 1926–27), which, I should point out, he had to publish himself. (I should also point out that the multivolume work I cited in connection with wind roses [*Der Kompaß,* Hamburg 1911–18] was published at the author's expense, as was the lifelong work I cited in connection with sponge hunting [*Die Spongien des Adriatischen Meeres,* Leipzig 1852]. Moreover, Nordenskjöld spent his entire fortune on *Periplus.* Is it not a veritable faith in the South that encourages such sacrifices for the Mediterranean?)

Just beyond the Catholic cemetery on the high promontory overlooking the Marina Grande on Capri there is a cemetery founded in 1878 as the Cimitero degli a-cattolici, or Non–Roman Catholic Cemetery. Most, though not all, of the people buried there come from the four corners of the earth. I jotted down some inscriptions on the gravestones: Harold Gomberg, *maestro di musica;* Eugene Vinke, *consul de Rotterdam;* Poul Geleff, *Den danske Socialdemokrati;* Baron Jacques Adelsward Ferson; Salvator Vuolo, *libero pensatore;* Oscar Kollar, Croatian-Hungarian Freemason; Ernest Neufeld, Berlin (his stone had a Star of David on it); Marie Vokurková, Prague; Pontus Leander, Göteborg; Norman Douglas, a Scottish travel writer who devoted much of his life to the "island of the sirens." *Ci-gît* more than one Russian: the centenarian Princess Olimpia Britkina, Moscow; Prince Nikita Kozinov, Saint Pe-

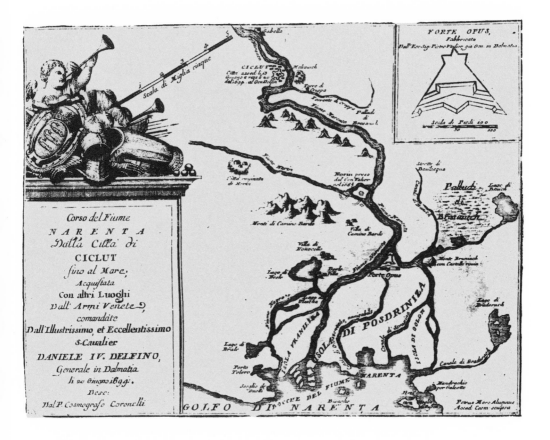

The mouth
of the Neretva.
Fr. Vincenzo
Coronelli. Venice,
1699.

tersburg; and a young geographer and poet whose modest stone reads only Tolya (the pet name for Anatoly). They all came as apostles of a faith in the South; they came to the Mediterranean to see Naples and die.

IT HAS ALWAYS BEEN Mediterranean etiquette to thank the people who help us to complete a task. Inscriptions on early maps displayed the names of benefactors in gilt letters. For my part I thank the librarians who located the books and atlases I needed and the photographers who reproduced the maps I have included. I am particularly grateful to the captains who navigated and the crews that manned the ships I sailed through the Adriatic and Mediterranean: they taught me what I could not read in libraries or find in atlases. But most of all I wish to thank the crew members of the *Hydra* and the *Dodekanesos,* who took me through the Cyclades and the Sporades and with whom I quickly found a common language. To quote Augustin Jal, "Though the words may differ, the language used by people of the sea has the same figures, the same energy, the same concision. . . . The practice of handling the same equipment, braving the same risks, and witnessing the same impressive spectacles has given sailors of all countries the same tropes. Their poetry is one; its means of expression cannot vary greatly" (*Glossaire nautique,* pp. 12–13). The helmsman of the *Hydra,* after explaining one or another sign on the map, would quote the following Ladino saying to me from the western reaches of the Mediterranean: *Dame el mazal e échame a la mar* (Grant me good fortune and throw me into the sea). Let me bring to a close the list of the Mediterranean anchors I have evoked in these pages with the anchor of destiny, of good and bad fortune (*agkyra . . . tas tykhas*) invoked by Euripides (*Helena,* 277).

TIME HAS ALTERED the meanings of many words, nautical and others. While sailing on the *Dodekanesos,* I called bread, according to classical usage, *artos;* the sailors called it *psomi.* I called water *hydôr;* they called it *nero.* For wine I used the word *oinos;* they used *krasi.* Bread, wine, and water have thus changed names, but the sea has remained the same: *thalassa.* As Jal the glossarist would say, the Mediterranean is one.

Designer:	Steve Renick
Compositor:	Integrated Composition Systems
Text:	11/12 Bembo
Display:	Bembo and Lombardic
Printer and binder:	Edwards Brothers, Inc.

PREDRAG MATVEJEVIĆ was born in 1932 in Mostar, Herzegovina, not far from the Mediterranean. A leading European public intellectual and writer, he has taught at the Universities of Zagreb and Paris (the Sorbonne) and is now Professor of Slavic Studies and East-Central Europe at the University of Rome (La Sapienza). His numerous books encompass literary and cultural criticism, history, and politics, always from a highly personal perspective.

MICHAEL HENRY HEIM, Chair of Slavic Languages and Literatures at the University of California, Los Angeles, is the award-winning translator of books from Russian, Czech, Croat, Serb, Hungarian, German, and French, by authors including Kundera, Hrabal, Kiš, Esterházy, Konrád, and Enszensberger.